The Fourth Estate at the Fourth Wall

The Fourth Estate at the Fourth Wall

Newspapers on Stage in July Monarchy France

Cary Hollinshead-Strick

NORTHWESTERN UNIVERSITY PRESS
EVANSTON, ILLINOIS

Northwestern University Press
www.nupress.northwestern.edu

Printed in the United States of America

10   9   8   7   6   5   4   3   2   1

Library of Congress Cataloging-in-Publication Data

Names: Hollinshead-Strick, Cary, author.
Title: The fourth estate at the fourth wall : newspapers on stage in July Monarchy
   France / Cary Hollinshead-Strick.
Description: Evanston, Illinois : Northwestern University Press, 2019. | Includes
   bibliographical references and index.
Identifiers: LCCN 2019011176| ISBN 9780810140356 (paper text : alk. paper) |
   ISBN 9780810140363 (cloth text : alk. paper) | ISBN 9780810140370 (e-book)
Subjects: LCSH: French drama—19th century—History and criticism. | Theater
   and society—France—History—19th century. | Press—France—History—19th
   century. | Press and journalism in literature. | France—History—Louis Philippe,
   1830–1848.
Classification: LCC PQ548 .H65 2019 | DDC 842.709—dc23
LC record available at https://lccn.loc.gov/2019011176

For Terence

And in memory of Elizabeth Berg and Joseph Strick

CONTENTS

ACKNOWLEDGMENTS

The Comparative Literature program at the University of Pennsylvania provided intellectual, social, and material support for the research that informs this book. Maurice Samuels made a nineteenth centuryist of me, and has been a generous mentor since the earliest days of this project. Gerald Prince has framed questions of academic work and academic life in consistently straightforward and enlightening ways. JoAnne Dubil is simply an unfailing model of grace. First Liliane Weissberg, then Rita Copeland, as chairs of Comparative Literature at Penn, provided guidance and support. Joan DeJean trained me as a research assistant and has been a friend and mentor ever since. After Penn, Jean-Marie Roulin helped me navigate another university culture in France. Françoise Mélonio provided intellectual clarity and practical guidance for the project, and Roger Chartier's comments at two key moments gave the book itself its initial impetus. A Bourse Marandon from La Société des Professeurs Français et Francophones d'Amérique (SPFFA) allowed for extended research time in Paris.

In a year spent at the Université Paris 7, Denis Diderot, Régis Salado, and José-Luis Diaz gave freely of their time and energies. The *Civilisation du journal* group, especially Marie-Ève Thérenty, helped me find my footing in research on vaudeville revues. Marilyn Himmesoëte introduced me to Anne Réach-Ngo, Julie Lambilliotte, Élodie Cassan, and Laurence Marie-Sacks, friends who have made the Bibliothèque nationale and various apartments, cafés, and conferences sociable places over the years. I owe an extra debt to Caroline Raulet-Marcel, also of this band, for proofreading my French. Guillaume Pinson and Olivier Bara have been both generous and patient with invitations to speak and write on topics covered here, and Amélie Calderone very kindly gave me access to her dissertation before it had been published as a book. Historians John Monroe and Albert Wu have clarified disciplinary expectations when that was needed.

Librarians at the Bibliothèque nationale, Tolbiac, Richelieu, and l'Arsenal, as well as at the Bibliothèque Historique de la Ville de Paris and at the Archives nationales have provided assistance for years. At the Maison de Balzac, Axel Radiguet managed the early editions of *César Birotteau* expertly. The staff of the library at the Société des auteurs et compositeurs dramatiques helped me to locate available information about performances.

At Northwestern University Press, editor in chief Gianna Mosser, acquisitions editor Trevor Perri, and creative director Marianne Jankowski kept book production smooth and friendly. Managing editor Anne Gendler balanced guidance and reassurance beautifully. Lori Meek Schuldt's careful editing saved me from all sorts of opacity, and Steven Moore's precision and expertise made the indexing process both fast and enlightening. The anonymous reviewers of the manuscript gave valuable advice.

Part of chapter 4 develops an argument which first appeared in "La campagne publicitaire de *L'Époque* en 1845 vue par le vaudeville," in Bara and Thérenty, *Presse et scène au XIXe siècle* (Médias 19, October 19, 2012, http://www.medias19.org/index.php?id=2884). Likewise, chapter 3 includes material that appeared in "Using *La Presse* to stage *La Vérité* in Delphine de Girardin's *L'École des journalistes*" (*Dix-Neuf* 7, no. 1 [2013]: 140–50). Both publishers have kindly granted permission to reprint that work.

In Paris, the crèche de la rue d'Estrées and the American University of Paris allowed small children and this project to grow simultaneously. At A.U.P., Alice Craven offered wise guidance from the start. She and then Geoff Gilbert, Rebekah Rast, and Jula Wildberger chaired the Department of Comparative Literature and English expertly, enabling interesting teaching assignments and consistent support for research-related travel. Provost Scott Sprenger, too, facilitated meaningful work and advancement. Feedback and encouragement from Elizabeth Kinne, Robert Payne, Hannah Westley, and, especially, Geoff Gilbert got this book written. The end-stage exchanges with Kerstin Carlson and Sneharika Roy were also indispensable.

Among the many colleagues whom I look forward to seeing at the Nineteenth-Century French Studies (NCFS) Colloquium, Jann Matlock pushed me to define what mattered in this book from the early stages. Patrick Bray has been a very generous guide to the field, and I am grateful for Sara Phenix and Raisa Rexer's wisdom and company. There really are too many NCFS friends to list, but without this community, the field would feel much lonelier.

On the home front, my grandmothers both appreciated musical theater, and I can only imagine that they would be tickled to know that I had been writing about vaudeville. My father's tastes in that category run to the anglophone, but we share an enthusiasm for silly but astute performances. My sisters, Sarah and Jane, have provided printing for delivery, couches to surf, and countless other necessities. My mother, Mary Berg Hollinshead, has been a model for how to do academia while remaining true to oneself.

Terence and Julien and Eleanor have been through all of it with me—drafts and deadlines, drudgery and discoveries. Heartfelt thanks to them, for all of their support and good cheer.

The Fourth Estate at the Fourth Wall

INTRODUCTION

In November 1837, a versatile young actress, Mademoiselle St-Albe, took the stage at the Théâtre de la Gaîté in the allegorical role of Publicity.[1] The vaudeville in which she was performing, *Le revolte des coucous*, was one of several occasional plays about the arrival of railroads and the fears of lost jobs that they brought with them.[2] In such moments of change, Publicity had a crucial role to play, as she explained in her first song of the night:

> Il faut qu'on me lise, / Qu'on fasse ou qu'on dise, / Chacun subira ma loi, / Ou dira pourquoi / Je sais bien que sur mon compte, / Quelques gens font des propos ! / À leur fureur que j'affronte / Je ne réponds que ces mots : / Craignez mon autorité ; / Je suis la publicité ! / Je parais tous les jours à plus de 30 mille exemplaires, tu vois si je puis t'être utile ?

> I'm required reading / Whatever anyone says or does / They end up submitting to me / If not, they'd better have an excuse / I know some say nasty things about me / I put up with their fury, simply replying / Fear my authority, I am publicity! / My daily circulation is over thirty thousand, I could be useful to you, don't you think?[3]

Publicity's confidence on the boards of the Théâtre de la Gaîté was justified by the remarkable transformation that her namesake had been undergoing in the 1830s, ever since the July 1830 revolution that ended the Restoration and installed Louis Philippe as ruler of what became known as the July Monarchy (sometimes referred to as the bourgeois monarchy).[4] Publicity started the nineteenth century as a political principle: that the actions of government should be visible to its constituents. By 1837, when Mlle St-Alme started singing about her circulation, a sea change was under way. Newspapers began to be financed by advertisement in 1836, and with their transformation, publicity took on the commercial meaning that it has today. Marc Martin, in his history of publicity in France, uses the names and functions of newspapers as well as evidence from Honoré de Balzac's *César Birotteau* to place the shift in meaning between 1835 and 1840, while pointing out that that the older and the newer usage coexisted well beyond that five-year spell.[5] This book will cover the period from 1836, when the advertisement-financed press began in France, to 1848, when the February Revolution changed the media regime, canceling theatrical and press censorship and allowing new newspapers to proliferate—for a time. The birth of the mass press occasioned a flurry of discussion on the uses of commercial publicity and a great number of stage and print performances that sought to correct for it, often in the interest of civic publicity. Theatrical personifications of concepts and institutions essential to July Monarchy society did, at least some of the time, fulfill the role that Enlightenment thinkers, including Germaine de Staël and her contemporaries, assigned to publicity: that of representing society to the powers that governed it and vice versa.[6] The plays, novels, and newspaper articles considered in the following pages negotiated the transitional period during which civic and commercial publicity coexisted. The sheer quantity and variety of jokes about the corrupting effects of commercial publicity that appeared on Parisian stages between 1836, which Marie-Ève Thérenty and Alain Vaillant have dubbed "Year One of the media era," and the end of the July Monarchy suggest that audiences remained uneasy about the influence of commercial publicity at least until the advent of the Second Republic in 1848.[7]

The Fourth Estate and Publicity

Since before the French Revolution, *publicité* had been seen as a way for citizens to keep track of government business. After the Revolution, publicity in the press was perceived as having a double role: it guaranteed that government abuses of power would be noticed and corrected, and it provided a way for citizens to make their own views known to one another. This watchdog role made the press even more important than the "official" branches of the government, for it was the communicational link with the constituents whose approval legitimized the government's very existence.[8] Referring to the press as the fourth estate reflects the structural importance it was understood to have in liberal society from the eighteenth century on. Montesquieu, in his *De l'esprit des lois*, names the first three estates as the executive, the legislative, and the judicial. Lucien Jaume suggests that the term "fourth estate" was first used in France in a rant by the Count of Salaberry, in 1827. Salaberry declaimed against "l'apparition d'un quatrième pouvoir qui demain sera plus puissant que les trois autres [. . .] son nom générique est la liberté, mais son nom propre est la license de la presse, et son nom de guerre est le journalisme" (The appearance of a fourth estate, which will soon be more powerful than the other three . . . its generic name is liberty, its proper name is freedom of the press and its nom de guerre is journalism).[9] Salaberry posited that what was called public opinion was just the opinions of newspapers being passed off as representative information, and that those very newspapers would divide the body politic if they were allowed free rein. His vision of the fourth estate as a divisive force is one that would lose influence with the advent of the July Monarchy but would recur periodically, particularly in the theater. In contrast, many of the doctrinaires, who had resisted the Restoration government's restrictions on the press, subscribed to the liberal view of the press as a necessary and productive fourth estate. The revolution of 1830 revalorized press publicity, with newspapers taking the lead during *les Trois Glorieuses* in resistance to restrictive press laws, and many journalists (or *publicistes*) becoming members of the July Monarchy government.[10] Their ascendancy to positions of power, along with the regime's origin as a reaction against the press-censoring *Ordonnances de juillet*, ensured that liberty of the press would be important to the political ideology of the 1830s.

Freedom of the press, like the model of constitutional monarchy that prevailed in 1830, was often associated with the British political system. The term "fourth estate," too, though it surfaced in France, probably found its most famous use in a passage from Thomas Carlyle, who recounted that, shortly after reporters had begun to be allowed to attend sessions of Parliament, "Burke said that there were three Estates in Parliament, but in the Reporters' Gallery yonder, there sat a fourth estate more important by far than them all."[11] In England, as in France, early evaluations of the desirability of such influence varied considerably. Elizabeth Eisenstein points out that in England prior to the nineteenth century, even the first three estates had somewhat varying meanings, with the fourth estate changing even more than the rest.[12]

One difference in attitude toward the press as a fourth estate was that in England, press reliance on commerce was thought to free it from the pressures of political factions, while in France, on the contrary, newspapers were imagined as the voices of political groups and were thought to be corrupted by too much support from business. There was consensus in 1830s France, however, that the British press was both freer and more commercial than its French counterpart. This freedom is why Mme de Staël praised English publicity, and this commercial success is why Émile de Girardin, one of the founders of the advertisement-financed press in France, took the *Times* of London as a model, declaring, in his prospectus for *La Presse*, that it would take inspiration from the economies of scale that the *Times* achieved through a combination of technology and advertising. To succeed, it would need to do so, in that producing a newspaper had recently become riskier and more expensive, with the passage of the September Laws of 1835.[13]

Because the July Monarchy had been founded partly in reaction against a proposed set of restrictive press laws, its early years were fairly permissive, but by 1835, when a Corsican nationalist named Fieschi tried to assassinate King Louis Philippe with an "infernal machine" of his own invention, the government reacted by making it more expensive to found a newspaper and making offenses against the king or government officials crimes for which editors would be jailed. Images and plays had to be submitted to censors for approval before their publication or performance. While the *cautionnement*, or deposit, required to found a newspaper had grown, the market for a less politicized press had also been reinforced. Before 1835, newspapers usually acted as representatives of party opinions. After the September Laws, both to steer clear of legal penalties and to reach broader audiences, they began to move away from clear political identifications.

This was the context in which the forty-franc press (*presse à quarante francs*, or the *presse à bon marché*) was invented. Two new newspapers, *La Presse* and *Le Siècle*, appeared simultaneously in July 1836, promising to use advertising revenues to halve newspaper subscription prices, which tended to be eighty francs a year. Their editors, Émile de Girardin and Armand Dutacq, had initially planned to collaborate, but when they could not agree, each founded his own newspaper.[14] The incipit for *La Presse*, written by Victor Hugo, proclaimed the newspaper's devotion to "la grande substitution des questions sociales aux questions politiques" (the great substitution of social questions for political ones).[15] To many, the already muzzled press appeared to have been put up for sale. Louis Blanc, still smarting from both the betrayal of the ideals of 1830 and the financial burden that the September Laws represented for his own newspaper, wrote that Girardin "venait de transposer en un trafic vulgaire ce qui est une magistrature et presque un sacerdoce" (had just transformed what was a public and nearly a sacred duty into a base transaction).[16]

Émile de Girardin, who already had a flamboyant reputation as a press entrepreneur, attracted more negative attention for his role in founding *La Presse* than Dutacq did with *Le Siècle* because he was so vehement in his insistence that relying on commercial publicity was the next necessary step in propagating civic publicity. Having founded a great number of affordable newspapers and published cheap educational materials before launching *La Presse*, Girardin was familiar with the economics of enlightening the masses. His first newspaper, *Le Voleur*, reprinted articles from other newspapers, often without their permission. In 1831, having failed to convince Casimir Périer to offer *Le Moniteur universel* for eighteen francs a year or five francs an issue, Girardin founded the *Journal des connaissances utiles*, whose annual subscription was only four francs. When the minister of education François Guizot's 1833 law requiring a primary school in every commune passed, Girardin published pedagogical materials, including affordable atlases and dictionaries.[17]

In his efforts to promote *La Presse*, Émile de Girardin extended the Enlightenment rhetoric of *publicité* as information sharing, by using the word to apply to advertisements. He argued that *annonces*, or print advertisements, not only reduced subscription prices but also freed newspapers' editorial positions from the will of their subscribers. In a dogmatic version of liberalism, which assumed that new subscribers needed to be educated before they would be truly fit for participation in the public sphere, he wrote:

> Déranger les opinions faites, contrarier les idées reçues, réformer
> des jugements arbitraires, c'est exercer sur l'esprit de l'abonné une

violence qu'il pardonne rarement, c'est le contraindre à douter de son infaillibilité, c'est troubler le repos de ses facultés intellectuelles et exiger d'elles un effort inaccoutumé, conséquemment pénible.[18]

To disturb set opinions, to contradict received ideas, to reform arbitrary judgments, is to do violence to the cleverness of the subscriber (who rarely forgives); it is to force him to doubt his infallibility, to trouble the repose of his intellectual faculties and to ask of them an unusual, and therefore annoying, effort.

Girardin's complaint was that in catering to the tastes of subscribers, newspapers were unable to elevate those tastes by publishing the ideas of great men (*supériorités*). His diatribe against subscribers' closed-mindedness lent credibility to his assertion that he was against flattering his readership (though most readers were likely to assume that they were among those capable of appreciating the *supériorités* that Girardin said the press had discouraged). Girardin was in favor of the idea of freedom of the press, but he had much to say about its abuses as it was being practiced.[19] Concerned that civic transparency and good new ideas had been obscured by factional agendas within the press, Girardin proposed signed articles and paid advertisement as ways to recuperate the possibility of a disinterested press. Girardin was so successful in making his idea known that his arguments probably contributed to the shift by which the word *publicité* came to include commercial advertising.[20]

Émile de Girardin instituted a second major innovation at *La Presse* in 1836. He started printing unpublished novels serially. The inclusion of novels, combined with the lowered subscription price, attracted new readers and kept their attention. Though Balzac's *La Vieille fille*, which is generally called the first serial novel, or *roman-feuilleton*, appeared in the "Variétés" column, subsequent novels in *La Presse* and elsewhere tended to be published in the bottom section of the first few newspaper pages, which was known as the *feuilleton* (its location on the page was referred to as the ground floor, or *rez-de-chaussée*). Even before the serial novel started to be published in the *feuilleton* of daily papers, though, the critics and society columnists whose work was published there were often accused of openness to publishing *réclames*, paid advertisements that were written into the article in which they appeared. *Feuilletonistes*, as these critics and society columnists were called, were also assumed to have an unchecked tendency to engage in *charlatanisme*, exaggerated praise of a product or performance, and *calomnie*, dissemination of false negative information about the same, or about well-known people. Such accusations against those who published in the *feuilleton* redoubled when newspapers started publishing literature as a promotional strategy. Though less likely to take bribes than society reporters or critics, novelists provided a product that was, itself, an incitement to buy the newspaper. They did so for both money and visibility. The very presence of novels in newspapers, coinciding as it did with the commercialization of *publicité*, made literature, particularly the serial novel, a commercial product.

Émile de Girardin had been excoriated by his fellow journalists for lowering subscription prices. Novelists who published serially were, in turn, taken firmly to task by literary critics for their cooperation with newspapers.[21] Political journalism before Girardin had been considered a public duty, and the Romantic movement had consecrated the poet as a spiritual leader of society.[22] Those who expected art and politics to lead the country in an entirely disinterested way disapproved of Girardin's insistence on the economic conditions of newspaper production and were troubled to see the novel so blatantly distributed according to commercial logic. Charles Augustin Sainte-Beuve's famous 1839 condemnation of "la littérature industrielle" was not restricted to literary concerns, for advertisement also affected the role of the new press as a social institution. According to Sainte-Beuve, "Les conséquences de l'annonce furent rapides et infinies. On eut beau vouloir séparer dans le journal ce qui restait consciencieux et libre de ce qui devenait public et vénal : la limite du filet fut bientôt franchie, la réclame servit de pont" (The consequences of advertisement were rapid and immeasurable. For all that the press wanted to separate what remained conscientious and free from what became public and venal, the line was quickly crossed; advertisement served as a bridge).[23] Sainte-Beuve portrayed the *feuilleton* as a river that could overflow its banks if not held in check by watchful critics like himself. He pointed out that theater, too, was in an industrial phase and that "de nos jours le bas fond remonte sans cesse, et devient vite le niveau commun, le reste s'écroulant ou s'abaissant" (these days the murky depths are rising constantly, and becoming the new standard, while the rest collapses or lowers itself).[24] His imagery was revisited by Émile Souvestre, a playwright complaining about the dominance of vaudevilles, when he quipped, "Open a theater and a sewer, at least the sewer you can close."[25] Closing the sewers had, of course, been a major hygiene initiative before and during the nineteenth century, while controlling the theaters, too, was thought to keep public passions regulated. Industry had dirtied the rivers of Paris in the first decades of the century. When Sainte-Beuve treated Balzac and Scribe as industrial writers, he was referring to their pursuit of gain and their promotional publicity practices, but he was also implying that they polluted the literature of their time. Balzac's and Scribe's strategic use of serialization and of the vaudeville form, their interest in authors' rights and the money that their protection represented, sat badly with the ideals of disinterested contributions to literature that Sainte-Beuve so visibly championed. He, like many critics and some playwrights, saw an Enlightenment ideal of social uplift via individual exercise of reason (in the press and the theater and their audiences) as threatened by the burgeoning of a mentality that put profits before principles. Such tensions between Enlightenment ideals and commercial interests were hardly new. Eighteenth-century historians have had rich debates about the extent to which prerevolutionary popular texts contested authority as part of an Enlightenment project or, on the contrary, did so out of what Robert Darnton has called a "Grub Street" mentality, because scandalous information sold well.[26] The teleology of the Revolution adds force to such debates, but both print culture and revolutions proceded apace in the nineteenth century, as did discussions of the effects of new media practices on systems of representation. In 1836, the editors who stood to benefit from relying on advertisements to finance the press claimed that theirs was an Enlightenment project. Opponents of such commercialization cried, "Industrial literature!" The competition between the older model of newspaper publishing, in which each paper published the considered opinion of a political group, and the newer one, which diluted and multiplied political positions to enlarge its readership, found an unfortunate embodiment in a duel between Émile de Girardin and Armand Carrel, editors of *La Presse* and *Le National*, respectively. Carrel accused Girardin of creating unfair competition, Girardin threatened to write about Carrel's liaison with a married woman, and a duel was declared. Both men were wounded, but Carrel died days later, as something of a martyr to an older version of journalistic principles.

Such conflicts played out not just between journalists who represented different attitudes toward press commercialization but also between writers who worked for the theater and those who worked for the press. There was overlap between these groups, with a number of newspaper critics writing plays from time to time and vice versa, but when plays staged the press, they tended to do so in ways that took advantage of the theater's physical, oral mode of communication. Likewise, journalists set themselves up as superior to the average theatergoer in their reviews of plays. Harold Mah's caution that the Enlightenment, however many discourses it may have contained or excluded, remained a broadly shared ideal, helps explain some of the wrangling between journalists and *vaudevillistes* who often competed to promote their own genre's contributions to the advancement of Enlightenment ideals.[27] Their productions share space at the bottom right of Pierre Bourdieu's graph of the literary field at the end of the nineteenth century; a position that indicates low cultural consecration and high profits.[28] The formats and periodicity of some of their practices, like the year-end revue, even echoed each other,[29] but as *feuilletonistes* reviewed vaudevilles, they dismissed stage "business" (a telling term for the funny and physical) as lowbrow. *Vaudevillistes*, in turn, teased journalists for not actually seeing the plays they reviewed. None of this jousting looks terribly enlightened at first glance, but each kind of writer was complaining about the distance that the other had taken from a preferred, more ideal, form. Vaudevilles, according to *feuilletonistes*, lacked the dramatic tension thought to elicit meliorative sympathy from audiences. Newspapers, according to *vaudevillistes*, failed at their ideal of conscientious reporting and informed judgment.[30] These concerns, lightly expressed as they often were, participated in a more generalized worry that, with the use of advertising to finance the press, commerce had tainted the entire structure of relations between civil society and government, even as it forced literature into a role of sales promotion. Pierre Rosanvallon points out, a propos of Guizot's concept of publicity, that publicity was to the political sphere what the market was to the economic sphere, but while the market could remain opaque to those involved in it, the press was supposed to increase transparency of relations between the social and the political for all who were engaged with it.[31]

The newspaper's change in status as a medium, from one of transparency to one of seduction of consumers, caused widespread concern about the value of the information it propagated. The new press made great efforts to proclaim the quality of its content, but the extent of its efforts at expansion made skeptics contend that attracting significant readership in a mixed society could only be achieved by appealing to the lowest common denominator. Playwrights, who were often past masters at doing whatever it took to attract large mixed crowds, proved particularly eager to deflate the claims of the new press. This enthusiasm was evidenced by the remarkable number of plays that staged the new press after 1836. Theatrical censorship, officially reestablished in 1835, was, for a while, abolished after the revolution of 1848. That change of regime, with its temporary freedom, marks the end point for this study. By the time the Second Empire established clear and repressive censorship, in 1852, vaudevilles relied less and less on songs, which had been prime opportunities for them to juxtapose known melodies with new words, one of their main modes of criticism.[32] Both journalists and censors had less leeway for interpretation of the rules concerning the theater after the July Monarchy, and, while discussion of restrictions on performance flourished, the dialogue between censors and playwrights, which has left interesting archival traces for the July Monarchy, dwindled.[33]

During the years between the birth of the advertisement-financed press and the end of the July Monarchy, Patrick Berthier estimates that an average of 311 new plays were produced each year.[34] To constitute the corpus of plays that stage the press on which this book is based, I looked through the play titles listed in Charles Beaumont Wicks's *The Parisian Stage* for references to newspapers, publicity, or popularity.[35] To include plays that were performed but not published, and to locate censors' reports for ones that did treat the press, I did the same with Odile Krakovitch's *Censure des repertoires des grands théâtres Parisiens (1835–1906)*.[36] Once an initial list had been constituted—and augmented with year-end vaudeville revues, which show up in a title search on the Bibliothèque nationale's catalog—I skimmed roughly a thousand plays to see which ones staged the press.

Having identified 144 plays that did so, I looked for reviews of them in five newspapers: *La Presse*, *Le Siècle*, and *Le Constitutionnel* (the most popular forty-franc dailies) and *La Quotidienne* and *Le Charivari* (for avowedly conservative and liberal perspectives, respectively). While not all plays were reviewed, the ones that were sometimes appeared in articles that mentioned similar works, which, in turn, provided more titles for the corpus of plays.

The widespread newspaper practice of running reviews of plays in Monday's *feuilleton* ensured that critics gave written accounts of the performances they had attended. Whereas the more prestigious comedies and dramas considered here often benefited from prefaces that discussed their reception when they were published, for vaudevilles and lighter comedies, *feuilletons* are often the only remaining source of eyewitness information about how audiences reacted to plays.[37] Because plays only ran as long as they were profitable, performance runs, too (which can be estimated from newspaper notices and, occasionally, tracked in the files of the Société des Auteurs et Compositeurs Dramatiques), are reasonable indicators of the popularity of any given play. Finally, the September Laws of 1835, which required that all plays be submitted to the censors before performance, expanded the archive considerably by conserving manuscripts of unpublished plays and keeping records (in the form of reports) of what sorts of content made censors nervous.

Given the difficulty of conclusive research on such ephemeral productions (not all plays were published, many have been lost, play titles are not always indicative of content), it seems safe to claim that more plays than the number identified for this book were, in fact, concerned with the press. Calculating from 144 plays about the press that were performed over 12.5 years (from July 1836 through the end of 1848), then, we can estimate that an average of 11.5 plays per year were about the press, or 3.7 percent of the 311 new plays per year that Berthier counts. Four percent, and perhaps even as many as 5 percent, of new plays would, I suspect, be a conservative estimate of the proportion of new dramatic productions that staged newspapers. (See appendix 1 for a list of plays.)

Press publicity was included in some genres of play, such as the year-end vaudeville revue, because it was part of recent events, and the revue's role was to provide commentary on the innovations of the passing year. In comedies and dramas, though, newspapers were included toward more specifically social and political ends. In comedies, newspapers frequently acted as "distorting mirrors"[38] not only allowing for dated and socially categorized exposition but also serving as an endless source of irony as they exposed characters' reliance on sensationalist journalism or made newspapers the instrument of plotters and the guide of dupes.[39] Staging the press became a trend that included everyone from the most prolific *vaudevillistes* to Balzac and Gérard de Nerval. The theater, across genres, provided extensive structural critique of press publicity and its effects, while the newspaper proved a marvelous prop, character, curtain decoration, and deus ex machina, according to the agenda of the playwright.

By foregrounding debates about the practice of press publicity and treating advertisements as an essential aspect of the culture they described, July Monarchy playwrights provided ironic material for the exercise of *esprit* and distinction in their audiences. In a world in which class divisions and interpretive competence were less predictably distributed than they had been, irony allowed spectators to aspire to the knowing disillusionment usually encouraged by plays that staged the press.[40]

Being duped was a particularly prevalent fear in a society that was increasingly concerned about the opacity of the information available to it. Robert Macaire, whose popularity had begun with Frédérick Lemaître's reinterpretation of his character in the 1823 melodrama *L'Auberge des Adrets*,[41] became the amoral theatrical hero of the early July Monarchy. His popularity was such that Lemaître, the actor who had reinvented him, rewrote *L'Auberge des Adrets* in collaboration with three playwrights, renaming it *Robert Macaire* and changing Macaire from a bandit in rags into an influential financier who subverted morals and mocked institutions. The personification of false information, Macaire could be counted on to represent the corrupt idea and the illegal scheme. When censorship was reestablished in 1835, *Robert Macaire* and *L'Auberge des Adrets* were two of the four plays banned from the theater indefinitely.[42]

In addition to outright cynicism, like Macaire's, parodic treatment of the current media was another common approach to amusing audiences who might otherwise react in all sorts of ways. "Comedy is impossible in 1836," said Stendhal in an article published in the *Revue de Paris*, for, he explained, audiences were made up of too great a variety of spectators. Because sophisticated and unsophisticated audience members did not laugh at the same things, the fellow-feeling (*sympathie réciproque*) between them was lost. For playwrights frustrated by such diversity of reception, Stendhal recommended novel writing, in which the author "deals with one spectator at a time."[43] Stendhal's discouraged analysis of the state of theater reception indicates that the ideal of theater as a populist celebration, outlined by Guizot in his preface to the works of Shakespeare, was in doubt. For Guizot (as for Friedrich Schiller a generation earlier),[44] times of peace and prosperity, such as the Elizabethan age, allowed different classes to mingle and be elevated together through identification with great drama. This was the logic behind such July Monarchy realities as the state subsidy attributed to the Comédie Française (then known as the Théâtre Français) and, in its negative version, censorship of plays.

The Fourth Wall and the Lessons of the Stage

Theoreticians from Denis Diderot to Guizot to Jürgen Habermas have seen audience identification with characters as the first step in drama's impact on social evolution. The "fourth wall"—a term associated with, though not exactly coined by, Diderot—imagines an invisible barrier separating the actors on stage from the audience. Diderot's idea was that audiences would be more moved by scenes performed as if actors had no awareness that they were performing before an audience. This book is concerned primarily with plays that crossed this imaginary fourth wall, often flamboyantly. Their aim was not, for the most part, to inspire emotional identification with characters (though some do) but rather to elicit thought and laughter. In vaudevilles, as in dramas whose setting had been changed to mollify censors, identification *of* (rather than with) characters constituted a significant part of the message a play could impart. The plays considered here often required audiences to negotiate anonymity or character identities made allegorical by choice or by censorship. Such plays about the press raised questions concerning who and what were socially knowable, and whether the press was contributing to that knowability or hindering it. Part of the definition of the vaudeville genre was that it put new lyrics to preexisting tunes. Describing the effect of this process on the experience of vaudeville performance, Olivier Bara points out that, "l'ironie se loge dans ce constant décalage entre la chanson connue et la chanson réécrite . . . les spectateurs du vaudeville se font presque co-auteurs de la pièce, participent à l'avènement de son sens momentané" (irony resides in this constant contrast between the known song and the rewritten song . . . vaudeville spectators almost become coauthors, participating in the creation of momentary meaning).[45] Such clever reuse of themes, often at the expense of the commercial press, forced audiences to practice the sort of recognition and reflexivity typical of civic publicity. Jacques Rancière has quite rightly questioned the assumptions behind the tradition of seeing the spectator as a passive observer.[46] In the case of nascent mass culture during the July Monarchy, not only were theater audiences active participants in completing the meanings of many of the performances they attended, but newspapers and novels, too, adopted the knowing mode of pastiche particular to vaudeville in order to encourage their readers to question the motives of those who promoted new media developments. Such critiques, while occasionally promoting outright cynicism, also used irony and humor to encourage reflective engagement with the fourth estate, however commercial its production was becoming.

Steven Mullaney, writing about Elizabethan popular drama, points out that "sometimes a complex form of cultural performance and production . . . can serve as a primary rather than a secondary forum for social thought. Sometimes . . . theatrical performance and reception enable and constitute a significant form of inquiry in and of themselves, a kind of critical social theory conducted by other means." Rephrasing a quotation from Tadeusz Kantor, Mullaney characterizes theater as "an answer to, rather than a representation of, reality."[47] Mullaney's book focuses on Shakespeare, but his argument can certainly be applied to popular drama of the nineteenth century, too. In fact, when dealing with popular drama that few people study, like the vaudeville, it can even reveal "answers to reality" that haven't been considered in nineteenth-century literary history.

What, then, can vaudeville teach us about the press at a key moment in its commercialization? Chapter 1 shows how vaudeville served as an important vulgarization of the liberal Enlightenment claims of the new press in a format that required neither literacy nor much income for access. By having personifications of new newspapers sing about the claims of the forty-franc press and engage in dialogue with other characters about how they did or didn't live up to the promises they made, year-end revues and other vaudevilles were able to explain those ideals and to question whether they were actually being served by the papers in question. Because vaudevilles were popular theater, with ticket prices accessible to most people who were employed, and because newspapers were sold by far more expensive annual subscription rather than by the issue during the July Monarchy, press innovations reached an even broader public via the theater than they did through papers themselves. The vaudeville revue and the newspaper *feuilleton* both gave periodic accounts of the cultural life of the capital. Because vaudevilles could be crude, and their jokes about the evolving media sphere were broad, newspaper responses to their critiques of new media practices were often condescending. Though they shared the prerogatives of timeliness and cleverness and were marked by regular periodicity, the differences in angle of approach between the *feuilleton* and the vaudeville revue reveal the expectations and priorities of each of the genres. The vaudevilles considered in chapter 1 were not satires of the press but rather send-ups. The humorous displacement that they practiced, one suited to times when competing media are concerned about a divided public, may account for the return of the vaudeville genre in the twenty-first century. In 2001 and again in 2017, Georges Lavaudant, director of the Odéon theater in Paris, staged vaudevilles by Feydeau, suggesting that he did so not for their social satire but for the disjointedness and excesses of the situations they presented—an approach that he feels appeals to our current moment, too.[48]

Chapter 2 traces the contours of debates about fake news that reached critical mass in 1838. One gap that worried July monarchy playwrights and censors alike was the space that could open up between true and false news about people's behavior as an ever more quickly produced and more gossip-hungry press was expanding. Less than two years after the introduction of the forty-franc press, the Théâtre Français launched a spate of dramas and comedies that focused on the potential for political clout inherent in a populist press. These plays illustrated diabolical synergies between the mechanisms of calumny, the spreading of false and malicious rumors, and the practices that made the new press successful. Partly because all plays were subject to preemptive censorship after 1835, the authors who wrote comedies and dramas about the double-edged sword that was press populism chose to set their plays long ago and far away, often in eighteenth-century London, which was understood to be a precursor for the media sphere of nineteenth-century Paris.

For those who didn't immediately understand that the dramas playing out in "London" were meant to reflect on the French media, parody plays and vaudevilles playing in the less prestigious theaters of the capital spelled out the mechanisms of popularity and journalistic misbehavior that the dramas discussed. Nineteenth-century vaudevilles are expert explainers of *how* the media phenomena that were so carefully staged "abroad" when performed at Paris's most prestigious theater, functioned in France in the 1830s.[49] Not only did parodic vaudevilles and year-end revues spell out the claims of calumny dramas, but the vaudeville genre itself also shaped the calumny plays to varying degrees. Delphine de Girardin wrote one act of her *L'École des journalistes* as a vaudeville (other acts were conceived of as comedies, tragedies, and farces) in an effort to appeal to as broad an audience as possible. Desnoyer and Labat, authors of *Richard Savage*, were greeted with skepticism at the Théâtre Français because they usually wrote vaudevilles for boulevard theaters, and Scribe's greatest formal innovation, which was reflected in his calumny plays among others, was arguably to have integrated techniques from vaudeville into comedy. Whether it was stylistically integrated into the plays in question or stood apart as separate commentary, then, vaudeville proved to be central to efforts to explain the risk and the power of increasing the pace at which information was disseminated.

Chapter 3 argues that vaudeville was a formative mode for the best-known antipress novel of the nineteenth century. In his preface to the second part of *Illusions perdues*, the part that lambastes the world of Parisian newspapers, Balzac said that the work was inspired by Scribe's vaudeville *Le Charlatanisme*,[50] and his pastiches within the novel suggest that his uses of vaudeville were not merely thematic. Read together with Balzac's earlier novel *César Birotteau*, *Illusions perdues* presents the reader with a variety of textual samples that exemplify the phenomena it is describing. Presented as evidence, these set pieces are also remarkably similar, structurally, to the ironic displays of cultural productions that made up much of the "business" of vaudeville performances. Such strategies, be they deployed on stage or on the page, caught audience attention effectively, but they could come to seem passé with time and the shifting of cultural reference points. As he invented the ingenious republication strategy that was the *Comédie humaine*, Balzac rewrote many of the passages in *Illusions perdues* that functioned the way that lines of vaudevilles did. He recast events and descriptions in less theatrical and more historical terms, preparing his text for a shift from current self-promotion to future status as literature located in historical time. He even wrote what he saw as the necessary innovations in paper technology into his novel, conjoining technological progress and aesthetic transition from the ephemeral to the lasting. By doing so, he wrote *Illusions perdues* from its status as a partly serialized novel into that of a bound book.

Chapter 4, which treats the materiality of newspapers on stage, demonstrates that the press's physical presentation was used to question its fourth estate claims. When the object on the July Monarchy vaudeville stage was a newspaper, it was usually there to comment on the pretentions of the press. When newspapers were enlarged to include more advertisement, playwrights covered the stage and its curtain with giant dailies. When expanding papers claimed to unite the body politic, plays showed naive readers retreating into isolation and prejudice on the basis of the fragmenting stories they read in the news.

Such exaggerated uses of newsprint as part of plots and décor drew attention to the press's status as a medium as opposed to its claims as an institution. It was, for such plays, no fourth estate, allowing governments and the governed to communicate. It was, instead, a medium like any other. As such, it could transmit the messages of anyone who paid the necessary fee. In 1845, such fee paying for advertising space was centralized by the Société Générale des Annonces, which sold exposure in a variety of publications through one company. Vaudevilles from 1845 suggested that such "coverage" was blocking communication between various characters. By putting newspapers between actors, not as conduits but as barriers, these plays physically disputed any pretense to transparency that newspapers might still make.

Balzac put the matter and the spirit of the forty-franc press into tension in *Illusions perdues*, while vaudevilles of the 1840s staged the matter of newspapers to question their spirit.[51] Such skepticism about Enlightenment claims and emphasis on physical circulation of text continued to trouble July Monarchy playwrights, though, especially those who had been maligned by calumnies spread in newspapers. Chapter 5 examines the ways that both Félix Pyat and Gérard de Nerval suffered from attacks penned by Jules Janin, the powerful drama critic for *Le Journal des débats*. Pyat did time in jail and Nerval in an asylum because of their reactions to Janin's treatment. Having lived those unpleasant consequences of trying to stand up to a press bully, both authors turned to publication of their plays in books as a longer-term form of revenge on their nemesis. Whereas Balzac pastiched Janin, Pyat and Nerval cited him directly to prove him wrong, taking their own plays from the stage, where Janin had maligned their productions, to the page, in longer volumes of their own work where they put their faith for eventual justification.

This book follows the interaction between theatrical and journalistic representations of the newly commercial press. It locates debates about whether advertisement is allowing for increased access to news or bringing it under the influence of business, about what the limits on slander should be, about how one can promote one's work while retaining its integrity, in plays and articles that often respond to the same external events. By reading a range of dramatic and journalistic perspectives on the commercialization of the press, we can identify not just the terms of the debate about that press's social role but also the priorities of participants doing the debating.

The Vaudeville Mode

Within the active and expanding field of research on literature and the press, relatively few scholars work on the theater, though first the *Civilisation du journal* project, in which Jean-Claude Yon, Patrick Berthier, and Olivier Bara were contributors, and now the Médias19 website, have been changing that. The latter includes an anthology, edited by Bara, of critical editions of plays about the press, and online journal issues, edited by Bara and Marie-Ève Thérenty, devoted to *Presse et scène au XIXe siècle* and to *Presse et Opéra au XVIII et XIXe siècles.*[52] Vaudeville takes center stage in a 2015 issue of the *Revue de l'histoire du théatre* devoted to the subgenre of the year-end vaudeville revue, and in a few chapters of Bury and Laplace-Claverie's volume devoted to theatrical criticism, *Le Miel et le fiel*, but on the whole, it remains an understudied genre.[53] Stéphanie Loncle's *Théâtre et libéralisme (Paris, 1830–1848)* takes vaudeville seriously, though she suggests that the generic distinctions that have shaped historical and sociological readings of plays are perhaps less interesting now than a consideration of how performance itself negotiated social relations in ways that failed to fit neatly into a liberal paradigm.[54] Her argument works nicely with my analysis of vaudeville's use of the spectacular to question the press's claims of liberal transparency. A 2016 volume edited by Olivier Bara and Jean-Claude Yon on Eugène Scribe is indicative of a renewal of research on his work, which includes some vaudeville, but even Scribe's less prestigious production remains at the more consecrated end of the plays considered here. Vaudeville, whose peak in popularity coincided exactly with the July Monarchy, staged newspapers more often than other dramatic genres did, so its critical neglect has hampered our ability to see a full range of reactions to the commercialization of the press.[55] The vaudeville mode, which entails recuperation of recent cultural productions for analysis and mockery as well as appeals to the spectator as the ultimate judge, took the new press's promotional techniques as yet another set of novelties to be mocked. Like vaudevilles, which framed the press to suit their own purposes, newspaper critics cited plays strategically to discredit or refute the claims that those plays made about the way the press worked. Their practice of putting the evidence before their reading audience, while meant to demonstrate their superior judgment, echoed the vaudeville strategy of turning criticisms of the press over to audiences for evaluation.

This strategy is consistent and inventive enough to be considered a mode, like Peter Brooks's melodramatic mode and the tragic mode that Rita Felski's edited volume explores.[56] The vaudeville mode works not through sympathetic identification with characters but rather through rowdily theatrical gags and sing-alongs. It joyfully breaches the fourth wall, an aesthetic convention in theater that has been credited with everything from the shaping of citizen subjectivities to the exercise of cathartic or cosmopolitan identification with the suffering of others.[57] The vaudevilles considered here do so in this interest of questioning the ways and means of a press increasingly willing to project itself as a fourth estate. If recent discussions of the Enlightenment have sometimes separated its networks from its ideas, its discourses from its books, this book is a look at how vaudevilles and the articles, novels, and plays that share their modes performed ideas about networks for critique. By doing so, they played an essential role in the shaping of what Guillaume Pinson has dubbed *l'imaginaire médiatique* (the media imaginary) of the nineteenth century.[58] Recent publications that make information from the censorship bureau and the playwrights' guild, the Société des Auteurs et Compositeurs Dramatiques (SACD), more easily available, as well as two dissertations (one on theater published in newspapers and another on theatricality in mid-nineteenth-century novels), suggest that this cross-pollination of theater, press, and novels is starting to receive the attention it deserves.[59] For not only did vaudevilles and *feuilletons* share certain formats, periodicities, and modes, but they also positioned themselves in relation to one another and to other theatrical genres and newspaper sections.[60] Paying attention to these strategic positionings reveals how humor tells truths about corrupt sources of information; how false information (or the threat of it) can control a media sphere; how ideas, when buffeted by sources of news whose authority is contested, sometime take refuge in older formats, such as books; and how even that happens in parallel with extraordinary experimentation with the aesthetic and political capacities of new media. While new media themselves look different today from how they looked in 1836, the questions they raise have remained remarkably similar.

Chapter 1

The Press Personified

Even after annual subscription prices had been lowered to forty francs, newspapers remained well beyond the means of most Parisians. An occasional trip to the theater, however, was not. Once there, audiences could laugh and sing along as actors playing the major new newspaper titles discussed their own behaviors. Actors in newsprint accessories and sashes emblazoned with the names of the papers they stood for brought debate about the priorities of the commercial press to audiences broader than those the press was able to reach directly. Vaudevilles personified the press and ideas associated with it, the better to question newspapers' claims. The popularity of such an approach reveals a significant overlap in readership and spectatorship: playwrights would not write jokes unless they thought their audiences would understand and be amused by their references. The capacity of spectators to interpret staged material, which Jacques Rancière has defended, was essential to the success of plays about newspapers.[1] Wherever audience members stood along the spectrum of engagement with the new press, their comprehension of jokes about it was necessary to the success of vaudevilles that treated the subject. The most popular theatrical genre of the July Monarchy, vaudeville was attentive to public tastes and concerns: plays that did not entertain folded quickly. The combination of vaudeville's commercial responsiveness, its focus on humorous critique (especially in year-end revues), and its uses of embodiment to make points about social institutions make it a particularly useful lens through which to examine popular response to the mediation proposed by the early mass press.

Vaudeville and the press had evolved in parallel since at least the seventeenth century. When Théophraste Renaudot founded his weekly *Gazette* in 1631, vaudevilles were subversive songs about the news of the day, which were often sung on the Pont Neuf in Paris. In the eighteenth century, vaudeville songs were integrated into plays, particularly those performed at theaters where speaking roles were not allowed. The system of *privilèges* allowed only a few theaters to stage plays that involved dialogue, restricting the rest to inventive combinations of pantomime, song, and written speech. Vaudevilles were popular attractions at the annual Saint-Germain and Saint Laurent fairs, where they avoided restrictions on speaking parts, first by having characters pull scrolls from one pocket, display them, and return them to the other pocket, and then by hanging *écriteaux*, panels with text on them, from the front of the stage.

Martine de Rougemont explains how this worked:

> Pour aider à comprendre les comédies à la muette ou en écriteaux, les forains les accompagnent de la musique des chansons connues, que l'on appelle vaudevilles . . . Les paroles des écriteaux sont adaptées à la coupe de ces chansons, elles en constituent des couplets nouveaux, qui allient le charme du familier et de l'inattendu. Pour aider le spectateur analphabète, ou simplement myope, quelqu'un chantera ces couplets : soit un acteur en scène ou en coulisses si la police le permet, soit des compères placés parmi le public et qui l'entraînent à chanter avec eux. Double intérêt : un texte est entendu, auquel chacun a le sentiment de participer.[2]

> To help audiences understand the plays that were silent or had text panels, troupes accompanied them with well-known tunes, which were referred to as vaudevilles. . . . The text on the panels was adapted to the lines of the songs, it provided new couplets, which mixed the charm of the familiar and the unexpected. To help the illiterate (or simply myopic) spectator, someone sang the new lyrics, either an actor on stage or in the wings if the police allowed it, or shills in the audience who got people to sing with them. Double advantage: a text was heard, and each spectator felt he had participated in it.

At such fairground theater, vaudeville established a tendency to recast the familiar in a skeptical mode by putting new lyrics to old tunes. Displaying texts and asking the audience to sing them encouraged participation not unlike the kind that would later be elicited by July Monarchy vaudevilles that brought newspapers on stage and asked audiences to consider their social roles.

With the Revolution, the restrictions due to the *privilège* system were lifted, and the vaudeville as a dramatic genre got its first permanent theater, the Théâtre du Vaudeville, which opened in 1792. Vaudevilles, which were now plays with dialogue and songs, whose new lyrics were sung to preexisting tunes, retained the irreverent attitude of their earlier form as well as the expectation of audience participation.[3] In the nineteenth century, this tradition continued, particularly in the form of year-end vaudeville revues, which commented on recent plays, joked about inventions of the previous twelve months, and critiqued or hailed press innovations and events.[4]

For press innovations were, themselves, considered worthy of coverage both in newspapers and in theatrical revues.[5] Vaudevilles were sometimes used to promote newly founded newspapers, but they as often commented on how such publications affected the shape of the public sphere, without seeking to condone or condemn them per se. Several year-end vaudeville revues included the use of advertisements to reduce subscription prices as one of the important events of 1836, even as they aired doubts about the consequences of such innovation. Comparing their commentary on the phenomenon to that of *Le Charivari*, a humorous center-left illustrated newspaper, which also covered it, reveals that a satirical newspaper and satirical plays could treat the same material similarly while still doing quite different work socially. *Le Charivari* of January 2 and 3, 1837, pointed out in its section on "VAUDEVILLE–PALAIS ROYAL–AMBIGU" that "ces trois théâtres sont les seuls qui aient sacrifié, cette année, à la mode des revues de fin d'année. L'an 1836 a été jugé le soir, à la lumière des quinquets, comme *Le Charivari* l'avait jugé le matin, à la première page de son numéro du 31 décembre" (these three theaters are the only ones who followed the trend of staging year-end revues this year. The year 1836 was judged in the evening by the light of the oil lamps, just as *Le Charivari* had judged it in the morning, on the first page of its December 31 issue).[6]

The first page of the December 31, 1836, issue of *Le Charivari* did, indeed, present a scene highly reminiscent of the openings of most vaudeville revues. The author of the article summons the year 1836 to appear before him and accuses her of being dull. The description of her appearance has a great deal in common with the sort of allegorical costuming practiced in vaudeville revues:

> Elle était vêtue d'une robe dont l'étoffe primitive avait disparu sous les différentes applications qu'on y avait faites. D'un côté, on voyait un exemplaire-spécimen de *la Presse*, journal à 40 francs ; de l'autre, le numéro du *Moniteur* où fut annoncée la défaite de Constantine ; elle portait par-devant une affiche de M. Musard et une annonce de M. Mozart, brevetés tous deux, l'un pour le bruit que fait sa musique, et l'autre pour le bruit que ne fait pas son papier. Sur l'autre face était étalée une énorme affiche de la Porte-St-Martin, qui montrait écrit en gros caractères : "Invention simple à l'usage des simples, par M. Balisson de Rougemont."[7]

> The original fabric of her dress had disappeared under examples of its uses. One side displayed the sample issue of *La Presse*, a 40-franc newspaper, the other showed the issue of the *Moniteur* that told of the defeat of Constantine. On her front she wore a poster for Musard and an advertisement for Mozart, patented, both of them, one for the noise made by his music and the other for the lack of noise made by his paper. Her back was covered by an enormous poster for the Porte-St-Martin theater, whose bold type touted a "Simple invention for simple people, by Balisson de Rougemont."

Vaudeville revues routinely staged the old and the new year as an old and a young woman, and they made a practice of costuming figures associated with the press in newspapers. The anonymous journalist for *Le Charivari* combined the two tendencies, dressing the personification of 1836 in newspapers and advertisements to proclaim the age of press publicity. What is more, the newspapers used to dress 1836 were specific numbers of named papers, one of them indicating a media innovation and the other a military loss. Such specificity did not characterize vaudeville images of the press. The poster cited at the end of the quoted passage, however, forgoes details to make fun of all the plays staged at the Porte Saint-Martin. Unlike the press, the theater is treated as an unchanging series of simple-minded entertainments. Individual issues of newspapers are contrasted against the generic treatment of yet another indistinguishable play by Balisson de Rougemont. This newspaper's description of year-end vaudeville revues privileged datelines and downplayed theatrical authorship. *Le Charivari*'s article also made a newspaper event the clincher in an argument about whether or not the year 1836 would be cursed for her misdeeds. The 1836 character, having stated, "J'aime mieux être maudite qu'oubliée" (I'd rather be cursed than forgotten), achieves her goal by pointing out that she killed Carrel. It was, however, Émile de Girardin who killed Armand Carrel in a duel over calumny (see introduction), but this death of one newspaper editor at the hands of another is the culminating example of the vices of 1836. The article concludes with "1836! Carrel!"[8]

Two of the vaudeville revues to which the *Charivari* journalist compared this article had also staged the press, but in their versions, characters representing *La Presse* and *Le Siècle* (at the Ambigu-comique) and the *feuilleton* and *La Gazette des tribunaux* (at the Palais-Royal) were personified by actors. As such they were put before theater audiences as institutions to be judged. Whereas *Le Charivari*'s article privileged the newspaper's ability to mark time by documenting events, the vaudevilles' newspaper characters proclaimed their editorial principles while playing on the more incongruous aspects of their social roles. In the Palais-Royal's revue (*L'Année sur la sellette* by Courcy, Bayard, and Théaulon), *La Gazette des tribunaux* has come to report on the trial of 1836 for her readers, who love a good adultery case, while Feuilleton advertises his *grand format* and forty-franc price and is teased for not always having seen the plays and events he covers in his columns.[9] With the birth of the serial novel (or *roman-feuilleton*) in 1836 and the increased emphasis on relatively nonpolitical parts of the new press, the *feuilleton* was a section in transition and was the subject (and sometimes location) of much debate about the role of commerce in the new press. At the end of 1836, both *Le Charivari* and *L'Année sur la sellette* deemed forty-franc subscriptions to have been a notable event of the year, but the newspaper tied its invention to an identifiable issue of *La Presse*, while the vaudeville had the *feuilleton* laud the logic of advertisement, reinforcing the idea that information published in the *rez-de-chaussée* would henceforth be entirely commercially determined.

Having declared itself to be treating the same events as the vaudeville revues, *Le Charivari* reports on them as news, while the vaudevilles analyze the social implications of commercializing the press. *Le Charivari* may have been one of the more contestatory publications of the period, but vaudevilles paid more attention to the institutional and social effects of commercial publicity.[10]

Vaudeville revues were expert at using temporarily anonymous figures to say revealing things about newspapers. Characters representing publications and social phenomena associated with the press appeared in costumes meant to recall or comment on their role in society, but definitive identification usually occurred during the dialogue. One of the annual revues mentioned in the *Charivari* article, Clairville and Delatour's *1836 dans la lune*, cast *La Presse* and *Le Siècle* as allegorical characters who represented both the news-papers in question and the entities for which they were named (the press and the century). The characters are young, as befits new inventions; La Presse is dressed in a paper printer's hat reminiscent of the *Trois Glorieuses* and subse-quent struggles over press freedom, while Le Siècle is clad "en argent," which could be money or silver.[11] When the play's narrator, Gaillard, asks La Presse whether she is the press of 1830, La Presse says that no, she is the press of 1836. When another character asks, "Est-ce que ce n'est pas la même chose" (Isn't that the same thing?), she responds:

> Non vraiment, la Presse de 1830 malgré son penchant pour la démo-cratie ne s'adressait qu'aux personnes riches, elle parlait du peuple aux gens qui ne la comprenaient, et qui avaient intérêt à ne la pas comprendre, moi je m'adresse à la classe ouvrière, je livre mon esprit aux personnes indigentes ; je distribue mes bienfaits dans la rue.[12]

> No, truly, for the press of 1830, despite its penchant for democracy, addressed itself only to the rich: it spoke of the people to those who did not understand them and had no interest in doing so. I address myself to the working class, I share my wit with poor people; I dis-tribute my benefits in the street.

Gaillard reacts by saying, "ce n'est pas beau" (that's not nice), and by arguing that such largesse "n'est guère propre à vous attirer l'estime, à vous donner de la considération" (is unlikely to attract esteem or consideration). He takes advantage of the press's allegorical onstage existence as a woman to accuse her of prostituting herself. This was an accusation frequently leveled against the new press (and particularly *La Presse*) because of its dependence on com-mercial publicity. Ambiguity over which press this is—the newspaper or the institution—allows the characters to air multiple perspectives on the advan-tages and dangers of the press's new commercial model.

For the scene is not a one-sided critique. La Presse has an answer for Gaillard: "Au contraire," she retorts, "ne vivons-nous pas à une époque de popularité. Conspiration, révolution, réputation, tout s'est fait dans la rue, c'est de là que sont sortis beaucoup de nos grands hommes et qui sait, peut-être quelques-unes de nos grandes dames" (do we not live in an age of popularity? Conspiracy, revolution, reputation, everything starts out in the street—that's where many of our great men and who knows, perhaps some of our great ladies, come from). She concludes her case with the argument that Émile de Girardin had put forth in response to critics of his new model for newspapers: advertising revenue allowed for the democratization of the press's readership, so more people had more access to a supposedly impartial mix of information.

In a sort of hymn to the fourth estate as imagined by Girardin, La Presse sings:

> Vous le savez la France était bien sombre, Notre Paris n'était qu'un noir tombeau, / Et tout un peuple allait mourir dans l'ombre. / Quand de la presse apparut le flambeau : / Et ce flambeau qui brillait à la ronde / Fut un soleil qui vous montra vos droits ; / De sa lumière il éclairait le monde, / De ses rayons il aveuglait les rois. / Et cependant j'étais encore si fière / Que je craignais de me mésallier / Je parlais bien pour la classe ouvrière, / Mais je fuyais le toit de l'ouvrier. / Je me donnais à prix d'or au plus riche / Que mon langage offensait bien souvent ; / Vous me voyez moins bégueule et moins chiche, / Au peuple seul j'appartiens maintenant . . . J'ai dans ses rangs, propagé mes lumières, / Je l'ai guidé, mes travaux l'ont instruit, / Et, si sa main brisa les réverbères, / C'est qu'il vit clair au milieu de la nuit.

> France was somber, you know, Paris was a dark tomb / And an entire population was going to die in ignorance. / When the light of the press appeared / And this torch that shone all around / was a sun that showed you your rights; / It lit up the world with its light, / With its rays it blinded kings. And yet, I was still so proud / That I was afraid of marrying beneath myself / I spoke for the working class / but avoided its home. / Expensive, I gave myself to the rich / who were often offended by my words; / I stand before you less prudish, less mean, / I belong to the people now. . . . I have spread my light among them, / I've guided them, my work has educated them, / And, if streetlights were broken by their hand, / It's because they could see through the dark.

For all her glorious self-promotion, though, La Presse is mocked for her forward ways by onlookers: "Tudieu ! Quelle gaillarde !" (Zounds! What a bawd!) says one, "ce pauvre Siècle aura toutes les peines du monde à la suivre" (poor Siècle will have a world of trouble following her). The nineteenth century's ability to keep up with its new media and the competition between the two newspapers whose invention launched its latest expansion are confounded. The figures in this scene perform the jumble into which press innovations have thrown information transmission. For the sophisticated spectator, the multiple meanings would seem clever. For the less acute, the basic claims of the new press are laid out in La Presse's song. Any audience confusion surrounding those claims was a potential indication that they had not been fulfilled, as was the laughter their critique elicited. The inherent polyvalence of allegorical figures allows both pedagogy about media and critiques of the press to coexist when newspapers are personified. This is a clever solution to the dilemma of how to amuse socially mixed audiences. If nothing else, characters who represented newspapers ensured that messages about the new role of the press were being delivered and debated by people, not just in print. Year-end vaudeville revues showed and told their audiences that what once would have been negotiated between citizens was now being debated between newspapers.

For the press in question is both categorically ambiguous (are these figures Girardin's *La Presse* and Dutacq's *Le Siècle*, or are they the press and the century?) and historically precise. The ambiguity, in addition to allowing for exposition, also gestures to the fact that much of the press did follow *La Presse*'s lead quite quickly, cutting their subscription prices and increasing advertising. La Presse's songs place this movement in time. This is not the heroic press of 1830, whose resistance to government censorship helped initiate the July Monarchy. It is the press of 1836, whose agenda is different and has to do with getting information to the people, teaching new members of the electorate. By endowing newspapers with bodies,[13] which they were then accused of using inappropriately, plays could critique the press's reliance on seduction, which operated through a combination of entertaining content and advertising's ability to create desire.[14]

What kept critical ambiguity interesting in vaudevilles was that audiences were expected to react to the jokes and songs they heard. The audience interaction that had been the heritage of the vaudeville since its performances at the *foire*, along with what Olivier Bara has referred to as vaudeville's "théâtralité joyeusement exhibée" (gleefully displayed theatricality) were especially marked in the vaudeville finales.[15] Though strategies such as explaining temporarily anonymous figures were part of the irony that sought to create audience complicity throughout vaudevilles, the vaudeville finale was the consecrated moment for the theater public to join in singing and to judge a play. These ensemble pieces, which were often conclusions drawn by several of the characters of revues, turned judgment over to spectators.

There were those, however, who insisted that vaudevilles, especially year-end revues, were unworthy of judgment. Chief among them were a certain number of theater critics writing for the new press.

Most theater critics reviewed vaudevilles with frequently stated reluctance, insisting on the similarity of such plays to one another and to well-worn models, and on their lack of literary merit. *Feuilletonistes* compared vaudevilles unfavorably with various parts of the newspaper. They called *prologues d'ouverture* (vaudevilles written for the openings of theaters) prospectuses, and presented end-of-year revues as second-rate imitations of *petits journaux*, or as *lanternes magiques* (magic lanterns), which projected whatever recent events were fed into them.[16]

Because annual vaudeville revues were both formulaic and concerned with recent trends, concurrent plays did tend to resemble one another. They had material in common. They also had material in common with the *feuilleton*, whose authors so enjoyed denigrating them. Newspaper critics, who earned their living giving accounts of dramatic successes and failures, could hardly resist taking a dismissive attitude toward jokey annual summaries of plays and innovations. Théophile Gautier, who wrote variants on the same complaints about vaudeville revues year after year, contended:

> Les revues ne sont et ne peuvent être qu'un ramassis de mots et de plaisanteries usés. C'est la mise en action de la quatrième page des journaux, moins les annonces médicales et les facéties industrielles dont le comique sérieux ne saurait être dépassé. Vous y voyez toujours figurer . . . tout ce qui a occupé les grands et petits feuilletons pendant cinquante-deux semaines. Vous conviendrez que cela n'est guère amusant, surtout pour nous autres qui avons fait les susdits feuilletons.[17]

> Revues are not and cannot be anything more than a collection of used-up puns and jokes. They are the fourth page of newspapers put in action, minus the medical ads and the industrial jokes whose serious comedy would be impossible to surpass. You always see what has been in the great and small *feuilletons* for fifty-two weeks. You must agree that it's hardly amusing, especially for those of us who wrote the *feuilletons* to begin with.

Gautier was the critic who most consistently insisted on all that vaudeville revues owed to *feuilletons*, but he was hardly alone in comparing the two to the former's detriment.[18] Eugène Guinot at *Le Siècle* said of a play that "les auteurs de la pièce, comme tous les vaudevillistes, n'ignorent rien de ce qui se publie ; ils dévorent les journaux, ils en font leur pâture" (the authors of the play, like all *vaudevillistes*, are aware of everything that is published; they devour the newspapers, they feed off them),[19] while Charles de Matharel, reviewing a vaudeville that treated the press for *Le Siècle*, wrote, "Ils (les journaux) donnent aussi chaque jour des idées aux auteurs dramatiques, qui, sans les journaux, seraient souvent bien à plaindre" (Every day the newspapers give ideas to playwrights, who would often be in dire straits without them).[20] In another column, Guinot told the story of an *auteur dramatique* (dramatic author) who nearly had a duel in a dispute over how long he was taking to read *Le Charivari* in a café. Guinot explained the author's slow progress by suggesting that he "cherchait sans doute des mots piquants pour ses pièces de théâtre" (was doubtless looking for clever barbs for his plays).[21] *Le Charivari* was understood to be a particularly rich source for vaudevillistes because of its comic and subversive tone and its combination of written and visual jokes. Matharel even wondered why revues were only *spirituel* (witty) once a year, when *Le Charivari* found enough material to be funny daily.[22]

Vaudeville revues were annual, and in the new press, *actualité* (topicality) was of prime importance, so saying that a vaudeville revue was old news was condemning it based on new criteria to which it could not correspond, bound as it was to "l'éternel cadre inventé il y a quelque cent ans pour les revues de fin d'année" (the eternal framework invented several hundred years ago for year-end revues).[23] Critics' judgment was sometimes questioned on the basis of the fact that they had to work fast to produce weekly theater reviews. They had little extra time to reflect on the plays they had seen. For critics, denigrating vaudevilles for their out-of-dateness had the advantage of associating *actualité* and accuracy, rather than supporting the inverse relationship between pace and judgment on the basis of which they themselves were sometimes criticized.[24] Critics presented vaudeville revues as the old media and, by implication, their own *feuilletons* as the new.

Critics insisted on the fixity of vaudeville revues' structure, not just to make them seem out-of-date and static but also to emphasize what they, as critics, brought to theater reviews. Again and again, critics compared vaudeville revues to *lanternes magiques*. The critic of *Le Constitutionnel* complained of year-end revues that "ce genre d'ouvrage exige peu d'invention : il ne s'agit que de trouver un cadre ingénieux où vous puissiez faire passer rapidement, comme les figures d'une lanterne magique, tous les ridicules du jour" (this sort of work requires little creativity: all you have to do is find an ingenious frame through which you can make all the follies of the day pass quickly, like the figures in a magic lantern).[25] Janin, too, said of a vaudeville, "Vous voyez tour à tour passer devant vous, comme dans une lanterne magique mal éclairée, toutes sortes de choses bien étonnées de se trouver ensemble" (You see, passing before you as in a badly lit magic lantern, all sorts of things that are astonished to find themselves together).[26]

The magic lantern comparison made vaudevilles seem childish and crude, and it emphasized the episodic character of vaudeville revues. In an article lamenting the state of theatrical literature, Eugène Guinot wrote, "Tout est haché et servi en vaudeville. . . . Dans ce temps où on ne lit plus, où l'on ne sait rien, où l'on se contente d'un peu de tout ce qui compose un gros rien, le vaudeville règne en maître absolu" (Everything is chopped up and served as vaudeville. . . . In this time when no one reads anymore, no one knows anything, and people are happy with a little of each which makes up a big nothing, the vaudeville reigns as absolute master).[27]

Whether they compared vaudeville revues to mincemeat or magic lanterns, critics were sure to point out that in vaudeville, coherence was lacking in favor of digestibility. Joseph-Marc Bailbé, in a study of the uses of magic lanterns, notes that Janin had also used the magic lantern as a plot device in his novella *Le Gâteau des rois*, probably out of respect for its efficacy as a simpler means of access to literature.[28] In Janin's novel, a boy sets out to save his family from starvation by putting on shows with his magic lantern. Most lanterns were simple devices in which a candle and a mirror projected light through a painted glass plate. They tended to show scenes from well-known stories. Sometimes text was included at the bottom of plates, but mostly it was up to the person operating the lantern to provide any narration deemed necessary. Like the stories most often painted on lantern plates, vaudeville revues followed minimal standard plots and privileged the visual. By calling vaudeville revues magic lanterns, though, *feuilletonistes* ignored the clever visual puns often included in vaudeville costumes and scenarios (not to mention the dialogue and songs), choosing instead to portray revues as entry-level art, amusing to the eyes of an uncultivated public but lacking the narrative and esprit that *feuilletonistes* brought to their version of dramatic reviews. *Feuilletons*, though they, like vaudevilles, reviewed a variety of plays, were held together by the wit of the *feuilletoniste*.[29]

Critics defended their turf on the grounds of both *actualité* and poetics. Successful July Monarchy critics, most notably Janin and Gautier, had immediately recognizable personal writing styles. Comparisons they made between vaudevilles and magic lanterns emphasized the added value of critical thought and of "spiritually" turned phrases in newspaper *feuilletons*. Critics still praised the gaiety and esprit of some vaudeville revues—it was often the only direct evaluation they offered—but as long as they compared vaudevilles to old news and magic lanterns, they relegated them to a role in the literary field which was structurally inferior to that of the *feuilleton*. The magic lantern retained its civic pedagogical appeal, as an 1869 image by Daumier attests (see figure 1.)[30] Here the magic-lantern vote (*scrutin*) that Marianne holds is the source of light that projects liberty (LIBERTÉ) for spectators to see. In the 1830s and 1840s, though, if vaudevilles were assumed to lack both currency and cleverness, they merited little consideration. Vaudevilles' continued success in theaters indicated broad support among audiences, but newspapers' consistent dismissal of them constituted a voluntary disavowal of the popular on the part of *feuilletonistes*.[31]

Such antagonism did not go unnoticed. In *Ah ! enfin !* a play written for the reopening of the Théâtre du Vaudeville in 1848, the personification of the theater complains, "Pourquoi me réveiller ? Je suis peu littéraire / Au dire des journaux, / Quand ils disent cela, / Vite, afin de leur plaire, / Je deviens litté-raire, / Et le public s'en va" (Why wake me up? According to the newspapers, I'm not very literary. When they say that, I quickly become more literary in order to please them, and the public flees).[32] To ensure that its new audience will remain engaged, this line is quickly followed by an outline of the theater's

Figure 1. Honoré Daumier, "Lanterne magique!"
Le Charivari, November 19, 1869, 3. Courtesy of
Bibliothèque nationale de France.

republican background and a version of "La Marseillaise" adapted to blame
critics for le Théâtre du Vaudeville's woes: "Allons enfants du Vaudeville. /
Le jour d'épreuve est arrivé ; / Contre nous du critique hostile / Le feuilleton
s'est soulevé, / Le feuilleton . . ." (Onward children of the vaudeville, the day
of proof is upon us. The hostile critic, the feuilleton has risen against us).
Reinstated as the French national anthem after the July 1830 revolution,
"La Marseillaise" had, at this point, become a popular way for audiences
to intervene in theatrical performances. When they decided that a jolt of
republican patriotism was in order, they simply demanded that the actors
stop their performance and sing "La Marseillaise."[33] The actress Rachel, who
was considered the queen of tragedy, declaimed the song, rather than singing
it, in 1848.[34] Explicit efforts to rally an audience at a theater's opening were
likely to include "La Marseillaise" one way or another. What is remarkable,
though, is that in this vaudeville's rewrite of the anthem, the enemy at the
gates is the *feuilleton*. Vaudeville, faced with critics who excluded it based on
their own literary criteria, not only claimed its popular nonliterary status but
used it to rally its audience. In this rewrite, the anthem's "la Patrie" becomes
"le Vaudeville," while "la tyrannie" raising a bloody standard becomes a hos-

tile critic wielding a *feuilleton*. Audiences weren't the only social body that could demand a moment of patriotism, though. Vaudevilles, too, could co-opt the formula, demanding that audiences join them in solidarity faced with the tyranny of newspaper critics. Reaching across the fourth wall in a send-up of the song of the moment, *Ah ! enfin!* seems to signal that there is no need to exact a "Marseillaise" from its actors: they know its significance so well that they can use it on behalf their theater. This usage opens the question of whether that is what other theaters were doing by having the song spoken or sung, but that is in keeping with the usual irreverent stance of a vaudeville joke. If the vaudeville version of the press was embodied in 1836 as an actress of questionable morals, by 1848 the press's most changed section, the *feuilleton*, had become the tyrant against whom citizens were to arm themselves.

The commercialization of the press in 1836 changed newspaper marketing practices very quickly. New forty-franc papers claimed that their increased readership was an indication that more people were gaining access to news and information. For new subscribers, this may have been the case, but vaudevilles were quick to point out that such claims were funded by advertisers and so could hardly be expected to remain impartial, and that the price of annual subscriptions was still well beyond the reach of most people in society. The structural similarities between newspaper and vaudeville reviews from early January reveal that the former were concerned with datelines and the latter with broader social effects. If vaudevilles were well placed to send up social phenomena, papers were liable to denigrate vaudeville revues as crude, old-fashioned, and out-of-date. Newspaper critics, or *feuilletonistes*, whose role was expanding with the growth of the press, defined their own esprit as more sophisticated than that of annual vaudeville revues. Several critics, such as Théophile Gautier, are still read to this day, though mostly in their capacity as novelists and poets. The genre and medium they were both appropriating and writing against, though it has been mostly forgotten today, was a popular and vibrant form of education and critique. The songs that characterized vaudevilles were set up for creative pastiche, and the embodied newspapers that danced across the stage were more entertaining to more people (including those who could not read) than the skillfull verbal jousts that critics wrote to counter their staged critiques.

Chapter 2

Do New Media Encourage Scandalmongering?
The View from 1838

Calomnie, or calumny, the spreading of false and malicious rumors, was memorably put to music by Gioachino Rossini, in Don Bazile's aria from *The Barber of Seville*. As a music teacher, Don Bazile uses terms from his own profession—*pianissimo . . . piano . . . rinforzando . . . crescendo*—to explain how poisonous information can catch the attention of the public and take flight. Rossini's opera was based on Pierre-Augustin Caron de Beaumarchais's play *Le Barbier de Seville*, the first work in his Figaro trilogy. Beaumarchais, who began his own career as a music teacher to King Louis XV's daughters, owed the enomous success of the trilogy in part to his musical tableaux, which, playing on the vaudeville tradition, put new words to existing tunes, inviting audience complicity even as he advanced his plots.[1] His focus on calumny proved to be a precursor for the work of *comédie-vaudevilles* in the 1830s and 1840s, as they grappled with explaining the pressures of an industrializing press to their audiences.

From 1838 to 1840, the Théâtre Français, as the Comédie Française was then known, produced a spate of vaudeville-influenced plays about calumny that suggested that changes in press practices might be encouraging the publication of slanderous information. Unlike the vaudevilles described in chapter 1, these were five-act plays, selected by the same prestigious national theater that Beaumarchais himself had courted assiduously. Their authors were, for the most part, respected playwrights, and the calumny plays they produced had the hallmarks of prestige, though their remaining connections to the vaudeville genre sometimes cast doubt on those pretentions.[2]

Two plays from 1838, Desnoyer and Labat's *Richard Savage* and Casimir Delavigne's *La Popularité*, and one from 1840, Eugène Scribe's *Le Verre d'eau ou les effets et les causes*, took eighteenth-century England as their setting. In eighteenth-century London, as it is presented in these plays, the press is free, and the reputations of noble ladies and their powerful consorts are in the hands of journalists, who can protect them or bring about their disgrace by publishing their secrets. Like *Chatterton*, Alfred de Vigny's Romantic hit of 1836, these dramas lament the incompatibility between noble poetic or political ideals and the Machiavellian ways of governments and of aristocratic society.[3] Unlike *Chatterton*, though, these plays make the press central to their analysis of the ways and means of influence.

Concern about how artists were to make a living after the age of noble patronage was already a major Romantic theme in the early 1830s, when Vigny's *Chatterton* demonstrated how a poet housed by an industrialist might starve, artistically and physically.[4] Inspired by the brief sad life of Thomas Chatterton, who died at the age of seventeen in London in 1770, Vigny's play made Chatterton an out-of-work poet living with John and Kitty Bell, a penny-pinching businessman and his angelic wife. When the play opened at the Théâtre Français in 1835, Marie Dorval, Vigny's lover at the time, played Kitty Bell, and fell spectacularly down an on-stage staircase each evening as she died of grief at Chatterton's suicide.[5] The actors of the Théâtre Français were not pleased to be joined by Dorval, who usually acted in less prestigious boulevard theaters. Wary of their reactions, she had practiced her staircase tumble in secret, counting on the play's success to validate the rather melodramatic gesture. Her plan worked: the play did succeed, and she was lauded by critics for her performance in it. In his version of the story of a doomed Romantic poet, Vigny used England (which he knew relatively well given his adaptations of Shakespeare and his English wife) as the land of unforgiving capitalism, and of social ambitions that privileged rank over elevation of the soul.

While Vigny's plot was part of a Romantic tradition which was by then accustomed to looking across the channel (Hugo's 1827 *Cromwell* and its preface are famous examples), it also participated in a growing sense that England was a current political and commercial powerhouse whose influence might not be as benign as its aesthetic and individual freedoms would suggest. One conservative critic asked how France could possibly want to imitate a country "pour qui l'argent est tout, et chez laquelle tout finit par un marché !!!" (for which money is everything, and where everything concludes with a deal!!!).[6] Politically, the July Monarchy already looked to its neighbor as a constitutional monarchy worth emulating, but, as recent scholars of revolutionary historiography have shown, the idea that London might also be emulated for its economic and industrial advances solidified with England's commercial success in the 1830s.[7]

Émile de Girardin, unlike his Romantic contemporaries, embraced the commercial successes of the British press. In his 1836 prospectus for *La Presse*, Girardin presented the *Times* of London as a business model for his new paper. Where Romantic dramas had sought pity for impoverished poets unable to earn a living with their art, 1838 calumny plays, staged after the birth of the forty-franc press, proposed to use the press's increasing ability to generate popularity (verging on what we would now call populism) to right the wrongs of a media and social sphere that they portrayed as stacked against artists and idealists.

Unlike the year-end revues and other vaudevilles that explained the risks of the commercial press to popular audiences, the more prestigious plays about the press considered in this chapter threatened to use the press's influence on public opinion to advance the interests of poets and politicians through spin and slander. Contemporaries saw the press as a double-edged sword. As Jacques-Charles Bailleul, a moderate lawyer during the Revolution and a sometime journalist for *Le Constitutionnel*, put it,

> Si la presse est une puissance, un pouvoir, comme nous l'avons rappelé plus haut, n'est-ce pas elle-même qui s'est investée de ces titres ? et si elle est fondée dans cette pretention, ne le doit-elle pas à l'abus qu'elle en a fait et qu'elle fait tous les jours ? . . . ce n'est que par le mal qu'elle fait qu'elle est un pouvoir. C'est une arme à deux tranchants ; serait-il impossible de constater que l'un de ces deux tranchants est bien autrement aiguisé, bien autrement acéré que l'autre ?[8]

> If the press is a power, an estate, as we called it above, isn't that because the press has given itself these titles? And if there is a basis for its pretention, isn't it the abuse of its power that the press practices every day? It is because of the harm that it does that the press is a power. It is a double-edged sword. Is it so impossible to say that one of those edges is sharper, steelier than the other?

Bailleul's question—about whether the power of the press might come from its abuses—is one that Desnoyer and Labat's, Delavigne's, and Scribe's calumny plays raised, too. Like *Chatterton*, their plays were set in eighteenth-century London, but whereas Vigny saw a society that was particularly harsh toward its poets, these playwrights saw a context in which entrepreneurial journalists could wield influence. On stage, journalists' power is grounded in their ability to destroy individual reputations by publishing calumnies, but they mostly use that threat to bring about virtuous ends. They do so by influencing popularity, a more ambiguous phenomenon than calumny, in that it designates group enthusiasm, whether that energy is used for good or for ill.

Desnoyer and Labat's *Richard Savage*

Desnoyer and Labat, both seasoned *vaudevillistes*, adapted their play, *Richard Savage*, a from a recent novel about the fate of the eponymous *poète maudit* (1697–1743),[9] to focus on his friend, Richard Steele (1672–1729), a pioneering journalist, while Delavigne, who had been celebrated as a liberal nationalist playwright in the early 1830s, personified various Parisian newspapers as characters in *La Popularité*, an eighteenth-century political drama, and set it in England under the reign of George II (1727–1760). Though the two plays were performed within weeks of each other, Desnoyer and Labat's play focused on the ways that press-based popularity could serve social transparency, while Delavigne's portrayal of the relationship between press coverage and popularity was primarily based on a pre-1830s vision of the press as a natural extension of political oratory.[10]

For Desnoyer and Labat, this press-based popularity is the defining attribute of Richard Steele, the ancestor of the modern *feuilletoniste* for whom they created a central role in their play. Richard Savage, Steele's poet/ playwright friend, is an illegitimate child of the woman who is now married to the Lord Mayor of London. In Desnoyer and Labat's version, Savage's too-public request for recognition from his mother leads him to be threatened with imprisonment for insanity.[11] His friend Steele, as a journalist, is able to rally bystanders to their cause when Savage is about to be carried off, but when the superior force of the Lord Mayor's troops overcomes this resistance, Savage kills the Lord Mayor. The journalist and the poet are sentenced to death until Savage's biological parents intervene to save them both. Barbara Cooper notes, in her edition of the play, that Desnoyer, one of its authors, had already been a coauthor of a play by which Émile de Girardin had declared his own existence as the illegitimate son of Alexandre de Girardin, a general, so the theme was one that connected to the world of the new press on several levels.[12]

In Desnoyer and Labat's play, Steele is both a feared newspaper critic and a loyal friend who, when the stakes are high, uses his ability to communicate with the people to ensure that a crime is prevented. When Steele brings a crowd to witness the attempts of the villain, Lord Mayor Lushington, to imprison his friend, the poet Richard Savage, as crazy, Lushington accuses him of creating scandal. Steele replies, "Le scandale, milord ! Vous voyez bien que ce n'est pas moi qui le cause," then, "au nom de cette loi qui nous protège tous, et devant laquelle le souverain lui-même s'incline avec respect, je vous défie d'attenter à la liberté d'un citoyen de Londres" (Scandal, my lord! Surely you can see that I'm not the cause of it . . . in the name of the law which protects us all, and before which even the sovereign bows with respect, I defy you to violate the liberty of a citizen of London!),[13] at which point the crowd of "peuple" he has brought along prevents Lushington's men from taking Savage away. The imperatives of public accountability Steele calls into play are reminiscent of the press's role as the fourth estate, a role whose positive portrayal here marks the play's politics as liberal. This journalist uses his influence, which derives from his mass readership, to protect individual rights, an end worthy of older liberal publicity. A critic uses his power correctly, while acknowledging that much of his influence comes from his ability to use it mean-spiritedly. Desnoyer and Labat read current press innovations against a British backdrop to protect their play from the censors, while nonetheless pointing out the virtues of a freer press. Doing so suggested to attentive audience members that theater censorship in France had driven public portrayals of the Parisian press to disguise themselves, a situation hardly indicative of a free society.

Jules Janin, who frequently articulated his vision of the critic's role, appreciated Desnoyer and Labat's representation of the power dynamics between a journalist and his readership. He wrote that "déjà Richard Steele se met à l'abri derrière son journal. Il sait très bien que de là lui vient sa force et qu'ainsi protégé il est inviolable" (already Richard Steele takes shelter behind his newspaper. He knows very well that it is the source of his power, and that its protection makes him inviolable).[14] Janin heartily approved of both the role of Richard Steele and the performance of the actor who played him. He was careful to point out that Addison and Steele were the forerunners of the current press, and said of Steele:

> Il est l'arbitre souverain de ce peuple qui le lit et l'écoute. Il lui dicte son esprit, il lui donne sa pensée, il lui impose ses préjugés, il le dispose à ses amours, il lui fait partager ses vengeances, il parle beaucoup plus haut et beaucoup plus loin que ne saurait parler l'avocat au barreau, le prédicateur dans sa chaire, l'orateur à sa tribune . . . il devient tout simplement un des pouvoirs de l'état, troisième ou quatrième pouvoir, peu lui importe, mais enfin un pouvoir. Admirable profession qu'Addison a trouvé, que le *Spectateur* a fondée, et dont Richard Steele était un des plus vifs, des plus ingénieux, des plus gais adeptes ![15]

> He is the sovereign arbiter for the people who read and listen to him. He dictates their wit, gives them their thoughts, he imposes his prejudices and inclines them towards what he loves, he has them share in his vengeances, he speaks louder and projects farther than the lawyer at the bar, the priest in his pulpit, or the orator at his stand could . . . he simply becomes one of those powers of the state, third or fourth power, he doesn't care, but a power. What an admirable profession! Invented by Addison, founded by the *Spectator*; Richard Steele was one of its liveliest, most ingenious and cheerful practitioners.

Janin's reference to the "people who read and listen to (journalists)" takes advantage of the theatrical nature of Desnoyer and Labat's representation (people are actually listening to it) to reinforce traditional continuities between the rhetoric of oratory and that of journalism.[16] As a permanently self-serving journalist (as we will see in chapter 5), Janin was well aware that the figure of the journalist as a public orator was more prestigious than that

of the journalist threatening wrongdoers with publishing slander, even though
that is exactly what Richard Steele does in the play *Richard Savage*.

La Popularité according to Delavigne

Like *Richard Savage*, Casimir Delavigne's *La Popularité* projected its commentary on the Parisian press into an earlier English context, and, like Desnoyer and Labat's play, Delavigne's emphasizes the extent to which a popular
newspaper can sway a fickle and divided crowd. Delavigne's plot is constructed around a young politician, Edward Lindsey, whose efforts to rally
support for a coalition government are challenged by his former girlfriend,
Lady Stafford, who is conspiring with the Jacobite rebellion, and by Godwin,
the corrupt populist journalist who threatens to expose her identity and to
calumny Lindsey's father. Godwin's execution of these threats does, indeed,
drive the former couple apart permanently and casts aspersions on the elder
Lindsey's name, though the audience is privy to the honorable motives behind
the slandered man's apparently problematic behavior. In addition to shifting
country and century for his meditation on the power of the press, though,
Delavigne also makes each of his characters a stand-in for a July Monarchy
Parisian newspaper, identifying them as such by giving them lines of dialogue
borrowed from the newspapers in question. Delphine de Girardin, in her
"Courrier de Paris" of December 8, 1838, describes *La Popularité* as "une
comédie politique . . . c'est un dialogue plus ou moins animé entre le *Journal
des débats*, le *Courrier français*, et la *Presse*, qui, pour sa part, a fourni à l'auteur plus d'un beau vers" (a political comedy . . . it is a more or less animated
dialogue between the *Journal des débats*, the *Courrier français*, and *La Presse*,
the last of which provided the author with material for more than one good
verse).[17] Though her husband's newspaper, *La Presse*, for which she writes a
column, is represented by the main character, Edward Lindsey, Girardin finds
"la politique des journaux déjà forte ennuyeuse à lire dans un bon fauteuil, au
coin d'un bon feu, nous la trouvons bien autrement pénible à entendre, assise
sur une mauvaise chaise dans cette botte de danse qu'on appellee une loge"
(press politics boring to read, even in a good armchair by a warm fire, we find
them even duller to listen to when sitting on an uncomfortable chair in one of
those dancing shoes that passes for a theater box).[18] Delavigne's vision of the
press, as reflected in *La Popularité*, remains divided by political allegiance and
modeled on in-person political rhetoric. To Delphine de Girardin, his vision
of the press is out of date and his nostalgia for it makes for a boring play.

   To the extent that there was critical consensus concerning *La Popularité*,
it was that though the verse was skillfully executed, the allegorical structure
gave the play a cold artificiality that limited its appeal. There is a certain irony
to this assessment, in that the popularity to which the title refers is gained
through effective oratory. Though newspapers within the plot are used to

further various causes, it is the rousing speeches of Edward/*La Presse* which seemed to promise him *popularité* to begin with. Delavigne, by making *La Presse* the hero of his play, acknowledged that the forty-franc press could indeed move large numbers of readers, but he also warned that the *popularité* it achieved was not loyal, and readers could easily enough transfer their affections to another newspaper, even to one with a very different political line. The fiercely Jacobite Lady Stafford/*La Quotidienne* declares the impossibility of her union with Édouard/*La Presse* in the following terms: "Je conspire ! Ce grand mot vous rattache aux destins d'un empire/ On a, comme Édouard, sa popularité : / Ce qu'on fait sera su, ce qu'on dit, répété ; / Tout semble à vos regards réfléchir votre gloire, / Et comme dans sa glace, on se voit dans l'histoire" (I conspire! This great word attaches you to the destiny of an empire / Like Edward, one gains popularity: / what one does will be known, what one says, repeated / Everything reflects your glory back to you / And, as in your mirror, you see yourself in history).[19] Reflected into history, press influence is very much a game of mirrors, in which Delavigne finds Jacobite and Chartist doubles for monarchist and liberal Parisian dailies. The libels that accompany their disagreements point to one widespread concern about the forty-franc press, but Delavigne's discomfort with nascent mass journalism is perhaps best revealed by his efforts to keep his allegory about it functioning according to a system in which newspapers still represented consistent points of view, and his relative failure to do so. *Le Constitutionnel*, an old-fashioned liberal paper whose political views were well aligned with Delavigne's, lauded the play and printed excerpts, while Delphine de Girardin at *La Presse* both decoded and mixed up Delavigne's system, on the one hand explaining it, on the other saying that Lady Stafford went from being *La Mode* to embodying *La Quotidienne*, a monarchist journal, within the course of the play.

Unlike Delphine de Girardin's column, with its vaudeville-esque efforts to educate readers about Delavigne's play while making fun of it at the same time, *La Quotidienne* found the play's defense of order to be pure flattery of the government. Though it was not a particularly successful play with the public, *La Popularité* was Delavigne's wobbly last stand in favor of newspapers with identifiable political allegiances. His old-fashioned approach to the media insisted that the most principled and eloquent voices ought to rule the crowd, even as his play's reception indicated disagreements within the press itself about the relevance of Delavigne's nostalgia for a time when coherent oratory could make a politician or a newspaper popular.

Scribe and Institutions

Eugène Scribe, the most successful playwright of Delavigne, Desnoyer, and Labat's generation, crossed the genres of comedy and vaudeville when he wrote plays about the workings of calumny and the machinations of the press in the 1830s and 1840s. Like his fellow dramatists, Scribe, too, set a play with a powerful pressman in eighteenth-century London. His *Le Verre d'eau, ou les effets et les causes*, takes place at the court of Queen Anne (1707–1714) and stages the struggle between Henry St. John, Viscount of Bolingbroke, head of the Tories, who wants peace with France and edits the *Examiner*, and the Duke of Marlborough, a general in the ongoing war and a Whig, whose wife is a self-interested friend of Queen Anne. The very title of the play declares that the key to its denouement is the queen's request for a glass of water. It is this small cause (a signal for a galant meeting) which triggers a chain of events that, along with Bolingbroke's management of public opinion, facilitates peace between France and England. The influence that comes into play is that of Bolingbroke's newspaper. This is a play that pretends to be about small causes with large effects, but, like *Richard Savage* and *La Popularité*, the effects are brought about by a political schemer who, as a newspaper editor, is able to manipulate the great ladies of the court into an outcome he favors. Claudine Grossir has recently pointed out that Scribe consistently used history as a pretext for his theatrical needs (in this case partly the small causes–large effects theme), and that critics such as Sainte-Beuve recognized this at the time.[20] All three of these plays, taken together, seem to suggest that when the press is influential and relatively free, as it was in London in the eighteenth century, calumny itself becomes a small causes–large effects phenomenon. Small errors in judgment on the part of highborn ladies—an affair, an affiliation with the Jacobites, a crush on a handsome soldier—make noblewomen and the politics in which they participate vulnerable to the threats of journalists who serve what are, here, mostly admirable causes through a threatening press.

As Beaumarchais's Don Basilio sang, calumny starts small and spreads. From 1838 to 1840, on the boards of the Comédie Française, playwrights imagined it spreading in London in the *Examiner* or the *Spectator*, at the hands of journalists whom they framed as mirrors for their French contemporaries. This was not just an evolution in the Romantic tendency to turn to England for examples of aesthetic freedom, nor was it simply a politic gesture toward the model of constitutional monarchy that England provided. It was also a wily way to avoid censorship of plays about the press, for commentary on current Parisian journalism, particularly if it had to do with the political establishment, tended to catch the censors' eye. Scribe's smooth ability to make his social commentary look light, to suggest critiques while retaining plausible deniability, and his reputation as a reasonable and successful man of the theater, all protected his plays to some extent from the censors' ire. Thus, he could produce, not only *La Calomnie* in 1840, but also *La Camaraderie ou la court echelle* (1837), *Les Indépendants* (1840), and *Le Puff* (1848), all of which staged a corrupt Parisian press while making only minor changes to accommodate censors' objections.[21] *La Calomnie*, if read in the context of

July Monarchy debates about limits on the freedom of the press, downplays the influence of libelous journalism. It begins with negative newspaper articles about several of the main characters, but the articles don't play a decisive role in the comedy: most of the play's calumny happens in conversations that circulate among visitors to a bathing resort in Dieppe. The protagonists who marry in the end, a government minister and his ward, are those who have learned to ignore calumny, who even see it as an uncomfortable but necessary corollary to leading an active life. This minimizing of the dangers of press misuse is consistent with Scribe's centrist approach to media innovations.

In fact, Scribe's dialogue, as Olivier Bara has pointed out, is frequently constructed so as to allow audiences to project their own interpretations on it.[22] Like the commercial press itself, his characters speak in terms just vague enough to allow a great variety of spectators to feel they are understanding the action in ways that remain informed by their own expectations. This may have helped Scribe's case with government representatives, but it seems to have frustrated theater critics, who were present for the audience reactions that Scribe's references elicited. Critics complained regularly that Scribe's commercially successful plays sought to seduce the audience, rather than to communicate any particular lesson or idea. When his *Les Indépendants*, of 1837, did not succeed, several critics seized the opportunity to air their grievances against the playwright. Jules Janin accused Scribe of pandering to the parterre. His review started by criticizing the relationships between the play's characters for being overly schematic:

> Car ces gens-là ne se parlent pas entre eux, ils ne parlent qu'au parterre. Ils font des mots non pas pour eux, non pas pour remplir et pour expliquer convenablement l'action dramatique, mais ils font des mots pour le parterre. Cette sorte d'esprit comique, qui ne reste pas dans la comédie qu'on joue, mais qui au contraire en sort à chaque instant et se précipite au-dehors comme fait l'écume du vin mousseux, doit avoir à tout prendre, la destinée de cette mousse fouettée qui n'enivre personne. La comédie ainsi faite, perd tout son caractère, toute son utilité, tout son intérêt. Vous n'avez plus devant les yeux des personnages en chair et en os qui se partagent avec acharnement la passion, l'amour, la haine, le ridicule, l'éclat de rire, les leçons de la comédie, vous avez tout au plus des marionnettes, des comédiens de bois, derrière lesquels un homme d'esprit parle au hasard, trop heureux de trouver, de temps à autre un mot qui fasse rire.[23]

> For these people do not speak between themselves, they speak to the pit. They make clever remarks, not for themselves, to fill out and explain the dramatic action, but rather for the pit. This sort of comic wit, which does not stay within the comedy being played but rather flies out like the froth of a sparkling wine, must share the destiny

of that froth, which excites no one. Comedy done this way loses all
of its character, all of its usefulness, all of its interest. You no longer
have before you people in flesh and blood who share passion, love,
hate, ridicule, who burst out laughing (the lessons of comedy). At
most, you have marionettes, wooden actors behind which a clever
man speaks at random, pleased, from time to time, to come up with
a barb that draws some laughs.

Besides, he says, the play was badly performed and the parterre was bored.
Scribe had, by abandoning character development in favor of political esprit,
made a vaudeville of his comedy.

Scribe's other, more successful plays about the uses of corruption and nepotism had also elicited critiques for what were usually characterized as unintentional appeals to the parterre; cases in which Scribe's general commentary was
taken by the audience to be referring to specific political positions or people.[24]
Thus *La Quotidienne* noted that lines from *La Camaraderie* which cast doubt
on the qualifications and the constancy of *députés* caused the audience to see
it as a *pièce d'opposition*, and so to applaud enthusiastically, even though the
critic did not, himself, treat *La Camaraderie* as a political play.[25] Janin, who
called *Le Puff*, of 1848, one of Scribe's most challenging plays, supported his
contention by saying, "Que de mots qui ont porté coup ! que d'allusions qu'il
n'a pas voulu faire et que le public a faites !" (So many phrases that hit home!
So many allusions he hadn't intended, but that the public saw!).[26] As long as
Scribe's allusions were veiled enough to seem unintentional, their impact could
be chalked up to politicized audiences rather than provocative playwrighting.

This was less possible with a play that failed, such as *Les Indépendants*. In
fact, in their accounts of its lack of success, several critics who had recently
been favorable toward *La Camaraderie* suggested that *Les Indépendants* had
been written and rehearsed hastily to serve a political agenda, an irresistible
irony given that the play chastises exactly such behavior.[27] *Le Constitutionnel*,
which had characterized *La Camaraderie* as benign,[28] reacted much more
strongly to its successor, *Les Indépendants*. While pointing out that Scribe
seemed to be recycling characters and even jokes, *Le Constitutionnel*'s critic
concluded with:

Un dernier reproche, un reproche bien autrement grave que tous ceux
qui précèdent, peut être adressé à l'auteur des *Indépendants*. Son
ouvrage frappe mal, il est vrai, mais il a l'intention de frapper sur tout
ce qui professe une opinion libre et fière, indépendante, tranchons le
mot. La satire n'atteint pas ce but, mais elle y vise. Et c'est ainsi que
les plus nobles sentiments se trouvent affublés en ridicules, et bafoués
en plein théâtre au profit de je ne sais quelle école littéraire, bâtarde
et musquée . . .[29]

A last reproach, and one of a different order of seriousness from the preceding ones, can be addressed to the author of *Les Indépendants*. His work misses its mark, it is true, but it has the intention to strike at anything that professes a free, proud, independent opinion, to speak plainly. The satire does not attain this goal, but it aims for it. And this is how the most noble sentiments are reduced to ridicule and flayed in the theater to the advantage of who knows what bastardized, musk-scented literary school.

Like this critic, censors and vaudeville parodists kept an eye on the implications of Scribe's critiques for the social institutions that he represented. For the most part, the light touch of his dialogues kept Scribe out of trouble, but on occasion he came a little too close to criticizing ministerial behavior for the censors' tastes, or his portrayals of literary corruption cried out for parody.

Jouhaud's Send-Up of *La Camaraderie*

Parody, as it turns out, is exactly the approach that vaudevilles specialized in. Whereas newspaper critics had to articulate what they (or audiences) saw in Scribe's plays to give an account of them, vaudeville parodists had other tools at their disposal. By following the logic of Scribe's *La Camaraderie* to an exaggerated conclusion, Auguste Jouhaud's *L'Anti-camaraderie*, of 1837, reveals what is at stake in Scribe's treatment of corruption. Whereas Scribe's play about a group of artists and writers who help promote one another was taken by many observers to be a send-up of Romantic *cénacles* (literary circles), Jouhaud's *L'Anti-camaraderie* had nothing to do with literary schools; its targets were critics, actresses, and anyone else whose supposedly sincere representations were influenced by undisclosed networks of money and favors.

Jouhaud's play is set in 1930, implying that the state of corruption in theater criticism of the 1830s is only going to get worse. Jouhaud's journalist, the Comte de Sottenville (Count of Dumbintown) writes his reviews entirely on the basis of preferences established by his powerful friends. When Rosemont, a playwright, obtains the support of the Comtesse, an arbiter of influence, the success of his plays is assured, at least in Sottenville's newspaper:

> COMTE. Monsieur Rosemont, j'ai rendu compte dans mon journal de votre dernier ouvrage, *Le Tyran sans le savoir*.
> ROSEMONT. Monsieur le comte a daigné assister à la représentation ? . . .
> COMTE. Je n'en ai pas eu le loisir . . .
> ROSEMONT. Monsieur le comte a donc daigné le lire ? . . .
> COMTE. Je m'en serais bien gardé . . . nous autres journalistes, avons-nous le temps de lire les ouvrages que nous analysons . . . avec de

l'habitude, et le nom de l'auteur, nous faisons un article qui brille par le vérité, l'impartialité et mille autres qualités.[30]

COUNT. Mr. Rosemont, I reviewed your latest work, *The Unwitting Tyrant*, in my newspaper.
ROSEMONT. Monsieur the Count deigned to attend the performance?
COUNT. I didn't have the time . . .
ROSEMONT. Monsieur the Count deigned to read it, then?
COUNT. I think not . . . we journalists hardly have time to read the works we review . . . with practice, and the name of the author, we produce articles that shine with truth, impartiality, and a thousand other qualities.

This is one among many of the Comte de Sottenville's *sottises*, exchanges that show his stupidity, each of which highlights an abuse of the power of the press. The journalist plans to discredit a couturiere who has been late with an order by publishing slanderous information about her, and routinely writes articles provocative enough to cause duels, knowing full well that his newspaper's *gérant* (editor) is much feared for his prowess at arms. As the representative of the *feuilletoniste* of the future, the Comte de Sottenville is not a promising prospect. Despite its claim to be set in the twentieth century, the parody takes every opportunity to define its era in ethical rather than chronological terms. When a marquis buys positive press coverage for the actress who is his mistress, she has an initial moment of confusion about one of the articles he has paid for. He responds, "Zéphirine, je vous croyais à la hauteur de notre siècle . . . j'étais loin de m'attendre à pareille réflexion de votre part . . . prendre à la lettre un article de journal ! Mais vous êtes de l'âge d'or, ma chère . . ." (Zéphirine, I thought you were in tune with our century . . . I certainly didn't expect such a reflection from you . . . taking a newspaper article literally! You are from the golden age, my dear . . .).[31] The "golden age" is not attached to specific dates; it is an idea of transparency which, the play implies, will be entirely anachronistic in a hundred years.[32] Jouhaud's parody vaudeville indicates the danger inherent in the behaviors Scribe stages: that newspapers will become the sole arbiters of popularity and that their corruption will erode public faith in the institutions of society. Scribe included of some of Jouhaud's lines from *L'Anti-Camaraderie* in his 1838 opera *La Figurante ou L'Amour et la danse*,[33] a decision that can be read as a sort of validation of the *vaudevilliste*'s exegesis of his play.

If Jouhaud looked to the future to extend Scribe's critique of media practices, he turned to the countryside to poke fun at Delavigne's *La Popularité*. The vaudeville that Jouhaud staged after Delavigne's play premiered downgraded the "British" intrigue of the drama to a story of rival factions in the French countryside. In his own *La Popularité*, Jouhaud tells the story of popularity accorded and then denied through a typographical error made by a newspaper called *Le Moniteur*. The newspaper is supposed to say that M. Dupont has been appointed mayor of a provincial town, but it mistakenly prints M. Dumont. The play's humor relies on M. Dumont's reactions to his unexpected and short-lived glory. To broaden the humor even more, each step of the imbroglio needs to be explained to M. Dumont's illiterate valet. According to Jouhaud's play, provincial types of limited literacy were little troubled by the relative popularity of the forty-franc press (they didn't read it). In his play, half of those who live in a remote village can't read to begin with, and the rest are more concerned with a typo that affects their local status than with conspiracies between liberal and monarchist newspapers or with the misbehavior of less political dailies.

Such down-to-earth analyses of the influence of the press operated at a certain remove from the press dramas and comedies staged at the Théâtre Français in 1838. Delavigne, for one, was not aiming for a popular audience with his play about popularity. He refused to have it printed in *Le Magasin théâtral* or other cheap series of published plays, but Jouhaud's parodic point was that Delavigne's play wouldn't have concerned a rural audience anyhow.[34] For such characters, it was by one letter in the official newspaper that popularity stuck to one person or another—and the newspaper itself, regardless of its political alignment, was considered authoritative. With the lower theatrical genres fully accepting the power of the press as such, Delavigne looked behind the times; he still saw popularity as an individual politician or newspaper's status, while *vaudevillistes* took the perspective that it was a media phenomenon, protean and, in contrast to calumny's music-like dissemination, increasingly text-based.

Another humorous play that made fun of Delavigne's drama also emphasized physical newsprint as the source of popularity. Like Jouhaud's *La Popularité*, the Cogniard brothers' *Rothomago*, a vaudeville revue of the year 1839, insisted on the paper that brought the news, rather than on the news itself. In *Rothomago*, the character La Popularité is silent and dressed entirely in newspapers. Hermione and Ruy Blas, personifications of competing plays, hope to engage La Popularité in conversation and, eventually, to win her for their theaters. While the popularity or unpopularity of recent plays had been a topic for vaudeville revues for the last century, this version of La Popularité is as silent as a page of newsprint.[35] The stage directions say that when her interlocutors try to talk with her, "La Popularité fait signe qu'elle n'a pas besoin de parler ; qu'on peut lire les journaux qui l'enveloppent" (Popularity gestures to the newspapers that envelop her to show that she doesn't need to talk).[36]

The scene includes two attitudes toward La Popularité. First, Hermione and Ruy Blas fight over her as a phenomenon that they, as plays, would like to elicit. Next, they treat her as another play (Delavigne's) rather than as the status that all plays hope to attain.

Reading La Popularité's costume aloud, Ruy Blas and Hermione say:

HERMIONE. Je trouve que les journaux ne l'habillent pas bien ; ceux de l'opposition surtout.

RUY BLAS. Où sont-ils ?

HERMIONE. Sur ses épaules.

RUY BLAS. Et tout près de son cœur j'aperçois *les Débats*. Chacun de ces journaux a fourni sa tirade ; lisons . . .

HERMIONE, *lisant*. "La liberté, c'est la lumière."

RUY BLAS, *lisant*. " La république, c'est le chaos. "

HERMIONE, *lisant ailleurs*. "Le royaliste a raison."

RUY BLAS. "Le républicain n'a pas tort ; le juste-milieu vaut encore mieux."[37]

HERMIONE. La popularité, c'est une comédie ; / La popularité, c'est une jonglerie.

RUY BLAS. La popularité, c'est le rêve des fous : / La popularité, c'est la gloire en gros sous ! Ah ça ! mais dites donc, ma belle camarade, / Votre pièce, entre nous, est une arlequinade.[38]

HERMIONE. I find her badly dressed in those papers, especially the opposition ones.

RUY BLAS. Where are they?

HERMIONE. On her shoulders.

RUY BLAS. And right near her heart I see *Le Journal des débats*. Each of these newspapers has provided a tirade; let's read them . . .

HERMIONE, *reading*. "Liberty is light."

RUY BLAS, *reading*. "The republic is chaos."

HERMIONE, *reading elsewhere*. "Royalists are right."

RUY BLAS. "Republicans are not wrong; the status quo is even better."

HERMIONE. Popularity is a comedy; / Popularity is a juggling act.

RUY BLAS. Popularity is a madman's dream: / Popularity is well-paid glory! Ah! say, my pretty colleague, / Between us, your play is as patched-together as Harlequin.

This particular critique of the play (that it was a performance made of patches) was one invited partly by Delavigne's use of British characters as stand-ins for Parisian papers and partly by his direct borrowing of sayings and bon mots from some of the papers he portrayed. An *arlequinade* was an apt term for this silent figure in a patchwork costume, like that of the commedia dell'arte's stock character Harlequin. In its doubled representation as the phenomenon of popularity, the figure stood as a silent commentary on the contributions that a noisy press could make to the popularity of a play.

The vaudeville revue's character La Popularité demonstrated that being literally covered by the press was now what indicated the popularity of a play, no matter how contradictory its reviews might be. Hermione and Ruy Blas's encounter with silent Popularity suggests that newspaper opinions are hard to engage with. Popularity itself, while silenced by its transition to newsprint, is nonetheless very much desired by completing plays, who conclude that each will have its turn as a popular success. Where Delavigne's play portrays press-generated popularity as a dangerous influence on electoral politics, the plays personified in *Rothomago* remain enthusiastic suitors of popularity, the phenomenon, even as they regret the silence and patchwork nature that the press has imposed on her. For vaudeville revues were pragmatic about the impact of press innovations on the theater. Even those that disapproved of the press's newly commercial turn recognized its importance.[39]

Vaudeville's clever reuse of a flawed new medium, which so often served as exegesis for its mechanisms, appealed to Delphine de Girardin, poet, *feuilletoniste*, playwright, and spouse of Émile de Girardin, founder of *La Presse*. She, too, wrote a calumny play for the Théâtre Français in 1838, but hers was set in France and was, rather exceptionally for the period, entirely refused performance by the censors. In her preface to the published version of her play, Delphine de Girardin explained that she had written each act of *L'École des journalistes* in a different genre, beginning with farce and passing through tragedy and drama, for, "la surprise est un enseignement" (surprise is a lesson).[40] She was worried about how to get her play's message about responsible journalism across in "(une époque) comme la nôtre où tous les rangs sont intervertis, où toutes les classes sont confondues ; ère d'envie où les grands s'abaissent pour être encore quelque chose, où les petits ne s'élèvent que parce qu'ils sont les petits, où la supériorité sans travers est comme un crime sans excuse, où l'on a besoin de se moquer pour admirer" (an age like ours in which all ranks are inverted, all classes mixed up; era of envy, in which the great lower themselves to remain relevant, in which the lowly only rise because they are lowly, in which unalloyed superiority is like an unpardonable crime; in which we have to make fun in order to admire).[41] Girardin's characterization of her age, which goes on for several pages, is given as an explanation for why she chose to use a different dramatic genre for each of her play's five acts. In a public increasingly perceived as divided, a variety of genres was meant to appeal to a variety of people.[42] Times of deep social divisions are times that raise the stakes of media reliability. Delphine de Girardin's play, which was set in contemporary Paris and referenced several recent instances of calumny, raised them too high for the taste of the censorship bureau.

In October 1839, the members of the selection committee for the Comédie Française had unanimously approved the play's performance, but the censors found that the play was too harsh a critique of journalism to be staged in a state-subsidized theater. The censor's report states, "Quelque abus que des écrivains puissent faire de la liberté d'écrire, ce n'est pas par l'abus de la liberté du théâtre, ce n'est pas en déversant le mépris sur toute une classe de personnes qu'il convient de combattre le mal que l'on veut corriger" (However much writers may abuse their freedom to write, it is not by abusing the freedom of the theater, or by loading scorn on a whole class of people that they should fight the problem they seek to correct).[43]

In *L'École des journalistes*, a newspaper called *La Vérité* publishes calumnies against an artist and slanders a political figure, leading to the suicide of the former and to strained family ties and a tarnished public image for the latter. Delphine de Girardin took it upon herself to explain how libelous rumors could come to be spread in the press, and to counter their impact by informing the public about the workings of news production. In her play, the article that starts to spread calumny about a minister had been relegated to the journalist's desk drawer until a pressing need for copy made it necessary. Press expansion itself, with the accompanying need to find advertisers and increase readership, created conditions in which printing inflammatory scandals could be a good business move. The censors objected to her portrayal of the press, but Girardin's play was probably also banned because the rumors that her characters so recklessly published were too similar to rumors that had circulated about the marital status of Adolphe Thiers, once and future prime minister, who was said to have been his mother-in-law's lover before he married her daughter.[44] Girardin casts the rumor that the daughter's fiancé had been the mother's lover as calumny, false and malicious information, in her play, but that was probably little comfort to the people about whom the story was being revived. Aside from Thiers, Girardin's play referred much more directly to a painter who had recently killed himself, le baron Gros, and to the power of a newspaper critic, "Griffaut", whose biting articles on the artist's work were said to have driven him to despair. As Amélie Calderone points out in her excellent critical edition of the play, not only was Eugène Briffault a critic, but Charles Brifaut had also been a Restoration-era censor, so Delphine de Girardin was taking particular risks by naming her critic character Griffaut.[45]

After her play had been accepted by the Théâtre Français, but before its performance there, Delphine de Girardin publicized it further by holding a reading for two hundred guests from the world of the theater and the press in her salon (figure 2). The next day the censors forbade its performance.[46]

Jules Janin, Alphonse Karr, and Honoré de Balzac attended Mme Girardin's reading and referred to it in *Le Journal des débats*, *Les Guêpes*, and *La Revue Parisienne*, respectively. They recognized the rumor about Thiers but contended that it was dangerous to overinterpret any theatrical character as referring to a political figure.[47] This was particularly true in that the use of public figures in plays was one of the most common motives for censorship. Even veiled references, when not veiled enough, were flagged for modification by censors wary of any negativity directed at those in power.

Girardin took advantage of her play's refusal by posing as a censored poet in the *feuilleton* of *La Presse*: the monologues from the play which Girardin chose to publish in her *feuilleton* were those spoken by the artist character who is cruelly criticized and eventually driven to suicide for lack of public

Figure 2. Delphine de Girardin's salon by Jean-Jacques Grandville, "Thé artistique assaisonné de grands hommes. 'Et vous, Honoré, en voulez-vous une tasse?' " (An artistic tea, flavored with celebrities. "And you, Honoré, would you like a cup?") Copyright © Maison de Balzac/Roger-Viollet.

acclaim. Like her husband, who promoted the forty-franc press as a vehicle for enlightenment, Delphine de Girardin insisted that *L'École des journalistes* was written for public edification.[48] Promoting it, as she did in *La Presse*, would, then, serve the dissemination of its lessons. For, as the vicomte de Launay (Delphine de Girardin's pseudonym) had written in the "Courrier de Paris" of April 12, 1839, "ce ne sont pas les journalistes que nous voulons persécuter, ce sont les abonnés que nous voulons instruire ; oui, nous rêvons de la régénération de la presse par l'*initiation* des abonnés" (We aren't trying to persecute journalists but rather to instruct subscribers; yes, we dream of regenerating the press by *initiating* its subscribers).[49] As part of her educational program for the newspaper-reading public, Girardin (as the vicomte de Launay) compared the persuasive power of newspapers to that of the theater. A propos of a typical newspaper subscriber, she wrote, "nous voulons lui apprendre comment dans les coulisses de ce théâtre on soulève la tempête populaire" (we want to teach him how behind the scenes of this theater, the popular storm is raised).[50]

For Delphine de Girardin, humor and legibility of references were essential to engaging an audience or readership. They got her in trouble with the censors, who found that her critiques exceeded "les termes de la satire dramatique" (the terms of dramatic satire) and that her portrait of the artist character, modeled on le baron Gros, was "trop clairement désigné" (too clearly designated).[51] Without giving the public something to recognize, though, be it gossip or jokes about the press, *L'École des journalistes* might not have been censored, but it also might have lost its purpose.

For the sense of complicity that Girardin said she was aiming for to work, her situations had to be familiar to at least part of her audience. Unlike Delavigne, Girardin was not nostalgic for an earlier age of political newspapers. Her play reports on new practices in journalism, using humor and allusion to warn of their risks. Her semi-veiled references to famous figures were a way to acknowledge the recirculation of all sorts of information (articles reprinted without permission, engravings reused in *canards*, rumors written up as society news) while imposing an edifying spin on the behavior depicted. She even opened the play with a vaudeville-esque gag that referred to *La Presse*'s new practices. An actor stumbles onto stage under the weight of an enormous roll of posters in a variety of colors which advertise *La Vérité*, the newspaper that has just been founded. A journalist character who is looking on remarks, "Voici des vérités de toutes les couleurs" (Here are truths of all different colors).[52] The posters, printed on paper in a variety of colors, were to be a wink at Émile de Girardin's contention that *La Presse*, thanks to its reliance on publicity, diffused the truth, regardless of the political affiliation (or *couleur*) of its sources. Though the play's interdiction meant that the joke was not performed as planned, the layout of the posters was included in the published edition of the play (figure 3).

According to Delphine de Girardin's play, truth is a many-colored thing, and calumnies can simply be misinterpretations of social behavior, published too quickly. If journalists would just attend a little more to the consequences of their actions, much harm could be avoided. Her play, like *Richard Savage* and *La Popularité*, acknowledges that the press can be misused, but it aims to instruct its audiences in the art of prevention.

When she published the play itself in volume form, Delphine de Girardin used the preface to explain, "Quant au sujet principal de cet ouvrage, il est puisé dans l'histoire même du journalisme . . . Les journaux seuls sont donc coupables des allusions que l'on peut trouver, c'est leur calomnie qui a fait la pièce" (As for the main subject of this work, it is taken from the very history of journalism . . . Newspapers alone are guilty of any allusions one might see, it is their calumny that served as the basis for the play).[53] The critic Paul Saint-Victor agreed, describing the play thus: "La Calomnie de Beaumarchais et de Rossini appliquée à une comédie toute entière . . . Le poëte ne flétrit pas les journalistes qu'il accuse : il les avertit, il les éclaire, il

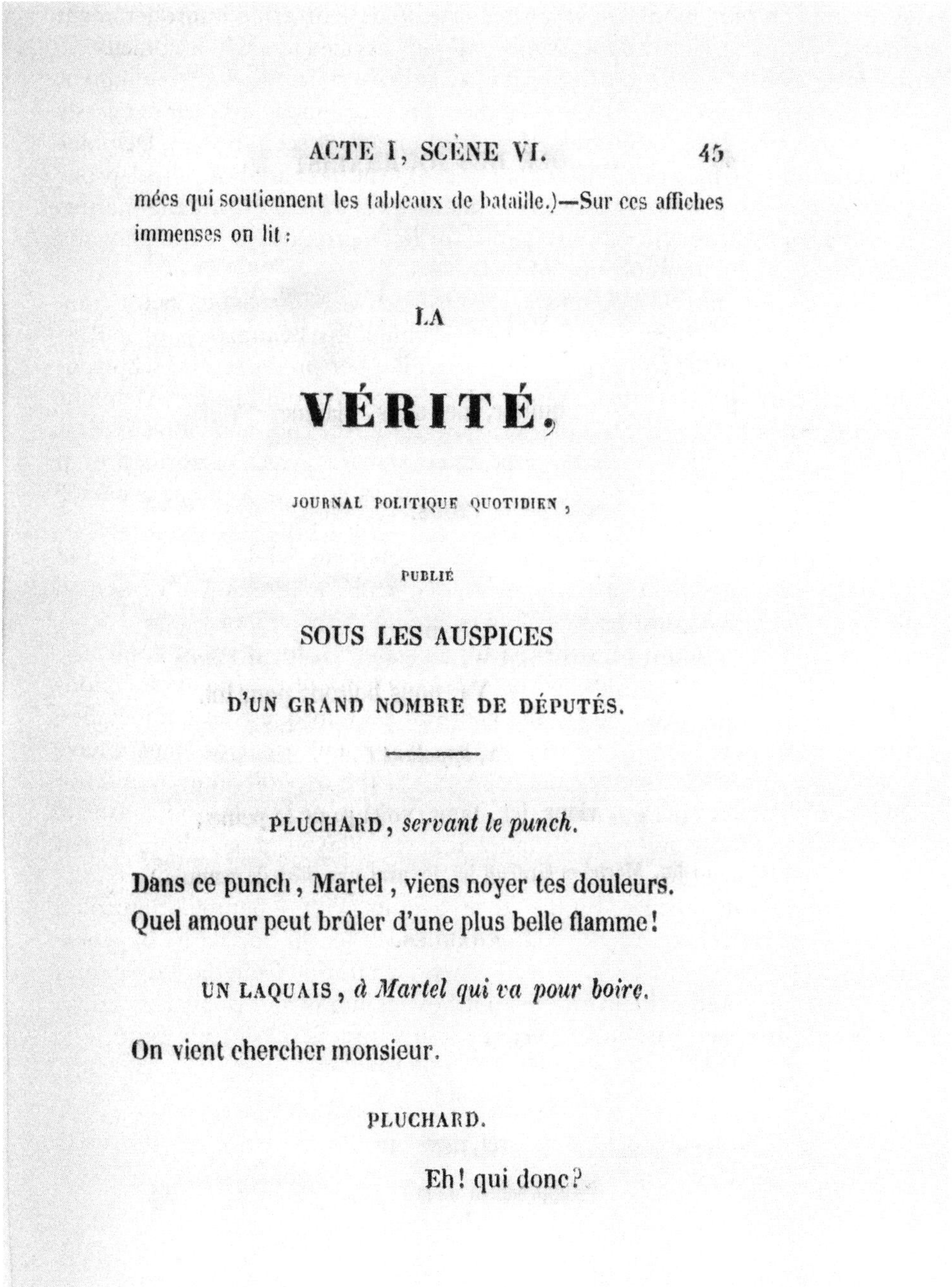

mées qui soutiennent les tableaux de bataille.)—Sur ces affiches
immenses on lit :

LA

VÉRITÉ,

JOURNAL POLITIQUE QUOTIDIEN ,

PUBLIÉ

SOUS LES AUSPICES

D'UN GRAND NOMBRE DE DÉPUTÉS.

————

PLUCHARD, *servant le punch.*

Dans ce punch, Martel , viens noyer tes douleurs.
Quel amour peut brûler d'une plus belle flamme !

UN LAQUAIS, *à Martel qui va pour boire.*

On vient chercher monsieur.

PLUCHARD.

Eh! qui donc?

Figure 3. Poster for *La Vérité.* Delphine de Girardin, *L'École des journalistes*, 2nd
ed. (Paris: Dumont, 1839), 44. Courtesy of Bibliothèque nationale de France.

les étonne en leur montrant la portée cruelle de leur arme imprudemment ajustée" (Beaumarchais and Rossini's Calumny applied to a whole comedy . . . the poet doesn't flay the journalists [he] accuses: he warns them, he enlightens them, he astonishes them by showing them the cruel impact of their carelessly adjusted arm).[54] Like the authors of the calumny plays set in Britain, Delphine de Girardin was interested in casting light on the potential of a libel-prone press. While the play itself warned of the dangers of press scandalmonering, its author sought to use the newspaper for both promotion of her play and education though amplification of its lessons.

This risk, when discussed on stage, is instructive. When Saint-Victor compared *L'École des journalistes* to "La Calomnie" by Beaumarchais or Rossini, that was meant to be a compliment. Like her predecessors, who cautiously explored the creative uses to which calumny could be put, Delphine de Girardin had made art out of a warning about the speed and effectiveness of slanderous speech when it was repeated in the press. Such performances of iffy press behavior, whether they happened on stage or in a salon, remained real-time proposals for collective reflection.[55] Dramas and comedies worked through concerns about press calumny and nepotism, while vaudevilles and parodies—some of them based on the very comedies in question—focused on the practices and inconsistencies of an emerging media regime.

Newspaper calumny was, then, a topical concern for dramas, comedies, and vaudevilles in the 1830s. While some elements of theatrical depictions of slander were determined by the genre of play in question (vaudevilles, for example, were more likely to dress people in newspaper, dramas to have characters speaking in verse), the debate over the uses of calumny did not consist of blanket condemnations of badmouthing people in print. Instead, plays explored how and why calumny happens. Playwrights identified what encouraged it (need for copy, political angling) and what its nefarious effects were, but they also focused on the advantages its skillful manipulation could confer. Those advantages could include influence over the popularity of people or ideas. Theater, if only because of its generic separation from the newspapers it considered, could explain and exhibit how calumny and popularity might relate to each other, particularly via newspaper practices.

Chapter 3

✦

From Beaumarchais to Scribe,
Balzac's Concrete Publicity

When Delphine de Girardin, a friend of Honoré de Balzac, read her play, *L'École des journalistes*, aloud for colleagues in 1839, contemporary critics such as Théophile Gautier and Jules Janin interpreted it as a continuation of the the antipress diatribe Balzac had launched a few months earlier with the publication of the second part of his *Illusions perdues*. Théodore Muret, whose review of Balzac's text appeared several months after its publication, wrote:

> En vérité, ces pauvres journaux ont du malheur. L'autre jour encore, une femme, qui pourtant est journaliste, continuait, en cinq actes et en vers, la croisade commencée par M. de Balzac sous la forme du roman . . . elle empruntait la plume d'Aristophane, et immolait en bloc et en détail, tous les écrivains de la presse périodique, excepté ceux de son journal. À défaut du théâtre, fermé à cette muse en colère, le trépied de son salon était l'Olympe d'où partaient ses foudres, Le journal aura la vie dure, s'il résiste à cette fameuse lecture de *L'École des journalistes* et au dernier roman de Balzac.[1]

> Honestly, these poor newspapers are unfortunate. Just the other day a woman, who is herself a journalist, continued, in five acts and in verse, the crusade that M. de Balzac started as a novel. She borrowed Aristophanes's pen to immolate, as a group and individually, everyone who writes for the periodical press, except those who write for her newspaper. In lieu of the theater, closed to this angry muse, her salon served as the Olympus from which she launched her thunderbolts. Newspapers are in for a hard time, if they resist this famous reading of *L'École des journalistes* and the latest novel from Balzac.

Jules Janin, in an article devoted to *L'École des journalistes*, agreed that its project was similar to Balzac's, and Théophile Gautier wrote to Gérard de

Nerval that Delphine de Girardin's play was Balzac's novel, "mis en pièces" (put in pieces/plays).[2]

While hundreds of plays staged the press in the years surrounding the publication of Balzac and Girardin's novel and play, few caused as much hue and cry as the second section of *Illusions perdues* did, and even fewer were banned from the stage as *L'École des journalistes* was. Balzac, like Delphine de Girardin, used some of the publicity strategies he criticized (notably advertising and calumny) within the very novel doing the criticizing, but he made sure to frame such practices historically in the version of his work that was printed in volumes and bound for posterity as part of the *Comédie humaine*. Balzac's theatrically informed critiques of press practices, had, in fact, been developing for some time when he wrote them into *Illusions perdues*. *César Birotteau*, which he began writing in 1834, was largely about publicity practices and drew heavily on Pierre-Augustin Caron de Beaumarchais's work for elements of its plot.

Whereas dramas examined the uses of negative publicity and comedies and vaudevilles plastered the stage with posters (as we will see further in chapter 4), Balzac's novels transcribed newspaper advertisements and articles supposedly verbatim, in a reality effect informed by the conventions of stage pastiche. The so-called documents included in Balzac's novels dealt mockingly with the fact of their press publication *and* declared themselves to be evidence for a future history of their age. By adapting theatrical practices of press critique for use in his novels, Balzac was able to self-consciously sensationalize and promote the books in question in their serial format, even as he looked forward to a more fixed and prestigious existence of these very samples of publicity as pseudoarchival material after they were included in the *Comédie Humaine*.

Finot as the *presse à quarante francs*: Updating Figaro

Andoche Finot, the unscrupulous editor for whom Lucien de Rubempré writes the article that sets his literary path toward journalism in *Illusions perdues*, was invented as part of Balzac's efforts to make *César Birotteau* comment on the conditions of its own circulation. The book was given away as a promotional bonus to readers who took out a subscription to *Le Figaro*. Association with such a title was an opportunity for Balzac to draw parallels between his own writing and that of Beaumarchais. *Le Mariage de Figaro* and *Les Deux amis ou le négociant de Lyon*, two plays by Beaumarchais, served as important references throughout the composition of *César Birotteau*, while Finot, the author of the prospectus which plays a central role in its plot, was introduced specifically to provide examples of post-1836 publicity.

Beaumarchais's plays treat questions of money and publicity with subtlety and humor, an approach that Balzac sought to emulate. In his promotional article about *César Birotteau*, Édouard Ourliac proposed to celebrate Balzac's novel as "un choeur d'opéra comique" (a comic opera chorus) or "un corps de ballet" would. Continuing the theatrical comparison, the prospectus that promoted *César Birotteau* as an example of the virtues of the *Association de la librairie et de la presse quotidienne* emphasized parallels between Balzac's work and that of Beaumarchais. Playing on the newspaper's name, it says:

> FIGARO et BALZAC ! Quels noms plus heureusement juxtaposés ! où trouver une similitude plus intime d'esprit, de pensées, de sentiments, d'individualisme, que celle qui existe entre Beaumarchais et M. de Balzac? Tous les deux, pleins de verve et d'originalité, ils ont tour à tour attaqué, blâmé, défendu les mœurs de leur époque, et leurs personnifications sont restées comme des types à jamais populaires.[3]

> FIGARO and BALZAC! What names could go better together? Where to find a deeper similarity of wit, of thought, of sentiment and individualism than that which exists between Beaumarchais and Balzac? Both of them, full of verve and originality, have attacked, blamed, defended the ways of their era, and their personifications have become perpetually popular types.

Pierre Laubriet has pointed out that Birotteau's oft-repeated diatribe against the current state of bankruptcy law owes much to a similar scene in Beaumarchais's *Les Deux amis*.[4] Like Beaumarchais, Balzac uses the scene to foreshadow Birotteau's upcoming disaster. When it arrives, Birotteau's bankruptcy is referred to as a "drame commercial" (commercial drama), which has "trois actes distincts . . . sa mise en scène pour le public et ses moyens cachés, il y a la représentation vue du parterre et la représentation vue des coulisses" (three distinct acts . . . its staging for the public and its hidden mechanisms, there is the performance seen from the audience and the performance seen from backstage).[5] Mme Madou's reaction to Birotteau's efforts, "demain, à la Halle je cornerai votre honneur. Ah ! Elle est rare, la farce !" (tomorrow at the market I'll be trumpeting your honor—a rare farce! *CB*, 376) suggests that the Parisian market parterre, used to fraudulent bankruptcies, was incredulous at César's exaggerated probity.

Financial dramas, though important in both *Illusions perdues* and *César Birotteau*, were but one version of Balzac's debt to Beaumarchais. By opening *César Birotteau* with a bourgeois measuring his wife's bedroom in anticipation of business success, Balzac seems to be updating *Le Mariage de Figaro* in accordance with nineteenth-century values.[6] Whereas Figaro and Suzanne must contend with the Comte d'Almaviva's interest in keeping Suzanne close to his bedroom, César and Constance need to elaborate a business plan. Birotteau's concern about his protégé Anselme Popinot helping him pay his debt in exchange for marrying his daughter is, again, an ironically updated version of Beaumarchais's examination of the appropriate conditions for providing a young woman's dowry.[7] Balzac also adjusted Beaumarchais's attitudes toward the economics of writing to suit the publishing conditions of the July Monarchy, making Finot a Figaro of the commercial press.

Like Figaro's monologue, which Roger Chartier has shown attacks the "régime de la librairie" (bookselling regime) and connects the liberty to publish with the legitimacy of writing, Finot's biography within the *Comédie humaine* is a commentary on the conditions for success in the age of the press.[8] In *César Birotteau*, Félix Gaudissart and Andoche Finot, the traveling salesman and the hack writer, are just starting careers in which they will become a theater director and the owner of a newspaper. Integrated into the novel once it became clear that *Le Figaro* would be promoting the book in its entirety, not serializing it, Finot develops in *César Birotteau* and *Illusions perdues* as a sort of forward-looking spokesman for the commercial press. As such, his character and actions provide a sketch of the strengths and weaknesses of *la presse à quarante francs* (the forty-franc press), according to Balzac.[9] In *Illusions perdues*, Lousteau characterizes Finot as "ce lourd garçon, sans esprit ni talent, mais avide, voulant la fortune à tout prix et habile en affaires" (this heavy-handed young man, lacking wit and talent, but avid for fortune at any price and a smooth businessman; *IP*, 379). The author of Popinot's prospectus for *L'Huile céphalique* in *César Birotteau*, Finot looks after the product's reputation using his contacts at newspapers and in the theater, for, "dans ce temps d'innocence, beaucoup de journalistes étaient comme les boeufs, ils ignoraient leurs forces" (in this age of innocence, many journalists were like oxen, they didn't know their strength; *CB*, 191). Having recently decided to "rester dans la littérature d'exploiteur" (stay in the literature of the exploiter; *CB*, 191), Finot was ahead of his time because he understood "l'effet de piston produit sur le public d'un article réitéré" (the inflated effect of a repeated article on the public; *CB*, 260).

To achieve this effect, Finot does everything in his power to get César Birotteau's *Huile céphalique* (hair oil) mentioned in the newspapers:

> Il corrompit avec des billets de spectacle les ouvriers qui, vers minuit achèvent les colonnes des journaux en prenant quelques articles dans les petits faits, toujours prêts, les en-cas du journal. Finot se trouvait alors dans l'imprimerie, occupé comme s'il avait un article à revoir. (*CB*, 259–60)

> He used theater tickets to corrupt the workers who topped up the newspaper columns around midnight, using little bits of text, always at hand, the filler of the newspaper. So Finot found himself at the press then, busy, as if he had an article to correct.

Finot's efforts are part of a national strategy. Gaudissart, the *commis voyageur* (traveling salesman), capitalizes on Finot's publicity by using mentions of the product in the newspaper to convince his provincial customers of its effectiveness: "Gaudissart s'armait des journaux pour détruire les préjugés" (Gaudissart armed himself with newspapers to destroy prejudices).[10] Meanwhile, Finot convinces more-sophisticated Parisian audiences of the oil's superiority by writing a vaudeville joke that helps people remember the falsity of the rival product's claims:

> Finot dirigea contre l'Huile de Macassar cette charmante plaisanterie qui faisait tant rire aux Funambules, quand Pierrot prend un vieux balai de crin dont on ne voit que les trous, y met de l'huile de Macassar, et rend ainsi le balai forestièrement touffu. Cette scène ironique excitait un rire universel. Dans cette campagne il devina lui, le premier, le pouvoir de l'Annonce, dont il fit un si grand et si savant usage. Trois mois après il fut rédacteur en chef d'un petit journal, qu'il finit par acheter et qui fut la base de sa fortune. (*CB*, 260)

> Finot launched that charming joke against the Huile de Macassar that drew so many laughs at the Funambules, where Pierrot takes an old horsehair broom, on which all you see are the holes, applies Huile de Macassar, and makes the broom bushy as a forest. This ironic scene elicited universal laughter. In this campaign he guessed, and he was the first to do so, the power of Advertisement, of which he would make such extensive and expert use. Three months later, he became editor in chief of a small newspaper that he eventually bought; it became the base of his fortune.

The novel refers to the vaudeville joke as though its readers may have seen it, making Parisians feel well informed, while Finot's multimedia strategy reassures merchants in the provinces, by assuring them that newspapers, too, advertise the oil. The written copy of the advertisement points out that the claims of the competitor, the *Huile de Macassar*, about making hair grow are false, presenting Birotteau's product, the *Huile céphalique*, as the rational alternative for those who aren't taken in by such claims. Finot has understood exactly how the relationship between the theater and the press can work for product promotion. He buys mentions in newspapers by distributing theater tickets and writes lines for the vaudeville workers see when they get there. By ensuring that the *Huile céphalique* will seem to be everywhere, Finot lays the foundation for his future in the press.

A Book in the Hand Is Worth Two in the Press

Having been associated with *la presse à quarante francs* since the serial publication of *La Vieille fille* in *La Presse* the year before, Balzac participated in a different form of publicity by publishing *César Birotteau* in collaboration with *Le Figaro*, a satirical literary newspaper. *Le Figaro* tried to compete with the large daily papers by giving away whole books in exchange for subscriptions, rather than buying novels and serializing them. *César Birotteau* was offered as a freebie to anyone who subscribed to either *Le Figaro*, for three months, or *l'Estafette*, an associated newspaper which reprinted articles from other papers, for six months.[11]

Thematically, *César Birotteau* was well suited to test such a structure of publicity. César Birotteau is a *parfumeur* who, having had commercial and then social success, is bankrupted by a combination of speculative real estate investment, the flight of a coinvestor, and the ill will of a former employee. Believing that his honor will be restored only if he repays all his creditors, Birotteau and his family work toward that end, helped by Popinot, who effectively exploits Birotteau's idea for a hair oil, the *Huile céphalique*. Madeleine (Ambrière) Fargeaud, who has analyzed potential sources for the hair oil's advertising prospectus, which is reproduced in the novel, contends that the book is primarily concerned with, "l'évolution du commerce artisanal que symbolise Birotteau au commerce industriel dont Popinot incarne le type, ainsi que l'irrésistible essor de la publicité" (the evolution from artisanal business, symbolized by Birotteau, to industrial business, of which Popinot embodies the type, along with the irresistible growth of publicity).[12] The origin of Birotteau's commercial success is that "il déploya, le premier d'entre les parfumeurs, ce luxe d'affiches, d'annonces et de moyens de publication que l'on nomme peut-être injustement charlatanisme" (he was the first among perfumers to distribute this luxuriant array of posters, ads, and means of publication that is, perhaps unjustly, referred to as charlatanism; *CB*, 71). This strategy was profitably combined with his wife's suggestion that they give a discount to merchants who bought large quantities of their product, which led to "bénéfices restreints quant à l'article, énormes par la quantité" (benefits that were limited for each article, but enormous given the quantities involved; *CB*, 75). In his description of the Birotteaus' tactics, Balzac could be describing the marketing strategy of *la presse à quarante francs*. Advanced as they may have been, though,[13] César's publicity techniques are only precursors to the marketing strategy that Popinot's friends Finot and Gaudissart implement to promote the *Huile céphalique*. Though he had, himself, been a pioneer in the earlier use of posters, when faced with the multiplicity and scale of Popinot's advertising, Birotteau is "incapable de mesurer la portée d'une pareille publicité" (incapable of taking account of the reach of such publicity; *CB*, 261).

César Birotteau, the novel, benefited from cross-promotion reminiscent of the *Huile céphalique*'s publicity campaign. During the time the book was being given away, *Le Figaro* frequently ran articles with titles such as, "La Littérature des annonces" and "Les annonces dans les grands journaux"[14] ("The Literature of Advertisement," "Advertisements in the Major Newspapers"). As specific publicity for *César Birotteau*, there were *annonces* (ads) at the head of the first column in the newspaper for as long as the book was being distributed, and both a detailed prospectus and a humorous article were devoted to its appearance. Meanwhile Cormon and Lagrange were writing a vaudeville based on the novel.[15] The prospectus for *L'Association de la librairie et de la presse quotidienne* (the structure set up to distribute books as incentives to subscribe to *Le Figaro*) was included in the first volume of *César Birotteau*'s first edition after the text of the novel, where it theorized the book's production and promotion extensively. The prospectus outlined the differences between reading a newspaper and reading a book, while the article told an adventure story about the production of the novel, accumulating fantastic details to insist on the integrity of the book as a nonserialized novel.

Pierre Laubriet has shown that descriptions of Finot were added during Balzac's exchanges of proofs with the printer in the winter of 1837. "Aussi une épreuve l'introduit-elle brusquement dans ce roman, muni d'un état-civil, physiquement dessiné et minutieusement analysé dans son être moral" (and so a set of proofs introduces him suddenly into the novel, with his civil status set, his physique drawn, and his moral being minutely analyzed).[16] In the same article, Laubriet says that Gaudissart, too, developed significantly in the last weeks of the work's composition. He suggests that both decisions were made in the context of Balzac's composition of *La Maison Nucingen* and in anticipation of Finot's role in the second part of *Illusions perdues*. The characters in *César Birotteau* who practice a new kind of publicity were developed after it became clear that the book would be distributed as part of a new promotional scheme. Although Balzac's portraits of Finot and Gaudissart as characters are not flattering, their products serve as metadiscourses which negotiate the promotion of Balzac's book.[17]

According to Balzac's description of Finot's techniques, which include insertion of *réclames* (paid advertisements written into articles) in newspapers, composition of a vaudeville joke, and distribution of prospectuses and pictures, publicity works best when the public is repeatedly exposed to a product. When Birotteau finally notices Popinot's innovations, he admires his successor for distributing engravings of Hero and Leander in gilt frames. "Il a inventé les cadres permanents, l'annonce éternelle !" (he has invented permanent frames, eternal advertisements! *CB*, 257), says Birotteau. This is just what Alphonse Karr, the publisher of *Le Figaro*, hoped to do by distributing a novel by Balzac as a complement to his newspaper. During the extended time it would take a subscriber to read and reflect on the book, the newspaper that provided that book would be on his or her mind, too. Unlike serializing novels, which kept readers in suspense in the interest of getting them to renew subscriptions, this publication strategy was portrayed as allowing reflection, which eventually led to purchase. *Le Figaro* cast itself as marketing to a readership of intellect and esprit whose decision to subscribe was a thoughtful one.

On December 15, 1837, when *César Birotteau* became available to the public, Édouard Ourliac published an article entitled "Malheurs et aventures de *César Birotteau* avant sa naissance" ("Misfortunes and Adventures of *César Birotteau* Before Its Birth") in *Le Figaro*. It announced *César Birotteau*'s recent completion and jokingly recounted the frenzy of corrections involved in producing the final text, which he called "un poème entier composé, écrit et corrigé à quinze reprises par M. de Balzac" (a whole poem composed, written, and corrected fifteen times over by M. de Balzac).[18] According to Ourliac's article, the proofs, once deciphered by typesetters, were stolen twice under dramatic circumstances in the week preceding publication. The first time, the thief abandoned them because he found them incomprehensible; the second time, the newspaper commissioned someone to hold up the stagecoach in which thieves were escaping with the latest version of the novel. Though obviously a spoof of an adventure story, Ourliac's article does emphasize the care taken to perfect the novel (in his description of the multiple exchanges of proofs), its integrity as a unified work, and *Le Figaro*'s commitment to protecting it as such (even if, according his piece, that meant reassembling proofs scattered on the road). While purely invented, Ourliac's anecdotes do emphasize *Le Figaro*'s proclivity toward maintaining a work's physical and artistic integrity. In the guise of a farce, Ourliac's article positioned *Le Figaro* as the right kind of editor for an author of chef d'oeuvres such as Balzac. Even the title of the article, by referring to *César Birotteau*'s adventures before its birth, reinforces the idea that the work is an aesthetic whole, despite its peripatetic route to publication. Unlike serially published novels, this one has been assembled and completed before its public distribution.[19]

Ourliac's article provided initial publicity for *César Birotteau* in the newspaper and was reprinted for delivery with the second volume of the book. The first volume included a prospectus explaining the combination of newspaper publication and novel distribution it represented. The prospectus, which is transcribed in appendix 2, was a two-page advertisement for the newly founded *Association de la librairie et de la presse quotidienne*, the publishing structure that proposed to distribute novels with subscriptions, rather than dividing them into *feuilletons*.[20] The division of roles that it proposes between the newspaper and the novel reveals a coincidence of pragmatic and aesthetic agendas. A propos of *Le Figaro*'s new distribution strategy, the prospectus reads:

> Mais pour que le succès fût certain . . . il fallait qu'il y eût entre le LIVRE et le JOURNAL une corrélation constante ; il ne fallait pas surtout que les livres médiocres vinssent se faire traîner à la remorque par le journal, et que l'allure franche et décidée de celui-ci fût alourdie par l'impopularité des ouvrages. Il fallait que le Livre, comme le Journal, eût sa valeur propre, et qu'ils possédassent l'un et l'autre leur principe de vitalité.

But in order to ensure success . . . there had to be constant correlation between the BOOK and the NEWSPAPER; it was essential that mediocre books not be dragged along by the newspaper, and that the frank, decisive spirit of the latter not be weighed down by unpopular works. The Book, like the Newspaper, had to have its own value, so that each possessed its own vital principle.

The temporalities of newspaper reading and book consumption were also portrayed as different but complementary:

Le Journal, acceptant les sujets à mesure qu'ils se présentent ; écrivant pour être utile aujourd'hui, pour être oublié demain, pour recommencer toujours, fraiera les voies de la Pensée, qui se recueille dans les livres, dont les effets sont plus durables, mais qui pour les produire a besoin de laborieuses études, de longues méditations. Ces rapports intimes des deux expressions de l'intelligence humaine . . . doivent avoir nécessairement pour résultat définitif l'agrandissement du domaine de la pensée : ce que le Journal ébauche, le Livre le finit ; ce qui n'était qu'un aperçu devient plus tard une formule habilement déduite. Le lecteur achèvera ainsi de comprendre dans le Livre ce qu'il n'avait fait que saisir dans le Journal.

The Newspaper, which accepts subjects as they present themselves and is written to be useful today and forgotten tomorrow, to restart again, will break the path for Thought, which gathers in books, whose effects are more durable, but whose production requires laborious study and long reflection. These intimate relations between two expressions of human intelligence must necessarily result in the enlargement of the domain of thought; that which the Newspaper sketches, the Book finishes; that which was just an insight becomes a skillfully deduced rule. The reader will finally understand via the Book, what he had just noticed in the Newspaper.

Laubriet suggests that the prospectus "pourrait bien être de la même main que celui de Finot" (could well be by the same hand that created Finot's),[21] without taking a firm position on whether Balzac wrote it or collaborated on its production. André Wurmser and Stéphane Vachon have also pointed out that Balzac not only used prefaces to some of his works to advertise the publication of other works but also sometimes wrote prospectuses for his own books anonymously or under assumed names.[22] Laubriet's coy-sounding turn of phrase indicates his expert awareness of the extent to which Balzac's portraits of pressmen played on his own very active participation in the world in which they operated.

In *Un grand homme de province à Paris*, the second section of *Illusions perdues*, Finot presides at the journalists' supper where Lucien de Rubempré writes his first newspaper article. Once again, Finot is the voice of the future of press development. His intervention spurs a dialogue that predicts the revolution of 1830 while playing on the 1839 ambiguity of the word *publicité*:

> — L'influence et le pouvoir du journal n'est qu'à son aurore, dit Finot, le journalisme est dans l'enfance, il grandira. Tout, dans dix ans d'ici, sera soumis à la publicité. La pensée éclairera tout, elle . . .
>   — Elle flétrira tout, dit Blondet en interrompent Finot.
>   — C'est un mot, dit Claude Vignon
>   — Elle fera des rois, dit Lousteau
>   — Et défera les monarchies, dit le diplomate.
>   — Aussi, dit Blondet, si la Presse n'existait point, faudrait-il ne pas l'inventer ; mais la voilà, nous en vivons.[23]

> "The influence and power of the newspaper are just dawning," said Finot. "Journalism is in its childhood, it will grow. Ten years from now everything will be submitted to publicity. Thought will enlighten all, it will . . ."
>   "It will wither everything," said Blondet, interrupting Finot.
>   "So to speak," said Claude Vignon
>   "It will make kings," said Lousteau
>   "And unmake monarchies," said the diplomat.
>   "Well," said Blondet, "if the press didn't exist, it would be better not to invent it, but here it is, and we live off it."

Blondet's conclusion would later become the final line of the *Monographie de la presse parisienne* in 1843. His prediction ("elle flétrira tout") is lent credibility by the behaviors of the journalists present in the scene. Given that Finot (the publicist character introduced during the writing of *César Birotteau*) has been presented as a strategic operator who is good at extracting the maximum profit out of any enterprise, his proclamation of the enlightenment function of publicity is ironically staged. Here, as Roland Chollet points out, "on ne s'étonnera pas que Girardin en ait avoué pour siennes quelques idées" (It would be unsurprising if Girardin had admitted some of these ideas as his own).[24]

Some of Girardin's positions are cited almost verbatim in this scene at Florine's supper, while other practices for which he was known are discussed more generally. Finot's pretentions to civic publicity, combined with his talent for commercial publicity, suggest that the combination of the two associated with Girardin is being criticized, while the discussion of collective authorship and the one of censorship within the supper scene are in agreement with Girardin's thoughts on those issues.[25]

Anonymity and Collective Authorship

Anonymous articles were the rule in the July Monarchy newspapers, which were assumed to represent collective opinions. Accordingly, only the *gérant* (editor) of a newspaper was legally responsible for the articles it published. Gilles Feyel has shown that Émile de Girardin was unusual in advocating signed articles in 1836. Such a position was consistent with *La Presse*'s declared freedom from party loyalty and emphasis on the publication of individual ideas. Most other editors and decision makers ignored the question of journalistic anonymity until 1848, when Republican lawmakers proposed trading signed articles for the abolition of the *cautionnement* (deposit) that newspapers had to pay to the government in order to be published. This idea of newspapers as forums for individuals rather than as voices for schools of thought was similar to Girardin's, but the law that eventually resulted from these debates in 1850 imposed both the barrier to publication that the *cautionnement* constituted and the signature of articles to ensure legal responsibility of individual journalists.[26] Until 1848, though, only the *gérant* (editor) was legally responsible for what a newspaper published.

When, in *Illusions perdues*, Finot objects that the journalists are exposing their corruption in front of subscribers, Blondet, one of the writers he employs, responds, "Tu es propriétaire d'un de ces entrepôts de venin, tu dois avoir peur ; mais moi, je me moque de toutes vos boutiques, quoique j'en vive !" (You are the owner of one of these venom exchanges, you should be afraid, but me, I don't care about all your boutiques, even if I make my living from them! *IP*, 322). Blondet is being realistic about what he risks, both legally and financially, compared with what Finot does as the *gérant*. The *gérant*, too, was something of a fiction, as revealed in Finot's dealings with Lousteau, who becomes the titular head of a newspaper that Finot is in fact financing and running. When Vignon cites Napoleon's dictum, "Les crimes collectifs n'engagent personne" (collective crimes commit no one; *IP*, 405), he may be recalling that Girardin, "Le Napoléon de la presse," had spoken in the same terms, contending that anonymity led to irresponsible reporting and gratuitous attacks, sometimes in the service of blackmail. In his 1838 article "De la liberté de la presse et du journalisme," Émile de Girardin voiced his concern about journalism propagating "un opinion qui n'appartient en propre à personne et dont la responsabilité pèse sur un être collectif" (an opinion that belongs to no one, the reponsability for which falls on a collective entity).[27] Differentiating between anonymous journalists and writers who signed their work, Girardin wrote, "Du journaliste il y a tout à craindre ; car il n'a pas la responsabilité du mal qu'il peut faire ; de l'écrivain il n'y a rien à redouter ; car il ne peut porter atteinte à la considération d'autrui sans nuire à la sienne" (There is everything to fear from the journalist, who is not responsible for the damage he can do; from the writer there is nothing to dread, for he cannot hurt the reputation of others without damaging his own).[28] Within

Balzac's scene at the journalists' supper, Vignon predicts that Lucien "com-mettra ces lâchetés anonymes qui, dans la guerre des idées, remplacent les stratagèmes, les pillages. . . . dans la guerre des *condottieri*" (will commit those acts of anonymous cowardice which, in the war of ideas, replace strategies, pillages . . . in the war of condottieri; *IP*, 407). Lucien fulfills the prediction, attacking Nathan and D'Arthez when he is told to and taking his revenge on Mme de Bargeton in an anonymous article.

Journalists' lack of accountability, combined with the new press's efforts to please the greatest possible number of potential subscribers, made actors of journalists. In *Illusions perdues*, Diderot's "Paradoxe sur le comédien," by which actors should study feelings to reproduce their manifestations on stage rather than actually seeking to feel a character's emotions, is proposed as a model for *feuilletonistes*. Impassive actors seeking to make expressions that will move the public are like the journalists who write from whatever point of view they need to in order to keep the public entertained.

When Lucien worries about the inconsistency of writing contradictory ar-ticles about the same novel, Coralie, his actress girlfriend, summarizes their parallel positions admirably:

> Fais de la critique, dit Coralie, amuse-toi ! Est-ce que je ne suis pas ce soir en Andalouse, demain ne me mettrai-je pas en bohémienne, un autre jour en homme ? Fais comme moi, donne-leur des grimaces pour leur argent, et vivons heureux. Lucien, épris du paradoxe, fit monter son esprit sur ce mulet capricieux, fils de Pégase et de l'ânesse de Balaam. Il se mit à galoper dans les champs de la pensée pendant sa promenade au Bois, et découvrit des beautés originales. (*IP*, 461)

> "Write criticism," said Coralie, "have fun! Do I not appear as an Andalusian tonight only to be a bohemian tomorrow and a man another day? Do what I do, make faces for their money and let's live happily." Lucien, caught up in the paradox, mounted his wit on this capricious mule, son of Pegasus and the she-donkey of Balaam. He galloped in the fields of thought during their outing in the Bois, and discovered some original beauties.

The "paradoxe sur le comédien" becomes that of the journalist, who, by writing anonymous and contradictory articles, will be playing his role in the new press.

Just before they watch the transformation that the stage undergoes as the footlights are put out, Lousteau tells Lucien that articles are always written at the last minute, requiring journalists to, "avoir de l'esprit . . . Absolument comme on allume un quinquet" (be clever . . . exactly as one lights a footlight; *IP*, 390). The journalist's role is spectacular, not material. The newspaper's dependence on popularity is such that,

pour gagner des abonnés, il inventera les fables les plus émouvantes, il fera la parade comme Bobèche. Le journal servirait son père tout cru à la croque au sel de ses plaisanteries, plutôt que de ne pas intéresser ou amuser son public. Ce sera l'acteur mettant les cendres de son fils dans l'urne pour pleurer véritablement. (*IP*, 405–6)

To attract subscribers, it will invent the most moving fables, it will hawk like Bobèche. The newspaper would serve its father raw, salted with its jokes, before it would fail to interest or amuse its public. It will be the actor putting the ashes of his son in the urn to be able to cry for real.

Journalism's Theatrical Commitment to Pleasing Spectators

Lucien's first newspaper article is both a critique of the priorities of liberal journalism and a promotional pastiche of a review by Jules Janin. Lucien's review of *L'Alcade dans l'embarras*, as a fictional sample of a successful theater review, makes fun of the gerontocracy of the Restoration, in the form of the Alcade of the play's title, and it credits Coralie and Florine's dancing with making a volcano of the parterre.

In his article, Lucien calls Bouffé's pompous elderly Alcade "digne d'être le ministre d'un roi constitutionnel" (worthy of being the minister of a constitutional king; *IP*, 396), combining praise for the skill of an actor who was young at the presumable time of the plot with an offhand critique of both gerontocracy and constitutional monarchy. Lucien depicts the audience's enthusiasm in charged terms:

L'auteur, qui, dit-on, a pour collaborateur un de nos grands poètes a visé le succès avec une fille amoureuse dans chaque main ; aussi a-t-il failli tuer de plaisir son parterre en émoi. Les jambes de ces deux filles semblaient avoir plus d'esprit que l'auteur. Néanmoins quand les deux rivales s'en allaient, on trouvait le dialogue spirituel, ce qui prouve assez victorieusement l'excellence de la pièce. L'auteur a été nommé au milieu des applaudissements qui ont donné des inquiétudes à l'architecte de la salle ; mais l'auteur, habitué aux mouvements du Vésuve aviné qui bout sous le lustre, ne tremblait pas : c'est M. de Cursy. (*IP*, 396)

The author who, they say, collaborated with one of our greatest poets, aimed at success with a lovestruck girl in each hand; and so, having moved the audience, he nearly killed them with pleasure. The legs of these two girls seemed even cleverer than the author. Nonetheless, when the two rivals left, the dialogue was found to be smart, which

definitively proves the excellence of the play. The author was named
amid applause that worried the theater's architect, but the author,
used to the movements of the cracked Vesuvius that bubbles under
the chandelier, did not tremble: it's M. de Cursy.

Chollet takes the "Vésuve aviné" to be a reference to the claque, which the
novel has already explained has been subsidized by the actresses' official
lovers. While he is doubtless correct that Balzac is imitating the style of *petits
journaux*, which would use such metaphors for paid shills, the reference to
an active volcano is also suggestive of the revolution of 1830.[29] Salvandy's
1830 declaration to the Duc d'Orléans, "C'est une fête toute napolitaine,
monseigneur ; nous dansons sur un volcan" (It's an entirely Neapolitan
party, Monseigneur, we are dancing on a volcano)[30] predicted the July days,
as Tocqueville's later variant on the formula predicted the revolution of 1848.
Volcanic parterres are hardly without political implications, even when what
has moved them is a pretty pair of legs. Coralie has already converted one
poet to journalism. Having leapt on stage and heard Coralie's declarations,
Lucien writes, "elle vous donne des désirs horribles, on a envie de sauter
dessus la scène et de lui offrir sa chaumière et son cœur, ou trente mille livres
de rente et sa plume" (she inspires terrible desires; you want to jump on
stage and offer her your heart and your cottage; or thirty thousand pounds
of income and your pen; *IP*, 397). Reactions to Lucien's article at Florine's
supper show that the liberal press appreciates a journalist who can stage his
enthusiasm.

   Lucien, having been told that the playwright is emulating Beaumarchais
and that the success or failure of the play will depend on the actresses and the
press, mentions the Comte d'Almaviva and various Figaros among the secondary characters in his article about the play, while saving his most compelling
prose for the seductions of the actresses. He concludes his article with the
suggestion that their dance is lascivious enough that it could worry the censors. Lucien's article focuses on exactly those elements of the play most likely
to move the crowd, passing lightly over its literary pretensions and adding a
hint of scandal with its line about censorship. In its success, Lucien's article
shows that promoting seduction is the first rule of dramatic criticism and that
relating such seduction to literature may be done in passing if a journalist is
clever about it. The presence of politics in his article, though, suggests that
such crowd-pleasing principles have their risks. The implication is that if
this is the sort of criticism liberal newspapers appreciate, such priorities will
eventually be politically destabilizing.

   Unlike most of the rest of the second section of *Illusions perdues*, Lucien's
article was included in the chapters published in *La Presse* before appearing in
volume form. Though Balzac's correspondence reveals little about the decision
to publish this scene in particular, a letter from Delphine de Girardin suggests

that Balzac, not the Girardins, set the limits of the excerpt. Toward the end of June 1839, Delphine de Girardin wrote, "Le chapitre qui suit les vers est un chef-d'oeuvre ; quel dommage qu'il ne soit point dans *La Presse*. Pourquoi ne nous avoir point donné Le Grand Homme ? Je le regrette, c'est charmant" (The chapter following the verses is a masterpiece; what a pity that it isn't in *La Presse*. Why not have given us Le Grand Homme? I wish it had been there, it is charming).[31] Balzac's correspondence casts little light on why only a chapter and a half of *Un grand homme de province à Paris* was sent to *La Presse*, but the excerpt itself, "Comment se font les petits journaux," was well chosen to act as a promotional gesture in favor of both the volume that was about to appear and of a new illustrated edition of *La Peau de chagrin*.

In Lucien's review of *L'Alcade dans l'embarras*, which, "fit révolution dans le journalisme par la révélation d'une manière neuve et originale" (created a revolution in journalism with its new and original manner; *IP*, 399), Balzac pastiches the style of Jules Janin, the famous critic of the *Journal des débats*. In 1830, Balzac had reviewed and "completed" Janin's *L'Âne mort et la femme guillotinée*, with Janin returning the favor by writing a clever review of *La Peau de chagrin*. The third paragraph of Janin's 1830 review begins, "Vous entendez un grand bruit ; on entre, on sort, on se heurte, on crie, on hurle, on joue, on s'enivre . . ." (You hear a great noise; people enter, they exit, they bump into each other, they cry out, they yell, they play, they get carried away . . .).[32] Lucien's review of *L'Alcade dans l'embarass* opens with, "On entre, on sort, on parle, on se promène, on cherche quelque chose et l'on ne trouve rien, tout est en rumeur. L'alcade a perdu sa fille et retrouvé son bonnet, mais le bonnet ne lui va pas . . ." (people enter, they exit, they speak, they walk, they look for something and find nothing, everything buzzes. The Alcade has lost his daughter and found his cap, but the cap doesn't suit him . . .).[33] Janin was often caricaturized wearing a *bonnet de coton* (cotton cap), in reference to his comfortable bourgeois existence.[34]

Having himself been a journalist in 1830, and having left that milieu with the publication of *La Peau de chagrin*, Balzac used Lucien's article to recall his earlier successful literary treatment of journalism. A new illustrated edition of *La Peau de chagrin* was coming out in bookstores just as Balzac printed his excerpt from *Un grand homme de province à Paris* in *La Presse*. The extract Balzac chose served both to promote Balzac's earlier book and to differentiate Balzac's post-1830 career from Janin's. Though Balzac commissioned Lucien's sonnets from Gautier, Delphine de Girardin, and Charles Lesailly, he wrote Lucien's article himself. In the context of the chapter published in *La Presse*, this was a bit of promotional bravado that recalled his jousts with Janin nine years earlier. Balzac showed that he, too, could write a *feuilleton* like Janin's, whereas journalists like Janin and the fictional Lucien, having written novels of merit, allowed themselves to be lured into the theatrical press, never to write good novels again.

Having masqueraded as a journalist again through the press publication of Lucien's article, Balzac declared himself a novelist, not a satirist, in his preface to *Un Grand homme de province à Paris*:

> Les journalistes ne pouvaient pas plus que les autres professions échapper à la juridiction de la comédie. Pour eux, peut-être eût-il fallu quelque nouvel Aristophane et non la plume d'un écrivain peu satirique ; mais ils inspirent à la littérature une si grande crainte, que ni le Théâtre, ni l'Iambe, ni le Roman, ni le Poème comique n'ont osé le trainer au tribunal où le ridicule *castigat ridendo mores*. Une seule fois M. Scribe essaya cette tâche dans sa petite pièce du *Charlatanisme*, qui fut moins un tableau qu'un portrait. Le plaisir que causa cette spirituelle ébauche fit concevoir à l'auteur le mérite d'une peinture plus ample.[35]

> Journalists could no more escape the jurisdiction of comedy than any other profession. For them, perhaps a new Aristophanes would have been necessary, rather than the pen of a not-very-satirical writer; but they frighten literature so much that neither Theater nor Iambs nor the Novel nor the Poem have dared to drag them before the tribunal where ridicule *castigat ridendo mores*. Just one time M. Scribe attempted this task in his little play, *Le Charlatanisme*, which was more of a portrait than a tableau. The pleasure this clever sketch elicited made the author see the merit of a larger-scale painting.

Aristophanes, as Romain Piana has pointed out, was often associated with vaudeville and caricature during the July Monarchy. Tradition held that once, when an actor refused to play a role that critiqued tyrants, Aristophanes colored his face for want of a mask and took the stage to play the risky part.[36] Balzac had played Aristophanes for a day by publishing his excerpt in *La Presse*, but his novel is the work of an "écrivain peu satirique" (not-very-satirical writer). Whereas Balzac had begrimed himself with the ink of newsprint to publicize his book and castigate the press, in the preface to his novel, Balzac is not Aristophanes.

Scribe

Instead he is a follower of Eugène Scribe, for each novel of the *Comédie humaine* is to a certain extent a vaudeville which prepares the audience for the greater work which is in preparation.[37] As the press excerpt was cropped to promote the volume, so the volume was prefaced to prepare for the masterwork. As Jean-Claude Yon points out, "le théâtre de Scribe est pour Balzac un modèle que l'écrivain veut certes dépasser en l'approfondissant, mais qu'en

aucun cas il ne méprise, comme le fait un Hugo ou un Gautier" (Scribe's theater is a model for Balzac, one that he wants to surpass by deepening it, surely,
but which he by no means disdains, as a Hugo or a Gautier did).[38] Scribe's
vaudeville, which portrays a journalist and a playwright trying to manipulate
public opinion to serve their competing interests, is a "spirituelle ébauche"
(clever sketch), which Balzac has developed into a painting, as Lucien's article is a lightweight demonstration within Balzac's more complete critique
of the priorities of the liberal press. Balzac's presentation of the various parts
of *Illusions perdues* is faithful to the program outlined in the prospectus for
César Birotteau, in which the newspaper provides an "aperçu" to be followed
by a book's, "formule habilement déduite" (formula skillfully deduced).[39] Like
most of the other novels that make up *La Comédie humaine*, each of the three
volumes of *Illusions perdues* was accompanied by a preface and divided into
chapters.[40] Balzac's individual novels were presented less showily in volume
form than they were in the press, but their prefaces and chapter titles insisted
on their existence as fragments of a future whole and sought to engage readers
with humor and polemics that appealed to multiple levels of interpretation.

In "Comment se font les petits journaux," the scene published in *La Presse*
in 1839, the text of the epigrams Lousteau writes against the baron Châtelet
is followed by, "Il est facile de voir que l'article était un tissu de personnalités
les plus drôles" (It is easy to see that the article was a web of in-jokes about
the funniest prominent people).[41] In successive versions of this passage, Balzac replaced his narrator's theatrical didacticism with historical commentary.
In the 1843 Furne version, the passage became, "L'article était un tissu de
personnalités comme on les faisait à cette époque" (the article was a web of
in-jokes about prominent people of the sort people wrote in that era), and for
the Furne corrigé, "L'article était un tissu de personnalités comme on les faisait
à cette époque, assez sottes, car ce genre fut étrangement perfectionné depuis,
notamment par *le Figaro*" (the article was a web of in-jokes about prominent
people of the sort people wrote in that era, pretty dumb ones, for this genre
has been strangely perfected since, especially by *le Figaro*).[42] Balzac made the
context of the articles written at Florine's supper increasingly historical and
decreasingly theatrical each time he revised the passage.

Practical considerations could have played a role in his decision. It would
doubtless have been provocative to print a direct attack on *Le Figaro* in
La Presse, but Balzac's progression toward historical citation of commercial
detail is consistent with his aim in *César Birotteau* to make historical *pièces
justificatives* (evidence) of prospectuses. In contrast, the press excerpt's theat-
ricalization of Lousteau's epigrams ("vous voyez que . . .": "you see that . . .")
keeps it in the immediacy of newspaper consumption. The *César Birotteau*
prospectus differentiated between the time of newspaper reading and that of
book reading. The framing of "Comment se font les petits journaux" suggests that Balzac was practicing the same distinction in his publication of the
extract and the volume of the second part of *Illusions perdues*. The excerpt

was a here-and-now condemnation of the ways of the theatrical press, published in the very *feuilleton* where such journalism usually appeared, and dressed up with didactic markers to point out the salient features of defamatory journalism. A take-home lesson was performed for readers of *La Presse*, and references to Girardin and Janin made the extract itself a cousin to the "tissus de personnalités" it described. The more extensive engagement with Girardin's and Janin's ideas that is practiced in the rest of *Illusions perdues* saves the novel itself from the fault of attacking "personnalités." Lucien's article is a bold and promotional tease when published in *La Presse*. Taken in the context of the rest of the novel, it makes Janin's practice a consequence of a system that encourages wide appeal, quick turnover, and anonymous reporting. The pastiche that appeared personal in the excerpt's press publication became a structural critique in the book.

In Balzac's global approach to the promise and perils of the press, theatrical journalism and overblown publicity are recuperable within a book because the temporality of its reading allows them to last and the reader to reflect. Likewise, using journalism to promote the book is a logical recourse in an age in which it will never reach its audience without some publicity. Balzac emphasizes the materiality of the book and the theatricality of the press to show that the press's temporality and marketing priorities conspire against responsible journalism. In doing so, he disagrees with Janin's contention that clever attacks can prepare public figures to weather the disagreements they face. Unlike Janin, who saw the post-1830 press as a heroic institution and as the source of the July Monarchy's greatest statesmen, Balzac thought that 1830 had made hypocrites of formerly opposition newspapers, and that such duplicity, combined with aggressive marketing and a lack of signatures on articles, ensured that the press's priority would increasingly be to appeal to the lowest common denominator in society. By promoting his works one way in the press, another in volume form, and yet another way in the *Comédie humaine*, Balzac tried to situate his arguments, rather than letting them be situated by critics or publishers.

Situating History on Paper

In the last section of *Illusions perdues*, having left David to his efforts to create a paper that will preserve Voltaire's works in less space, Lucien meets Carlos Herrera, who claims to put Voltaire's ideas into practice. Herrera proposes to make Lucien his secretary, illustrating his suggestion with the strange story of Biren, the goldsmith-turned-secretary who chewed paper while he worked. Biren, though he was sentenced to death for eating a treaty, escaped and eventually married a duchess from whom he had sought pardon when he accidentally ate a contract. Given that, as Chollet puts it, Biren's story, "n'est pas non plus sans d'étroites et ironiques connotations avec le thème de l'inventeur du papier" (is not without close ironic ties to the theme of the inventor of paper), I argue that the paper chewer is not cannibalistic, consuming the body of a writer projected onto paper, as Françoise van Rossum-Guyon, would have it, but rather theatrical.[43] David's chewing prefigures invention, while Lucien's writing constitutes a loss of principles. By ingesting contracts and treaties, Biren internalizes the political and economic relations between people so as better to get around them, even if he does so unintentionally. His story is of a piece with Herrera/Vautrin's admonition to "mettez en dehors votre beauté, vos grâces, votre esprit, votre poésie. Si vous vous permettez des petites infamies, que ce soit entre quatre murs. Dès lors vous ne serez plus coupable de faire tache sur les décorations de ce grand théâtre appelé le monde" (show off your beauty, your grace, your cleverness and poetry. If you allow yourself small infamies, keep them within four walls. That way you will no longer be guilty of staining the decorations of this great theater called society; *IP*, 700).

Vautrin provides the next round of Lucien's initial career in Paris. He assigns Lucien his final role as text, telling him, in *Splendeurs et misères des courtisanes*, "Je suis l'auteur tu seras le drame ; si tu ne réussis pas, c'est moi qui serai sifflé" (I will be the author, you will be the drama; if you do not succeed, I will be whistled at).[44] The discretion Vautrin encourages Lucien to learn is contrary to both the visibility that the liberal press pretended to bring to society and the calumnies and scandals that it actually published. Herrera calls, "Tâchez d'être riches !" (Try to be rich!), the maxim of the era, in a near quote of Guizot's, "Enrichissez-vous !" (Enrich yourself!). Guizot's ideals of the theater as a place of communal uplift and the press as an institution of transparency had been thoroughly disproven by Lucien's first stay in Paris. Vautrin's reduction of social priorities to the accumulation and protection of property reduce even what was supposed to be a suggestion of social mobility to a set of arbitrary rules for preserving the status quo.[45] For Guizot, accumulation of wealth was a proof of competence and should be rewarded with eligibility for inclusion among decision makers. Vautrin's doctrine of splendid appearances supported by secret behavior decouples income from merit, but not from success. Projected appearances regulate social relations. Lucien, having seen journalists publishing calumnies anonymously to attract readers, had imitated elements of their behavior without understanding the principles behind it. As a worldly dramaturge Herrera is more effective than the journalists Lucien has encountered so far. Having been transformed by Vautrin into a drama after their first encounter, Lucien declares in his final suicide note to his protector that, "vous avez voulu faire (de moi) un personnage plus grand que je ne pouvais l'être" (you wanted to make of me a character larger than I could be).[46] Lucien can no more survive as a projection of Vautrin's than he could as a journalist with illusions.

The year 1839, when *Un grand homme de province à Paris* (the part of *Illusions perdues* that treats the press) was published, was also the year the daguerrotype was invented. Philippe Ortel, in *L'écran de le représentation*, identifies this as a moment that split projection from touch in aesthetics; photography became the opposite of weaving.[47] Lucien's dependence on other people's impressions of him is in marked contrast to David's faith in his own ideas. Chardon, Lucien, and Ève's last name, takes its most material form as an ingredient for David's paper in Angoulême, and its most virtual in a sonnet written to mock Lucien's pretentions in Paris.

In Angoulême, David will make paper of "orties et chardons" (nettles and thistles) hoping to become "le Jacquard de la papeterie" (the Jacquard of papermaking), for "je suis sûr de donner à la papéterie française le privilège dont jouit notre littérature, en faire un monopole pour notre pays" (I am sure to give French papermaking the status our literature enjoys, to create a monopoly for our country; *IP*, 583), while in Paris, Lucien will suffer over a sonnet that calls him the "Chardon du parterre" (Thistle of the pit); a barb that plays on his botanical nonnoble name and his frequentation of the theater. Ève and Lucien Chardon both give up their patronym, but Ève does so to join David in making paper, while Lucien's efforts to assume his mother's maiden name draw out the worst in the Parisian press. David weaves and Lucien projects (or is projected). The one preserves literature, the other contributes to the depradations of the press. The aesthetic split Ortel discusses falls between printed novels and performed journalism within *Illusions perdues*.

Roland Chollet, in *Balzac journaliste*, points out that Balzac was convinced that literature could only reach its public by commercial means and that any artist who wanted to be effective had to engage with the economic imperatives of his profession. Balzac's great project of 1830–1833, the *Société d'abonnement général*, would have provided affordable new novels to the provincial elite. Though a lack of financing kept Balzac from trying his plan, Chollet reminds us that it was fruitful in other ways:

> Retenons que le projet de *Société d'abonnement général* atteste chez Balzac journaliste . . . la permanence et le renouvellement d'un effort de réflexion sur son métier, sur la situation de l'écrivain dans la société, sur le roman moderne et son destinataire, déstinataire réel quoique lecteur encore potentiel, démandeur qui s'ignore, et qu'il faut non seulement connaître, mais atteindre et éclairer.[48]

> Let us remember that Balzac the journalist's plans for the *Société d'abonnement general* testify to the permanence and renewal of an effort at reflection about his profession, about the writer's place in society, about the modern novel and its destinataire (person to whom it was directed), a real destinataire even if a still-potential reader, a source of demand who doesn't know he is one, and whom one must not only know, but also reach and enlighten.

After 1836, press publicaton was an essential way to reach readers. In the novels considered here, whose composition reflects the concerns Chollet identifies in Balzac's efforts at founding the *Société d'abonnement général*, a prospectus or a digression is never just a prospectus or digression. Instead, they are performative proposals for reconciling the practice of publicity with institutions worth preserving. The prospectuses included in *César Birotteau* and Lucien's article about *L'Alcade dans l'embarras* import the advertising mode, with its rhetoric of seduction, into the reflective book medium, where its causes and effects can be examined at leisure.[49] Unlike the set pieces which make books present as such, descriptions of Finot's publicity techniques and Lucien's adventures in journalism gradually expose the codes and priorities of July Monarchy journalism. Its theatricality, which is shown to have much in common with advertising and acting's emphasis on appearances, is critiqued within the plot, even as it is exaggerated when parts of the book are published in the press.

Scholars have examined Balzac's use and transformation of the melodramatic mode and have analyzed the theatricality of his *Scènes de la vie parisienne*.[50] A few have analyzed his plays. I argue that between their inclusion of advertisement and their exploitation of its effects, *Illusions perdues* and *César Birotteau* describe and practice the vaudeville mode, in all of its heterogeneity and critical verve. Whereas vaudeville's double meanings were simultaneously pedagogical for some members of their audiences and ironic for others, Balzac's novels were oriented toward different readerships at different times in accordance with their publication formats. In response to the question Balzac posed in his foreword, "comment plaire à la fois au poète, au philosophe et aux masses qui veulent la poésie et la philosophie sous de saisissantes images ?" (how to please the poet, the philosopher and the the masses who want poetry and philosophy in the form of captivating images?),[51] one of Balzac's practical solutions was to set the press up as a theater in which a showy version of his critiques attracted readers.

Such readers might then be inspired to take the time to read individual novels or even the whole of the *Comédie humaine*. Balzac's final insistence on textuality as a condition for reflection keeps his most interesting meditations on press theatricality in books, not plays. Nonetheless, like Scribe, who transformed vaudeville into comedy over the course of his career, Balzac took vaudeville material and made his comedy of it. The textuality of his procedure made a mosaic of his masterwork.[52] If the theatricality of its promotion temporarily made the reader a spectator, it also invited him or her to reflect on the implications of the support by which he or she experienced the novel.

When Balzac invented his Émile de Girardin-like character, Finot, as an updated Figaro, he didn't just describe the current state of publishing by redoing Figaro's monologue on bookselling and liberty of expression. His novels also performed the principles of the commercial press that they described, first

by explaining the virtues of promotional artwork in *César Birotteau*, which
was published as promotional volumes, and then by pastiching publicity via
feuilleton in the part of *Illusions perdues* published in the *feuilleton*. In successive editions of these novels and then of the *Comédie humaine* itself, though,
Balzac differentatied theatrical promotion from physical, historical documentation, with the former discussed as a contemporary phenomenon to be set
down for fuller consideration, now and in the future, by the latter. Media,
be they newsprint, book pages, or lines of vaudeville, are cleverly examined
as supports for different agendas with different temporalities. Balzac's prose
about journalism is thematized and performed in terms borrowed from the
theater but written toward material history to outlast dramatic conventions.

Chapter 4

Papers That Block the Light

To benefit fully from publicity revenues, newspapers needed room to print advertisements. The size of July Monarchy newspapers was regulated by the government, which increased the standard size of papers in 1837 and then again in 1845. To comment on these increases in format, vaudevilles covered Parisian stages with newspapers so giant that they obscured the audience's view of the actors. One year-end revue of 1836 staged *L'Univers pittoresque*, which was "soixante pieds carrés" (sixty square feet).[1] Other 1845 vaudevilles staged *L'Immensité*, which disappeared into clouds on stage, and *La Plaine Saint-Denis* (named after the plain on which Paris is situated), "format nouveau, facile à parcourir . . . en voiture . . . des allées sont ménagées entre les colonnes, et un chemin de traverse est réservé pour descendre au feuilleton" (new format, easy to skim . . . in a carriage . . . paths have been organized between the columns, and a shortcut has been reserved for going down to the *feuilleton*).[2]

Pretending that an onstage newspaper was as big as the world it represented allowed playwrights to suggest that the advertisement that was supposedly financing more widespread enlightenment was in fact blocking audiences' views of the play and, by analogy, obscuring newspaper readers' view of the events that they wanted to read about. As the forty-franc press gained traction in 1837, papers grew to a dimension of 400 by 560 millimeters (roughly 16 by 22 inches). In 1845 they added a fifth page and grew to 430 by 600 millimeters (about 17 by 24 inches).[3]

In that same year, 1845, the Société Générale des Annonces was founded to consolidate advertising contracts so that one agency (the SGA) could sell ad space in a set of different newspapers with each contract. A new newspaper, *L'Époque*, also burst onto the scene. *L'Époque*, which claimed to offer the content of ten newspapers in one (figure 4), sought to take advantage of the increased size of dailies and to compete with *La Presse* and *Le Siècle*. Its extraordinary efforts at publicity included sending a scantily clad charioteer through the streets of Paris in a vehicle emblazoned with the paper's title, and papering the town with posters and prospectuses.[4]

Figure 4. Publicity panel for *L'Époque.* Copyright ©
Musée Carnavalet/Roger-Viollet.

The theater exploited the materiality of newsprint to make fun of the
effects of newspaper enlargement and its increase in visibility. Holding up
a newspaper on stage became a pretext for critical commentary, which was
usually spoken in comedies and acted out in vaudevilles. In comedies, newspapers served as props on which the characters rely for everything from moral
direction to faulty election results. Rather than enlightening the reading members of the body politic, the stage versions of newspapers scare and mislead
their readers, making them behave badly in ways that set up comic situations. In vaudevilles, unsurprisingly, the humor is more directly physical, with
newsprint, the stuff of the fourth estate, often being made to stand in for the
theater's fourth wall. Piercing the paper, rather than reading it, is the gesture
that allows for enlightenment of theater audiences.

Before the invention of the forty-franc press, the newspaper ideal was to
be an *organe d'opinion* (organ of public opinion). Comedies and vaudevilles
retained the bodily metaphor as they set out to make fun of the press. Having
given up on representing consistent and identifiable political points of view,
newspapers are treated—mockingly—as the souls and hearts of characters,
rather than as members of the body politic.

Body Parts

In the comedies considered in this section, the plot varies little. Two young lovers cannot get married because one of their parents (nearly always the young lady's father or guardian) disagrees with their union or has another match in mind for his child. The reasons for disagreement vary, but in each of these cases the influence of newspapers further delays the inevitable granting of permission to wed the sweetheart which concludes the play. The newspaper is an obstacle because its ideas are too enthusiastically followed by certain characters, most often the father figures, and those characters usually speak of their paper as a physical or spiritual part of themselves. Rather than participating thoughtfully in the body politic on the basis of what they read, the subscribers in these comedies are isolated by their adherence to every detail of the articles they peruse. In Dumersan and Lurieu's *Le Pensionnaire*, M. Locard, the first of four tenants in an apartment building to read a shared newspaper, complains, "Quand je ne lis pas mon journal, le premier, je suis comme un corps sans âme" (When I don't read my newspaper first, I'm like a body without a soul).[5] Not only does Locard rely on his newspaper for ideas, but it matters to him that he be the first occupant of his building to read the paper, as if such priority somehow increases his degree of agreement with the paper's editorial positions. His belief that a partial purchase and an early turn at reading constitute a political existence is made to look ridiculous.

Like his middle-class counterpart Locard, the aristocratic Baron de Morivaux from Dumanoir's *Un Système* relies blindly, even physically, on his newspaper. He says, "Je me priverais plutôt de mon déjeuner que de mes débats" (I would rather deprive myself of lunch than of my debates) and believes "un journal à vingt lieues de Paris est une conversation quotidienne qu'on se procure encore avec la Capitale" (a newspaper at twenty leagues from Paris is a daily conversation that one procures with the capital).[6] The fact that the conversation is unidirectional is apparently of no importance to the baron. He objects to marriage in general, citing "un article extrait de la *Gazette des tribunaux*, un procès conjugal" (an article from the *Gazette des tribunaux*, a marriage trial)[7] as evidence for his point of view and then spends the rest of the play being proven wrong by his niece and her suitor, who marry happily at the end.

Dumanoir's *Un Système* sends up the Baron de Morivaux's false sense of engagement with the capital via his paper, but it also explores current concerns about the wisdom of judicial transparency as practiced by the *Gazette des tribunaux*. If making people aware of divorces predisposes them to question the institution of marriage, these plays suggest, then perhaps it would be better not to share such information so widely.[8] Likewise, in the play entitled *La Gazette des tribunaux*, a Parisian subscriber to the judicial newspaper becomes so terrified by all the crimes it reports that he moves to the country and lives under lock and key. Surely, the play seems to ask, publishing court proceedings is not meant to drive people from the city? Information spread too widely becomes a threat to the very ideals of civic engagement it was presumably meant to encourage.

Another extended joke at the expense of the deluded newspaper reader, Hippolyte Auger's *Mlle Bernard, ou l'autorité paternelle*, of 1838, sets the young protagonists the task of convincing a recalcitrant father to honor their feelings rather than following the abstract and anonymous counsels of his newspaper. The play opens with M. Truchet pulling out his newspaper and remarking, "L'auteur de cet article a raison : on élève mal les enfants aujourd'hui (The author of this article is right, today's children are badly brought up).[9] The rest of the plot depends largely on Truchet's shifting interpretation and exercise of paternal authority. His future daughter-in-law, who manages the situation so as to convince him to allow her marriage with his son, tries to put his dependence in perspective:

> TRUCHET. Tenez . . . un bon journal est une bonne chose . . . et le mien est excellent.
> MADEMOISELLE BERNARD. Chacun en dit autant du sien . . . parce qu'il le choisit selon ses opinions.
> TRUCHET. N'est-ce pas tout naturel ? . . .
> AIR : *Un homme pour faire un tableau*. Ainsi d'un esprit corrupteur / L'âme n'est jamais obsédée ; / On est soi-même son auteur, / On se maintient dans son idée ; / En tout, pour tout du même avis . . .
> MADEMOISELLE BERNARD, *l'interrompant*. Mais à ce compte-là, sans rire, / On peut s'en épargner le prix , / Ou fermer les yeux pour le lire. (1.3.781)

> TRUCHET. See here . . . a good newspaper is a good thing . . . and mine is excellent.
> MADEMOISELLE BERNARD. Everyone says the same of his own . . . because he's chosen it according to his opinion.
> TRUCHET. Isn't that natural? . . .
> TUNE: *A Man to Make a Painting*. This way the soul is never obsessed / By a corrupting spirit; / You're your own author, / You stick to your ideas; / About everything, always of the same opinion . . .
> MADEMOISELLE BERNARD, *interrupting him*. But in that case, seriously, / You could spare yourself the expense, / Or close your eyes to read the paper.

Truchet's blindness to his own situation when he insists that his loyalty to his newspaper protects him from any corrupting spirit, and even makes him more himself, is funny. As it happens, the article he is reading about paternal authority has a hole in it, one that Mlle Bernard fills in with her own interpretation. The article, read aloud by Truchet, says, "'Dieu a sa foudre, le prince a son sceptre, et le père . . .' il y a un trou dans le papier . . . aidez-moi à deviner . . . le père a . . .' MADEMOISELLE BERNARD. Eh ! monsieur Truchet ! le père a son cœur" (1.3.781) (God has his lightning, the prince has his scepter, and the father . . . There's a hole in the paper . . . help me guess . . . the father has . . . MADEMOISELLE BERNARD. Oh, Mr. Truchet, the father has his heart!). Mlle Bernard's solution to the hole in the newspaper is an unlikely one, given the gist of the rest of the sentence (earlier M. Truchet had proposed the more likely "un père a sa canne" [the father has his cane]), but her response is the one advocated by the play. Luckily for the young couple, M. Truchet, being used to adopting the opinions of others, accepts Mlle Bernard's improbable deviation from the newspaper's line. Good sense and good behavior prevail over the influence of the press, and once again a comedy makes fun of an overly naive reader, who mistakenly believes that in subscribing to a newspaper he has become his own author. The ways of the heart and the hearth were the domain of comedy. In *Mlle Bernard*, blind confidence in a newspaper appears as a potential obstacle to their smooth operation.

The hole in M. Truchet's newspaper participates in a pattern of piercings that enact concerns about newspapers obscuring access to enlightenment, rather than facilitating it. One of the most popular year-end revues of the 1840s, *Les Pommes de terres malades* (Rotten Potatoes), of 1845, compared the ubiquitous advertisements for the new newspaper, *L'Époque*, to the clouds that had contributed to the potato famine currently ravaging Europe. To connect publicity and opacity, its authors, Dumanoir and Clairville, had a character poke a hole in one of the advertising posters as part of a risqué joke. This was not only a critical move with regard to the newspaper's publicity but also a reinvention of one of the most famous gestures of the Romantic stage, the one in which Alexandre Dumas's Antony breaks a windowpane to reach the object of his affections. In *Antony*, which ran for 130 performances at the Théâtre de la Porte Saint-Martin in 1831, the broken window was a metaphor both for the hero's violent refusal of social convention and for an extension of that refusal across the fourth wall (itself a dramatic convention.) If Antony could break through to Adèle d'Hervey, refusing the respect for class ties that led to her marriage, their passion could inspire audiences to sympathize with such a refusal.[10] In *Les Pommes de terre malades*, the year-end vaudeville revue considered here, advertising posters cover buildings and need to be pierced for characters to communicate with each other. Where *Antony* innovated by evacuating the morality from melodrama (and thus privileging passion over social convention—a move that set Romantic drama apart), *Les Pommes de terre malades* defined a new epoch by portraying all commentary, however negative, to be a form of promotion within the new media sphere.

As a vaudeville revue, *Les Pommes de terre malades* was required to send up the events of the year that was drawing to a close. Its authors, Dumanoir and Clairville, focused on the two major innovations in press marketing

Figure 5. Sainville [Étienne François Marie
Morel] as the King of the Potatoes. Draner [Jules
Joseph Georges Renard], *Les Pommes de terre
malades, revue de Dumanoir et Clairville*, 1845.
Courtesy of Bibliothèque nationale de France. [11]

of 1845, the creation of the Société Générale d'Annonces and the launch
of *L'Époque*, to shape their jokes and dialogue.[12] Dumanoir and Claireville
treated the multiplication of advertisements for *L'Époque* as a plague that
had made the hero of the play, the king of potatoes (see figure 5) sick. Cloudy
weather had been contributing to the potato blight that destroyed crops
across Europe (most famously in Ireland) in 1845, so the idea that all this
publicity for a new newspaper darkened the environment dangerously had
immediate ominous echoes. The dark spots that appear on Pomme de terre 1e
(Potato the first) are direct references to the effects of mildew on potatoes, but
they are also associated with the newsprint with which much of the scenery
is covered.[13]

    Not all of the newspapers in the play were made of paper, though. Perhaps
to further emphasize the materiality of *L'Époque* as newsprint, *Le Soleil*, a
competing newspaper, was personified by an actor. Le Soleil plays the standard vaudeville role of the master of ceremonies for a parade of recent events.
He proposes to lift Pomme de terre out of his funk by showing him "tout ce

que la Société générale des annonces couvre d'or et de gloire, à trente centimes la ligne" (all that the Société Générale des Annonces covers with gold and glory, at thirty centimes a line).[14] The SGA was a consolidator of advertising contracts; Dumanoir and Claireville had their potato characters refer to it as the organization that determined what was worth seeing in Paris. Within the play, Le Soleil's inability to distract Pomme de terre from *L'Époque*'s coverage not only reflects the reality of the two newspapers' respective success as of the end of 1845 (for both were, indeed, real newspapers), but it is also a performance of light (metaphorically ideas and information) failing to break through the haze of advertisement that covers the city.[15] In fact, the one breakthrough that occurs in the play takes the form of a joke, which brought down the house when the play was performed.

When the prime minister Tubercule's second-story window is covered by a poster for *L'Époque*, Pomme de terre encourages him to break through the advertisement so that the president and prime minister can communicate (and so that the audience can see Tubercule). The stage directions read: "Il passe à travers l'affiche sa tête et son bras droit : le bras se trouve dans la lettre O du mot Époque, et la tête dans la lettre suivante, Q" (He pokes his head and his right arm through the poster: the arm winds up in the O of the word Époque, and the head in the next letter, Q). Pomme de terre calls attention to the joke: "Quel tableau ! . . . Il a fourré son bras dans l'O ! . . . Et son nez . . . dans une autre lettre !" (What a sketch! . . . He's stuck his arm in the O, and his nose . . . in another letter!).[16]

Several *feuilletonistes* reported that this joke at the expense of those who always had their "nez fourré dans un journal" (nose stuck in a newspaper) elicited great hilarity.[17] In the gag, the "Q" of the newspaper's title is a pun on the word *cul*, or ass. When Tubercule sticks his head into the Q/*cul* of *L'Époque*, he is putting his face in the title's ass to look out at the audience. With their joke, Dumanoir and Claireville, the playwrights, made a body of the title as it appeared on posters, the better to suggest that *L'Époque*'s success stemmed from its ability to solicit desire or curiosity (here marked as unorthodox) via massive advertisement. The humor is both ribald and wry, for in 1845 the number of people who would have given a great deal to have their *époque* traversed by a healthy tuber was large.

From Glass to Paper

In Dumas's *Antony*, the eponymous hero clears an obstacle by breaking through a panel, and in the process references a word considered inappropriate for the stage (*mouchoir*, or handkerchief): in *Les Pommes de terre malade*, Tubercule clears the way for communication by ripping through a poster, and in so doing sticks his nose in the title's ass. Parodies of Dumas's drama had often played on the homology between *verre* (glass) and *vers* (verse or, sometimes conveniently, worms), taking advantage of the playwright's dramatic use of the physical material of a broken window to make fun of his poetics. *Les Pommes de terre malades* is not close enough to *Antony* in any other way to be considered a parody of it, but it, too, uses the materiality of a printed letter (Q) to bring down an overpromoted title. It also replaces glass with paper—a less transparent (but cheaper) material.[18]

At least one critic speculated that *Les Pommes de terre malades*, by being outrageously critical of *L'Époque*, was "encore pour ce journal une sorte de prospectus" (yet another form of prospectus for this paper).[19] If so, it was an effective one: the year-end revue ran for eighty-two performances, nearly three times as many as most such plays.[20]

The scale of the advertising campaign for *L'Époque* and the success of the vaudeville revue that mocked it indicate that by 1845, the year of its performance, ubiquity and shock value had come to be associated with this new consolidated newspaper. In *Les Pommes de terre malades*, it is publicity that trumps all—much to the detriment of the reigning source of sustenance. If the Romantic theater allowed Antony to make glass its feeble barrier, nearly a convention in its friability, July Monarchy vaudeville obsessed over the uses of newsprint, and over the importance of seeing through it.

The same critic who wondered whether the piercing of *L'Époque*'s title wasn't a form of publicity also objected to the title of *Les Pommes de terre malades*, saying, "il faut avoir l'esprit furieusement tourné à la gaieté pour avoir trouvé un texte intarissable de bonnes et de mauvaises plaisanteries, dans un fléau qui a réduit à la misère et à la famine huit ou neuf millions d'individus en Europe ; jusqu'ici on n'avait pas imaginé de chercher des sujets de vaudeville dans une calamité publique" (You have to be terribly lighthearted to base a voluble script full of good and bad jokes on a plague which has reduced eight or nine million people in Europe to misery and famine; until now, people hadn't thought of using public calamities as subject matter for vaudevilles).[21] The provocative humor to which this critic objects probably contributed significantly to the vaudeville's success. As was so often the case with vaudevilles about the press, this one performed (and pastiched) the very practices it was critiquing, presenting them to the audience for evaluation. It conflated massive commercial promotion of a new paper with an agricultural plague, but it did so in terms surprising enough to beg the question of whether it wasn't participating in the very publicity campaign it made fun of. Coinciding, as it did, with the consolidation of the press advertising market under the SGA, the success of *Les Pommes de terre malades* suggests that negative publicity, which had been so unwelcome in the *presse d'opinion* that it sometimes occasioned duels,[22] was starting to seem useful to newspapers as a means of making themselves known. If this is the case, it is quite possible that even the most seemingly critical vaudevilles about the press are in fact involved in promotional schemes.

It is no accident that *L'Époque* is treated as an overwhelming material presence in *Les Pommes de terre malades*. If its credibility is unreliable, then the paper is no more than a very widespread medium. This is how George Sand saw it. She published her socialist novel, *Le Péché de Monsieur Antoine*, in the first issues of *L'Époque*. In the preface that she added to the novel's publication in volume form, Sand explained that opposition newspapers, "n'avaient malheureusement pas assez de lecteurs pour donner une publicité satisfaisante à l'idée qu'on tenait à émettre" (unfortunately didn't have enough subscribers to provide sufficient publicity for the idea I was trying to communicate); for the most part, newspapers that had the means to publish serial novels were not socialist, which led to a paradoxical situation in which "les journaux conservateurs devenaient donc l'asile des romans socialistes" (conservative newspapers became the refuge of socialist novels).[23] As for *L'Époque*, it took advantage of the fame of its contributor. Among the posters covering the scenery of *Les Pommes de terre malades*, several exhort characters and audiences, "Lisez *L'Époque* ! Lisez *Le Péché de M. Antoine* !" (Read *L'Époque*! Read *The Sin of Mr. Antoine*!) The play added a few jokes about Monsieur or Madame Sand,[24] and the novelist and the newspaper both benefited from their arrangement.

A somewhat earlier curtain raiser performed at the Théâtre de la Gaîté suggests that the critic who had suspicions about the motives behind the critique of *Les Pommes de terre malades* was starting to reason like a vaudeville impresario. In *L'Ombre du Nicolet*, the ghost of Nicolet, the former director of the Théâtre de la Gaîté, explains that all criticism, be it positive or negative, is good for a play. In response to another character's concerns about newspaper reviews, Nicolet's ghost proclaims:

> Les journaux . . . On les fait beaucoup plus méchants qu'ils ne sont . . . D'ailleurs . . . est-ce que tu penses, pauvre fou, échapper à la critique, lorsqu'elle n'épargne pas même les plus hauts personnages de la terre. . . . La critique, si elle est juste et loyale, aie le bon esprit d'en profiter, de réparer le lendemain les fautes de la veille. . . . Et suppose même qu'elle soit injuste et malveillante. . . . cela n'est jamais arrivé ; mais enfin, tout est possible, cela peut arriver. . . . Et bien ! même alors, la critique te fera vivre encore !!! Un bon feuilleton bien méchant, bien spirituel, qui dira beaucoup de mal de ton théâtre, fera songer au public que tu as un théâtre, et si monsieur tel ou tel . . . je nomme personne, parce que j'en aurais trop à nommer, si monsieur tel ou tel n'avait pas eu le bonheur d'avoir quelques ennemis, si on ne l'avait pas critiqué dans les journaux, qui diable saurait qu'il a jamais existé ?[25]

> Newspapers . . . they are made out to be much meaner than they really are . . . Besides . . . do you, poor loony, think that you can escape criticism when it doesn't even spare the greatest figures on earth? . . . If

criticism is fair and loyal, be clever enough to take advantage of it, to use tomorrow to fix today's faults . . . and suppose that it is unfair and malicious . . . that's never happened, but anything is possible, it could . . . well, even then, criticism will still help you survive!! A good mean *feuilleton*, nice and clever, that says all sorts of bad things about your theater, will remind the public that you have a theater, and if Mr. so and so or so and so . . . I won't name anyone, because there would be too many to name, if Mr. so and so hadn't had the good fortune of having several enemies, if he hadn't been criticized in the newspapers, who the devil would even know that he had ever existed?

Nicolet's evaluation is clearly tongue-in-cheek with respect to the critics watching his play. When he says that critics have never been unfair, "Cela n'est jamais arrivé,"[26] he means exactly the opposite, but his point, that even negative publicity can be helpful in theater, is crucial to an evaluation of the critic's role. Unlike plays that condemned critics for making a profit on their opinions, the judgments on which their influence is based, *L'Ombre de Nicolet* dismisses the idea that it even matters what their opinions are. According to Nicolet, the *feuilleton* is one more advertisement; one shouldn't expect it to be more disinterested than the commercial advertisements that surround it.[27]

Newspapers Play the Game

The *feuilletoniste* who covered *L'Ombre de Nicolet* for the *Constitutionnel* showed readers the physical reality of Nicolet's contention that all critiques could be used for publicity by conflating one of the subtitles of his *feuilleton* with a theater *affiche* (poster). First, in his remarks on *L'Ombre de Nicolet*, he reminded his readers that "un prologue d'ouverture est un véritable prospectus" (an opening night curtain-raiser is really a prospectus).[28] In his summary of the play he pointed out that Nicolet, the very successful former director of the Gaité, insisted on vaunting even the most caustic journalists, and continued to say that when the current director frowned at this idea:

> Nicolet insiste, et en homme de sens lui conseille de profiter des épi-grammes du feuilleton. . . . Le directeur pourtant reprend courage et fait porter aux journaux l'annonce de la réouverture par la première représentation de
>
> LE PETIT CHAPEAU[29]

Nicolet insists and, as a man of good sense, advises him to take advantage of the *feuilleton*'s epigrams . . . The director, encouraged, has

someone run to the newspapers with the poster announcing the theater's reopening with the first performance of

THE LITTLE HAT

Le Petit Chapeau is the title of the play for which *L'Ombre de Nicolet* was
the curtain-raiser. It is also the next work this critic reviews in his column,
so its title, though presented as part of a description of a fictional director's
publicity efforts, is also the subtitle that introduces the next subsection of the
feuilleton. The play's advertisement is the *feuilleton*'s section heading.

This is a direct physical incitement to the newspaper reader to consider
the *feuilleton*'s role as publicity for theater. Given that the curtain-raiser the
article has just described contends that all publicity, positive or negative, is
good publicity for a theater, the *feuilletoniste* seems to be acknowledging his
article's complicity in promoting plays. Both stage critiques of press publicity,
such as *Les Pommes de terre malades*, and newspaper discussions of their own
role in promoting theater, whether what they say is positive or negative, draw
attention to the materiality of newsprint and the increasingly promotional,
rather than critical, role that appearing in print is playing.[30]

Cross-referentiality between *feuilletons* and plays was facilitated by the
fact that a number of writers wrote for both the theater and the press. This
overlap could lead to debates carried out over periods of several months in
multiple newspapers and on stage. One such multisupport discussion began
with Alexandre Dumas's 1836 drama *Kean*, based on the life of the great
British actor Edmund Kean. The play drew extensive press coverage for its
remarks on journalism, even though they were, for the most part, limited to
one speech in which Kean tries to dissuade Miss Anna Damby from trying a
career in theater. *La Quotidienne* pointed out that the play's negative representation of the press had been oversold:

> On avait déjà menacé la presse d'une diatribe violente fulminée dans
> cette pièce, du haut des planches de Variétés contre la critique dra-
> matique. Les auteurs procédaient par la voie de l'allusion, et devaient
> donner les étrivières aux feuilletonistes français sur le dos des repor-
> ters anglais. Mais il paraît que les auteurs, les directeurs, et les acteurs
> ont, comme on dit, mis de l'eau dans leur vin, et que Kean ne se
> regimbera pas contre ses critiques ; M. Dumas vient de nous en don-
> ner l'assurance, dans un de ses feuilletons, car il est bon qu'on sache
> que M. Dumas est aussi feuilletoniste . . .[31]

The press had been menaced with a fulminating, violent diatribe
against drama critics pronounced from the height of the Variété's
boards in this play. Authors were going to proceed by allusions, and

to dress down French journalists at the expense of English reporters. But it sounds as though the authors, the directors, and the actors watered their wine, so to speak, and that Kean will not rebel against his critics. M. Dumas has just assured us of this in one of his *feuilletons*, for it is worth knowing that M. Dumas is also a *feuilletoniste* . . .

In his speech against the press, Kean warns of its dangers for actresses, while pointing out nonetheless that newspaper accounts are all that remains of an actor's art once he is gone. A number of *feuilletonistes* took issue with the play for its glorification of Kean's colorful biography and questioned the accuracy of its evaluation of his genius on stage. *La Quotidienne*, having announced that the play would not be too harsh on critics, nonetheless was indignant at the speech that finally appeared, pointing out that Kean owed quite a lot to positive newspaper publicity, as did Dumas. Jules Janin took the same argument even farther in the *Journal des débats*, objecting:

> Cela va bien au théâtre de déclamer contre la critique ! Le théâtre ne vit que par la critique ; sans la critique le théâtre serait mort aujourd'hui. C'est qu'aujourd'hui la critique a plus d'esprit, plus de style, plus d'invention que le théâtre. Hors de la critique, il n'y a ni théâtre, ni comédien ; la critique est la reine absolue de ces gloires éphémères, de ces inventions puériles, de ces imaginations perverties ; elle n'a qu'à retirer elle-même son appui tout-puissant, que deviendront les théâtres et ses froids déclamateurs ?[32]

> It suits the theater to declaim against criticism! The theater survives thanks to criticism; without it the theater would be dead today. It's that today criticism has more wit and style, more creativity, than the theater does. Without criticism there is no theater, no actor; criticism is the absolute queen of these ephemeral glories, of these puerile inventions, of these perverted imaginations; all she has to do is withdraw her all-powerful support—what would become of the theater and its frigid declaimers?

Janin, one of the most prominent critics of the time, was an ardent supporter of the new press, and perhaps an even more enthusiastic promoter of himself and his own writing (as we shall see in chapter 5).

J.T., at *La Quotidienne*, having written the preemptive article cited earlier, quoted the anticritic passage in *Kean* once the play was performed as evidence that Dumas had failed to do any damage: "M Dumas a cru devoir fulminer une petite imprécation contre les journalistes ; nous nous croyons si peu atteints par l'attaque, que nous allons la citer comme un des morceaux les mieux écrits de la pièce, quoique ce ne soit pas celui qui fait le plus d'effet" (M. Dumas felt he had to fulminate a little imprecation against journalists;

we feel ourselves so little concerned by his attack that we are going to cite it as one of the best-written passages of the play, though it was not the one that had the greatest effect).³³ Apparently pleased with the effect of his strategy, the same critic tried it again when faced with Louise Colet's tirade against critics in *La Jeunesse de Goethe* three years later: "Afin de prouver à Mme Colet que nous n'avons pas de rancune, pour la manière un peu hargneuse dont elle nous rudoie, nous allons citer le portrait qu'elle fait du critique, et les traits de satire qu'elle fait lancer par Goethe contre son ami Schlegel" (To prove to Mme Colet that we are not bitter about the way she roughs us up, we will cite her portrait of the critic and the satirical points she has Goethe launch against his friend Schlegel).³⁴

Whether or not newspaper critics cited anti-*feuilletoniste* passages from plays in their reviews, they made sure to retain their own joking but influential position as judges. In 1841, the *Constitutionnel*'s critic identified a representation of newspapers in *Les Fées de Paris* as exaggerated, saying of a character that "le sentiment n'avait aucune prise sur (son) cœur ; mais la peur du journaliste est un moyen plus efficace . . . Il paraît que le journaliste est un Croquemitaine, un Gargantua intellectuel qui dévore les députés tout aussi bien que les vaudevillistes" (sentiment had no influence on his heart, but the fear of journalists is a more effective means. . . . Apparently the journalist is a bogeyman, an intellectual Gargantua who devours deputies and vaudevillistes alike).³⁵ For all his irony, though, the critic took palpable pleasure in handing down a benevolent judgment, saying that Bayard, the author of the play in question, is protected by his talent: "Faites toujours d'aussi jolis ouvrages, Monsieur Bayard, et n'ayez pas peur du journaliste" (Keep producing works as nice as this one, Monsieur Bayard, and don't be afraid of journalists).³⁶ Safely ensconced as Gargantua (and not as Panurge's sheep, with which Sarcey would later associate critics), critics nonetheless found it unacceptable to have criticisms addressed directly to them without the veil of fiction.³⁷

Critics React to Breaking the Fourth Wall

Feuilletonistes, who often dispatched with unflattering images of journalists in plays by joking about them, citing them, or evaluating the style or morality of the performance in which they appeared, reacted more forcefully when actors addressed audiences directly. In 1843 and 1844, *Mlle Déjazet au sérail* and *La Tante Bazu*, which played at the Palais-Royal and the Gymnase, respectively, elicited unusually vehement reviews for their addresses to the audience; a fact made more remarkable by their status as minor comedies at medium-sized theaters. Nothing in *feuilletonistes*' practice required that these plays even be covered in the press.

When *La Tante Bazu* opened at the Gymnase, ending on what *Le Charivari* called an "*engueulement*, contre les journaux qui se sont permis de critiquer les productions remarquables des Prémaray, des Duchatelard, des Léonard et autres pseudonymes ou anonymes" (*chewing out* of the newspapers who took the liberty to criticize the remarkable productions of Prémarays, Duchatelards, Léonards, and other anonymous authors or pseudonyms), it prompted the reviewer to conclude, sarcastically, that, "M. Lardenay a bien fait de laver la tête à ces paltoquets de feuilletonistes" (M. Lardenay was right to let those good for nothing *feuilletonistes* have it).[38] J.T., at *La Quotidienne*, was incapable of such a remove. He wrote:

> Il y a dans cette pièce une intention d'étude de mœurs qui vaut la peine d'être remarquée. Mais, pour aujourd'hui, nous nous bornerons à blâmer l'inconvenance d'un acteur qui se permet d'interrompre son rôle et de sortir de la pièce, pour dénoncer la presse, comme si ce n'était pas assez des lois de septembre et des réquisitoires de M Poirson, par l'organe d'un de ses acteurs . . . Il nous semble qu'une pareille infraction aux lois sur la police du théâtre, qui défendent aux acteurs de rien dire sur la scène en dehors de leur rôle, ne devrait être tolérée, à moins que M. le Préfet de Police n'ait autorisé cette attaque contre l'indépendance de la critique, qu'on paraît vouloir intimider par tous les moyens possibles.[39]

> There was clearly a noteworthy intention to do a social study behind this play. For today, though, we will limit ourselves to condemning the inappropriateness of an actor interrupting his role and departing from the script to denounce the press, as if the September Laws and M. Poirson's indictments weren't enough, by the instrument of one of its actors . . . Its seems to us that such an infraction of the laws regulating the theater, which forbid actors from saying anything outside of their role on stage, should not be tolerated, unless the Prefect of Police has authorized this attack against the independence of criticism, which people do seem interested in intimidating by all possible means.

Given this critic's concern with intimidation of *feuilletonistes*, it is remarkable that he called for forceful repression of a speech made directly to the parterre. He would have authors and actors intimidated in the interest of dramatic convention, while critics were to be protected from verbal abuse. This article did appear in the very conservative *Quotidienne*, but the level of reaction this particular play's attack on critics elicited was nonetheless exceptional. As we have seen, plays frequently criticized critics, and usually critics simply evaluated the plays in question from whichever point of view seemed most apt to establish their own superior judgment. Critical comments on *La Tante Bazu* indicate real uneasiness with any nonfictional interaction between actors and the public.

Direct accusation of critics in the theater temporarily deprived them of their means of self-defense and made them look bad in a very public place. They found themselves in a position like the one ridiculed in *Paris dans la comète*, a vaudeville revue of 1843. One character pointed out that an advertisement marked AVIS AUX VOLEURS (Warning to Thieves) was "un avis maladroit : / Car lorsqu'un passant, par mégarde, / Regarde cet affiche, on croit / Que cette affiche le regarde" (An awkward warning, for when a hapless passerby looks at the poster, people will think that it concerns him).[40] Being seen to be taken in by an unflattering poster could happen to anyone. Critics who were seen watching harangues against critics had been explicitly targeted.

If the fear of the critic was direct address across the fourth wall, the fear of the playwright was a too-cynical public, unwilling to be moved by critiques that were frank about the promotional uses of criticism. Such concerns surface in the work of even the most established of playwrights. Eugène Scribe gained critical acclaim in 1848 with a comedy about the uses of publicity, *Le Puff*. Contemporaries called it "un acte de bon citoyen" (the act of a good citizen).[41] Several *feuilletonistes* reminded their readers that Mr. Puff had been a character in Richard Brinsley Sheridan's *School for Scandal*, a bit of erudition which, like the calumny plays of chapter 2, implied a genealogy of publicity starting in seventeenth-century England and extending to 1848 France. *Le Puff*'s connection to Sheridan was an oblique reminder that commercial publicity had an extensive track record across the channel. According to critics, the uses of puff had nonetheless had devastating effects on the critical faculties of the Parisian public. Charles de Matharel, at *Le Siècle*, having outlined all of the sorts of fraudulent publicity encompassed in the term "puff," concluded his explanation with a rhetorical question, "Et croyez-vous qu'il y a des oies qui se laissent prendre à ce gluau ? Énormement : le nombre est infiniment petit des gens qui affrontent la fatigue d'avoir une opinion et de juger par eux-mêmes" (And do you think there are still geese who are caught with this glue? There are a great many of them: the number of people who take on the fatigue of having their own opinion and defending it is infinitely small).[42] *Le Charivari*, too, took a negative point of view toward the sophistication of the public. It objected that *Le Puff* had not helped matters, chastising Scribe, "Il ne faut pas faire l'Académie plus ignorante, l'administration plus niaise et le public plus sottement credule qu'ils ne le sont. Restons, à cet égard, dans la vérité : elle est déjà assez fâcheuse" (You mustn't make the Academy more ignorant, the administration sillier, and the public more stupidly gullible than they are. For such matters, stick to the truth, it's already regrettable enough).[43]

Is Anyone Disinterested?

Critics went beyond simply lamenting the passivity of an easily duped public. In their reviews of *Le Puff* and of other works that portrayed the July Monarchy as the age of ubiquitous unreliable publicity, they asked their readers to reflect on the implications of such opacity for the production of the very newspapers they were reading. Rolle of *Le Constitutionnel* pointed out that such an all-encompassing portrait of a publicity-based society put him in an awkward position as a critic, for, when evaluating *Le Puff*,

> que dirai-je ? Si je loue l'esprit qui brille dans la comédie de M. Scribe, les combinaisons ingénieuses qui s'y montrent ; si je vante l'élégance du style . . . que va penser M. Scribe, qui ne croit pas qu'on dise aujourd'hui un seul mot de vérité ? . . . il s'écriera ; c'est un puff![44]

> what can I say? If I praise the brilliant wit of M. Scribe's comedy, his ingenious combinations and elegant style, what will M. Scribe, who thinks that today we don't write a single true word, think? He will cry, it's a puff!

The all-publicity-is-good-publicity approach revealed by *Les Pommes de terre malades* and *L'Ombre de Nicolet*, then, crossed genres and media but caused significant anxiety about how to promote audience engagement if it became accepted wisdom that all communication was trying to sell something, rather than to convince an audience of an idea. And indeed, one of the most interactive elements of vaudeville revues, the vaudeville finale, or sing-along summary at the end of the play, would disappear from the genre, along with the other songs, not long after the end of the July Monarchy.

Eugène Labiche, who was just beginning his career in the 1840s (and whose later success would help mark the end of the vaudeville aesthetic), made vaudeville's codified appeal to the audience self-reflexive by emphasizing its uniformity. The four main characters in his *Le Club Champenois* of 1848 each sang a couplet:

> Ta di da da . . . indulgent tribunal
> Ta di da da . . . Un arrêt trop sévère . . .
> Ta di da da . . . toujours impartial
> Ta di da da . . . La faveur du parterre.
> Ta di da da . . . Le pauvre auteur
> Ta di da da . . . Son espérance
> Ta di da da . . . Sa frayeur
> Ta di da da . . . Espoir flatteur
> Ta di da da . . . Votre indulgence . . .[45]

> Ta di da da . . . indulgent tribunal
> Ta di da da . . . too tough a judgment . . .
> Ta di da da . . . always impartial
> Ta di da da . . . the favor of the audience.

Ta di da da . . . the poor author
Ta di da da . . . his hopes
Ta di da da . . . his fears
Ta di da da . . . flattering wish
Ta di da da . . . your indulgence . . .

Although appeals to the audience were formulaic, they nonetheless recalled the fact that the verdicts of the audience determined the run of the play.[46] Vaudevilles that included newspapers empowered the audience to judge the press.

Labiche's standard version of the vaudeville finale does, however, point to a real limit on the genre's ability to encourage critical engagement with the shifting ideals of the press. If the standardized format of the vaudeville is itself becoming boring to audiences, then its time as a vehicle for critical commentary may be passing. For all that promotion and critique could coexist in vaudevilles without necessarily preventing reflection, audience disengagement would mean the death of the genre. July Monarchy playwrights managed to integrate elements of vaudeville's structure with other genres, often as part of an effort to draw audiences into interpretation of the plays they were watching. Already in 1838, Tournemine, the author of *La révolte de coucous*, wrote concerns about an increasingly jaded public into the dialogue between Monsieur Public and La Vogue:

> M. PUBLIC. Oui, je ne dis pas ; mais j'ai vu tant de choses !.. je crois que je commence à me blaser . . . je suis moins gai, moins curieux, moins . . . flâneur ; je perds de ma bonhomie habituelle, je deviens difficile . . . philosophe . . . misanthrope, même.
> LA VOGUE, *vivement.* Vous !.. l'homme de toutes les époques !..le public !.. par exemple !..
> M. PUBLIC. Oh ! c'est vrai ! je raisonne. Je réfléchis maintenant, et cela m'attriste : car on a besoin d'illusions, et le monde n'est pas beau quand on le voit ce qu'il est !.[47]

> MR. PUBLIC. Yes, I know, but I've seen so much! . . . I think I'm getting blasé . . . I'm less gay, less curious, less . . . flaneur; I'm losing my usual cheeriness, I'm becoming difficult, philosophical, misanthropic, even.
> VOGUE, *vehemently,* You! The man of all ages! The public! Now, really!
> MR. PUBLIC. Oh, it's true! I reason, I think now, and it makes me sad. We need illusions, and the world is not beautiful when one sees how it is!

The play in which this scene takes place is one in which stagecoach drivers are protesting the planned extension of a railroad to their city. It ends on a

promise of harmony in which former *coucou* drivers will be employed by
the railroad, begging the question of whether this is being proffered as one
of the illusions the world is currently lacking. What happens to those whose
livelihoods are threatened by new technology is a real social question. The fact
that characters such as La Vogue, M. Public, and (as cited at the beginning
of the introduction) La Publicité have a hand in determining the conditions
of this transition suggests that real economic and social consequences are
nonetheless being produced by new media practices. As is often the case in
vaudevilles, this play raises the question and prods the audience to consider
the credibility of official responses to it, without declaring an opinion as to
the virtues and dangers of such progress. It does, however, show public disengagement in a negative light, for even the most cynical of *vaudevillistes* had
to acknowledge that a public whose attention he could no longer attract was
an audience lost.[48]

On Parisian stages of the 1830s and 1840s, advertisements obscured sight
lines, and the sensationalism they encouraged corrupted newspaper-reading
characters. Commercial publicity's formative influence on the press was not
vaunted as a new broadening of access to information by plays (except in the
most ironically physical of senses) but was instead displayed and attacked,
cited and pastiched. While newspapers participated in the jousting that plays
initiated, evaluating and pastiching the theater's claims in turn, critics balked
when actors addressed audiences directly. Face-to-face communication across
the fourth wall apparently retained a charge greater than that which could be
achieved though more-mediated commentary on the evolving nature of the
press. As long as vaudevilles and comedies retained access to such influence,
their "take" on press developments had to be reckoned with by newspapers
that aspired to expand their own audiences. If anything, the risk for playwrights was that if they propagated too much cynicism, all their criticism
would look like old hat to spectators they had trained to see it as such. Conflating the fourth estate and the fourth wall by breaking through newsprint
or by addressing critics directly (ignoring the fourth wall to speak to the
producers of the fourth estate), plays had to push the limits of their own
medium's conventions in order to highlight material concerns about the ways
of the new rival, the press.

When newspaper publicity started to be consolidated and managed by the
Société Générale d'Annonces in 1845, plays came up with clever ways to point
out the disadvantages of counting on a medium in thrall to advertisement
for one's information about the world. Their efforts, along with newspapers'
counterparries, reveal an increasing awareness that, in a media sphere less
and less formatted by the political lines of papers and the generic licenses
of theaters, all publicity, however shockingly negative it might be, was good
publicity as long as it called public attention to a play or a title. The danger
in this new media situation became audience fatigue. A shocked audience was

far better than a blasé one. By stretching what one could say about current communication practices and how one could say it, vaudevilles and *feuilletons* began to worry about what would happen if audiences simply checked out of their debates, no longer caring so much about how they knew what they knew about the politics of their society.

Chapter 5

Paper as Moral Fiber

If vaudevilles and *feuilletons* pastiched each other in strategic combinations of promotion and critique, books, too, and authors aspiring to publish them borrowed citational techniques from the stage and the press to serve their own ends. By writing a pastiche of Jules Janin in *Illusions perdues*, Honoré de Balzac took advantage of the powerful theater critic's distinctive style to create readerly complicity while differentiating his own novel from Janin's journalism. This chapter focuses on two more-extreme cases of simultaneously critical and self-serving approaches to Janin's reviews: (1) Gérard de Nerval's republication of an article by Janin as he integrated *Léo Burckardt* (1839) into *Lorély* (1860), and (2) Félix Pyat's use of a legal battle as partial inspiration for *Le Chiffonnier de Paris*, which he wrote first as a play (1847) and then as a novel (1880).[1] Nerval and Pyat were both friends with Janin early in their careers, but disagreements with Janin may have contributed to one of Nerval's early mental breakdowns, and Pyat's public clash with the critic resulted in the former doing jail time. Nerval's and Pyat's methods for coping with Janin's betrayals and the way that those methods informed the republication of their dramatic works suggest that Janin's outsize influence in the world of the theater and the press had to be encapsulated, brought under another rule, for narrative reinvention of plays he had panned to seem plausible. To shore up the credibility and durability of their own counterattacks on Janin and the practices he represented, Nerval and Pyat, like Balzac in *Illusions perdues*, emphasized the paper on which their very words were printed.

Jules Janin is not the kind of author one tends to read *en filigrane*, between the lines, as a watermark within a literary text. He was prolific, successful, and corrupt. His longtime position as the theater critic at the *Journal des débats* gave him enormous influence in the world of Parisian letters. When he contributed a preface for a book, it cost twice the going rate, if not more.[2] Margaret Miner has quite rightly characterized his style as abject, in that it is uncomfortably chatty; too personal and too plentiful.[3] This style, combined with his tendency to promote critics and denigrate authors, and to pooh-pooh any deontological concerns raised about sensationalist journalism, made him a prime (if risky) target for pastiche by authors who had complaints against newspapers. Nerval and Pyat battled Janin on stage, in the press, and in the courts when he engaged in personal attacks against them, but they finally had to settle their accounts in the longer-term format of the books into which they eventually integrated their plays. As each author moved from contestatory stage performances, which questioned the legitimacy of the press, toward the historical record that the printed page represented, recording Janin's bad behavior by quoting him became a way of setting the record straight.

Nerval's *Léo Burckart*, a play that focuses on the difficulty of moving from journalism to political praxis, was republished as part of *Lorely*, a book whose preface sent up Janin and situated its own project in the context of Johannes Gutenberg's discovery of movable type. Pyat's *Chiffonnier de Paris*, the great person-paper play of the 1840s, was republished thirty years later as a richly illustrated novel of 920 pages, a physical *pavé* (tome) devoted to revolutionary principles that would keep stone *pavés* (cobbles) from settling too comfortably into roadbeds.[4] In both cases, efforts to pin Janin's positions down on paper that could be recontextualized shaped Nerval's and Pyat's repackaging of their plays for posterity.

Léo Burckart, Nerval's 1839 drama about the current state of the press, staged two journalists: Burckart himself, a respected author of political articles, who is asked to participate in politics and quickly finds himself compromised by the machinations the job requires; and his *feuilletoniste* colleague, Paulus, who introduces himself to Burckart as "un journaliste de très-mince importance ; j'écris comme vous dans *la Gazette germanique* ; un simple filet typographique sépare vos puissantes idées politiques de mes humbles observations morales, archéologiques, et quelquefois littéraires" (a journalist of slight importance; like you, I write for the *Germanic Gazette*; a simple printed line separates your powerful political ideas from my humble observations about morality, archeology, and sometimes literature).[5] Paulus opens the play by telling Burckart that one of his articles has caused the newspaper for which they both write to be seized and its editor to be thrown in jail. The *feuilletoniste* says, "On parle beaucoup de vous, monsieur ! Pour un article de vous, tout un pays est en rumeur ; pour un livre de vous, toute l'Allemagne s'agite" (People are talking about you, sir! One of your articles and a country murmurs, a book from you, and Germany moves!).[6]

Paulus plays the Mephistopheles to Burckart's Faust. Burckart gains political power, and Paulus, serving as his secretary, gets Burckart access to a secret society, where he witnesses a murder and hears his own death sentence from antigovernment conspirators. Having been well and truly compromised by his efforts to put ideas into practice, Léo Burckart, speaking of the prince he serves, says, "Cette plume était un sceptre plus réel que le sien . . . et j'ai peur, en la reprenant, d'en avoir usé le prestige" (This pen was a scepter more real than his . . . and I am afraid as I take it back up that I have worn out its prestige!).[7] In *la presse à quarante francs* (the forty-franc press), the *feuilleton*'s commercial success contributed to the large circulation that made new newspapers powerful, and it did so as part of a transition that decreased the political independence of columnists. Burckart's beginnings as a political writer and Paulus's as a *feuilletoniste* attach their behavior and dilemmas to those of the political article and the *feuilleton*.

Burckart's excellent motives and principles, while producing good copy at the beginning of the play, create political situations that force him to betray those principles. The prince in whose service Burkart experiences this disconnect recruits him by saying, "Vous savez qu'il y a des paroles qui tuent, et que, grâce à la presse, l'intelligence marche aujourd'hui sur la terre, comme ce héros antique qui semait les dents de dragon ! Or vous avez laissé tomber la parole sur une terre fertile ; si bien qu'elle perce le sol de tous côtés" (You know that there are words that kill, and that thanks to the press, intelligence walks the earth today like that hero of antiquity who sowed dragons' teeth. You let words fall on fertile soil, so much so that now they are poking through the ground on all sides).[8] Nerval's play suggests that journalists, however heroic they may appear, eventually discover that ideas, like the dragon's teeth sown by Jason and Cadmus, are as likely to cause senseless infighting as they are to create well-ordered armies. Words become bodies, yet again, and bodies who are disinclined to work together. The journalist who survives Burckart's experiment in governance is Paulus, the clever *feuilletoniste*, who, as Ross Chambers has pointed out, understands the language appropriate to a changing political scene. For, as Chambers puts it, "Dans les conditions politiques des années 30, en France, le droit à la parole publique ne s'obtient ni par la franchise ni par le secret, mais par une forme d'énonciation en même temps affirmative et réticente, qui en fin de compte déroute les catégories" (In the political conditions of 1830s France, the right to public speech is obtained neither by frankness nor by secrecy, but rather by a form of enunciation which is simultaneously affirmative and reticent, which finally confounds all categories).[9]

Nerval, himself a *feuilletoniste*, portrays Paulus, his *feuilletoniste* character, as prone to sullying the actions of Burckart, the political journalist and then politician. Paulus is nonetheless the one character who emerges unscathed at the end of the play. *Léo Burckart*'s own history as a censored and then staged dramatic work bore out the accuracy of the play's portrayal of the arbitrary relationship between press and government. In such a context, better to be Mephistopheles, the savvy go-between *feuilletoniste*, than Faust, the striving author-turned-politician.[10]

If *La Presse* was Balzac's chosen space in which to advertise and perform the lessons of his upcoming segment of *Illusions perdues*, the courtroom became the stage for Nerval's promotion of *Léo Burkart*. Censors who were concerned that the play would upset Franco-German relations delayed its production. They assumed that the model for its action was Karl Ludwig Sand's murder of the playwright August von Kotzebue in 1819. Sand was a radical student and Kotzebue a popular dramatist sometimes credited with the birth of melodrama. The death of the latter was used as an excuse to crack down on press freedom in Germany, a situation that might well have reminded the censors too much of the way that Louis Philippe had passed restrictive press laws in France after Giuseppe Fieschi's assassination attempt on him in 1835.

Although Nerval denied that *Léo Burckart* was a direct account of Kotzebue's assassination, and even provided another news item as his model, the assumption that a parallel was being drawn would have made a public censorship trial a particularly apropos introduction for a work accused of rehashing an incident that led to censorship elsewhere.[11] Unfortunately, the months that the trial took (rehearsals of *Léo Burckart* were stopped between January and April 1839) cost the play its place at the Théâtre de la Renaissance, where it had been scheduled to follow Victor Hugo's *Ruy Blas*. Nerval finally brought his play to the Théâtre de la Porte Saint-Martin, where its director Félix Harel squeezed it in without quite managing to deliver the scenery or the costumes that he had promised. By the time *Léo Burkart* was staged, to good reviews and small audiences, the play's fate had started to resemble the unfortunate consequences of moving from print to politics that its plot described. Its ideas and dialogue did not reach the audience they merited because they were misconstrued by the powers that be and then badly presented because of the resulting delay. As was perhaps fitting for a drama whose author was best known for his precocious translation of Johann Wolfgang von Goethe's *Faust*, *Léo Burkart*, too, became a work to be read.

In *Lorely*, the volume of writings on Germany into which *Léo Burckart* would eventually be integrated, Nerval took on his own diabolical *feuilletoniste* colleague, Janin, while simultaneously insisting on print technology as a misunderstood force of potentially creative progress. Separating a bad practitioner from a promising practice required citing an article by Janin in a way that linked it to scandal and connecting *Léo Burckart* to a tradition of misunderstood genius that was, Nerval implies, better explained in book form than on stage or in newspapers.

In *Lorely*, Nerval discusses which parts of Goethe's *Faust* came from popular legend and which were Goethe's own invention. Nerval's account of the legend has Faust, a goldsmith, as a collaborator with Gutenberg in the invention of the printing press. According to Nerval, tradition has it that Faust rescued a manuscript of Homer which monks were scratching out in order to reuse it to copy a current religious work. In doing so, Faust noticed that the seals with which the manuscript was marked could be reused any number of times, and the idea of reusable type was born. Nerval speculates that Faust's association with the devil could simply have been the monks' explanation of his behavior based on his desire to save a pagan author (the Homer that was being erased) and on the undermining of religious authority that the invention of the printing press would bring. Means and ends are always central to Faust stories, but Nerval's version gives pride of place to the medium through which Faust discovers a new technique and relates it to the impact that his innovation will have.

Nerval's dramatic meditations on print culture also took on a historical scale, though. His 1851 play, *L'Imagier d'Harlem*, turned again to the history of print, to Gutenberg and his circle, for its subject matter, this time bringing Laurent Coster to the fore and comparing his discoveries with those of Galileo Galilei and Christopher Columbus. In an effort to ease its arrival on stage, Nerval wrote to Jules Janin:

> Le personnage principal qui selon les légendes locales de chaque pays est Faust ou Guttenberg ou Laurent Coster n'a été pour nous qu'un type général de l'inventeur d'une grande chose contrarié par le mauvais esprit. . . . la pièce est religieuse au fond . . . c'est la Providence qui favorise les lumières et le progrès que le Diable voudrait supprimer . . . Il y a beaucoup de Faust dans la pièce et même beaucoup du deuxième Faust ce qui ne contribue pas à l'éclaircir. Mais vous savez que c'est une manie chez moi. Rappelez-vous Léo Burckart de la même Porte Saint Martin et soyez-moi bon.[12]

> The main character who, according to each country's local legends, is Faust or Gutenberg or Laurent Coster was, for me, nothing more than a type—the inventor of something grand impeded by meanspiritedness. . . . The play is fundamentally religious . . . Providence favors the enlightenment and progress that the devil wants to abolish. There is a great deal of Faust in the play and even a great deal of the second part of Faust, which doesn't help its clarity. But you know that this is a mania of mine. Remember Léo Burckart at this same theater and be kind to me.

Janin was not kind to Nerval in his review. It wasn't the first time that he had disappointed his friend. When Nerval was admitted to Dr. Blanche's clinic for convalescence from his first bout of madness, in 1841, Janin had published an article that spread the news of Nerval's status and praised his works with the implicit assumption that he wouldn't be writing any more of them. In the same article, Janin told the story of a discussion in which he and Nerval were both involved just before Nerval's crisis. While the other writers present discussed plagiarism as the way of the world, a nearly necessary step in the diffusion of texts as soon as they have been published, Nerval, according to Janin, would have none of it. Jonathan Strauss posits that "for Janin and his friends, *contrefaçon* is acceptable because it simply replicates the disappropriation, even the self-disappropriation, that is the essence of thought and writing, whereas for Nerval the struggle against piracy is a struggle against death, against the loss of self implicit in authorship . . . Nerval persistently rebelled against the idea that an author must necessarily lose his works, and an autobiographer his carefully constructed self, to the abstract universality of language."[13] Nerval's mental illness was, in this case, exacerbated by his solitary defense of the connection between an author and his work. His investment in maintaining that close relationship between self and literary production is reflected in the autobiographical tendencies that shape his treatment of Janin's repurposed article in the preface of *Lorely*.[14] The (perhaps closer than usual) identification between self and work that Nerval practiced, located his writing on a spectrum that seems to have emerged in the 1840s between *Cœur* (Heart) as an orienting principle for some people and their writing, and *Esprit* (Spirit) as a competing one. Nerval's complicated identification with his text seems to land him on the *cœur* side, whereas Janin was famous for his *esprit désinvolte* (cavalier wit).

In Nerval's letter to Janin about *L'Imagier d'Harlem*, it is the *mauvais esprit* (evil spirit) which works against inventors. A similarly problematic corrosive spirit animates Balzac's Lucien as he writes for competing Parisian newspapers and sends his debts on to David and Ève. In a revealing 1839 comedy, *La Jeunesse de Goethe*, Louise Colet imagined a a scene reminiscent of *Faust* staged between Goethe, Schlegel, and Johann Kaspar Lavater. The author and the critic compete for a certain Charlotte's affections by debating the merits of their respective professions, with the theologian serving as judge. Colet had Lavater judge in favor of Goethe, the author, over Schlegel, the critic, in the following terms: "Comme on plaint l'indigent, moi, je plains le railleur ; / Car l'esprit est souvent l'indigence du cœur" (As one pities the poor man, I pity the wit; for cleverness is often indigence of heart)[15] Schlegel crows that the public "vous juge selon moi car il ne vous lit guere" (Judges you according to me, for they hardly read you),[16] but Goethe gets Charlotte in the end. However influential the critic, it is the author who makes a happy marriage. When she wrote *La Jeunesse de Goethe*, Colet was having a relatively widely known affair with Victor Cousin. Just months after the play was performed, the critic Alphonse Karr published an insinuation that the child she was expecting was not her husband's, and she came to Karr's door with a kitchen knife to take revenge by stabbing him. Karr managed to disarm her, and he presented his apology for his "Acte de mauvais goût" in an article that followed their encounter.[17]

In 1841, when Nerval reproached Janin for publishing his similarly indiscreet account of Nerval's breakdown (which Nerval referred to as an obituary), Janin made no such amends. When Janin's piece was intitially published in the *Journal des débats*, Nerval was still in the asylum. After Nerval had recovered sufficiently, he wrote a personal letter to Janin, reproaching his friend bitterly for his betrayal. Nerval asked that Janin publish a refutation that he (Nerval) had written. Janin does not appear to have done so. Eleven years later, then, when *Lorely* was published, Nerval refuted Janin's assertion that his writing days were over by using Janin's *article nécrologique* to make up most of the preface to *Lorely*, a volume whose very bulk proved that Janin had been premature in his announcement of the end of his friend's career. Nerval contextualized Janin's article in his preface by relating it to the effects he had experienced with regard to his own reputation, but he also folded in barbs that referred to a recent scandal Janin himself had faced. Referring to Janin's article, he wrote:

> Cet éloge, qui traversa l'Europe et ma chère Allemagne . . . m'avait rempli tour à tour de joie et de mélancolie . . . Quand j'ai traversé de nouveau les vieilles forêts de pins et de chênes et les cités bienveillantes où m'attendaient des amis inconnus, je ne pouvais parvenir à leur persuader que j'étais moi-même. On disait : "Il est mort, quel dommage ! Une vive intelligence, bonne surtout, sympathique à notre Allemagne, comme à une seconde mère, et que nous apprécions seulement depuis son dernier instant illustré par Jules Janin . . . Et vous qui passez parmi nous, pourquoi dérobez-vous la seule chose qu'il ait laissée après lui, un peu de gloire autour d'un nom . . ." Voilà ce que m'avaient valu les douze colonnes du *Journal des Débats*, seul toléré par les chancelleries.[18]

> This eulogy, which crossed Europe and my beloved Germany, had filled me with joy and melancholy by turns . . . when I returned to the old oak and pine forests and the welcoming cities where unknown friends awaited me, I couldn't persuade them that I was myself. People said, "He's dead, what a shame! A bright mind, and kind, too, sympathetic to our Germany as to a second mother, and who we've only been able to appreciate since his last moments were illustrated by Jules Janin . . . And you who pass among us, why do you steal the only thing that he has left behind him, the glory of a name . . ." There's what twelve columns from *Le Journal des débats* (the only paper the chancelleries tolerate) got me.

According to Nerval, even those who know him have doubts, "et dans les villes où j'étais connu personnellement, on ne m'accueillait pas sans quelque crainte en songeant aux vieilles légendes germaniques des vampires et des morts-fiancés. Vous jugez si c'est possible que, là même, quelque *bourgeois* m'accordât sa fille *borgne ou bossue*. C'est la conviction de cette impossibilité qui m'a poussé vers l'Orient" (and in the cities where I was known, I was greeted with some trepidation, as my hosts thought of old Germanic legends of vampires and of dead fiancés. I ask you, then, what bourgeois would grant me his daughter, however blind or hunchbacked. The conviction of this impossibility pushed me toward the Orient).[19]

Nerval says that Janin's assertions about his madness and probable demise have been so widely believed that he himself is treated like a supernatural imposter—a role that has a certain cachet in a volume called *Lorely*, after "la fée du Rhin" (fairy of the Rhine). Patrick Bray has demonstrated that Nerval's "Généalogie," composed during his recuperation from the crisis depicted in the *article nécrologique*, situated the author in a background that included spirits of towers and bridges, and that the very document on which it was written created possibilities for a "spatialized subjectivity" that became a formative element of Nerval's aesthetic.[20] The "power of the subject to surpass its temporal and spatial limitations," affirmed in the "Génealogie" and questioned in *Sylvie*, is, in the *article nécrologiqe*-made-preface, recuperated from its damaging time in the news. Not only has Nerval, through Janin's mistaken evaluations of his longevity, gained something in common with the figurehead of his collection of articles and plays, but he has also, through the social misunderstandings occasioned by the article, been moved to travel more, and to produce other volumes.

Even Nerval's complaint about the difficulty of finding a wife when one is thought to be an impostor has a certain sting to it, in that Janin's own marriage had, not long after he published the *article nécrologique*, been the cause of a scandal. In 1841, Janin, whose early love life had been tumultuous, married Adèle Huet. He used his column in the *Journal des débats* to revel in his conjugal bliss, irritating a good number of his fellow critics by calling the article in which he announced his good fortune "le mariage du critique" (the marriage of The Critic) rather than "le mariage d'un critique" (the marriage of a critic).[21] This bit of hubris, combined with Janin's saccharine account of the joys that awaited him, led more than one of his competitors to accuse him of treating his marriage bed like the stage of a play. Certainly the story of his courtship as he told it had much of the boulevard comedy about it. He had had trouble convincing his respectable in-laws that a critic's salary could provide appropriately for their daughter, and he had needed character witnesses and letters from bankers, but the whole affair, of course, was ending happily. In fact, the scandal that surrounded Janin's public presentation of his marriage was such that a vaudeville play was written about it, modified by the censor, and then performed.

Submitted to the censor under the title *Le Mariage du feuilleton et de la raison*, the play was eventually authorized as *Le Feuilleton et la raison*, with all reference to their marriage replaced with a plot in which Le Feuilleton and La Raison (Reason) form a limited liability company.[22] Unfortunately, no censor's report exists for *Le Mariage du feuilleton et de la raison*, but the censors' corrections (visible on the submitted manuscript) were probably inspired by a desire to avoid reigniting a scandal that had surrounded the article that Jules Janin published in October 1841 on the day of his marriage. Hippolyte Rolle, in a biting article written for *Le National*, had accused Janin of publishing a prospectus for his wife and of making his marriage bed the stage of a boulevard theater.

While the censored vaudeville attenuated its participation in such attacks by allegorizing both Janin and his wife, it nonetheless realized some elements of Rolle's nasty diagnosis by proposing to stage an allegorical wedding which referred to theirs, and to the scandal that surrounded it.[23] For a minor unpublished play, Dennery and Clairville's vaudeville received more attention than usual in the press. In its rubric "Théâtres, fêtes, concerts," *La Presse* kept track of the vaudeville's fate. On December 21, 1841, the day's notes included the following: "On répète en ce moment, à l'Ambigu, un vaudeville intitulé: *Le Mariage du critique*. Nous ignorons quelle peut être cette pièce, mais il y a dans le titre qu'on lui donne au moins un grave inconvénient" (At the Ambigu there are rehearsals for a vaudeville entitled *The Critic's Marriage*. We know nothing about this play, but the title it has been given is highly inappropriate).[24] Four days later it was referred to as "la petite inconvenance dont nous avons parlé ; le *Mariage du critique*" (the little indiscretion we mentioned, *The Critic's Marriage*).[25] Finally, on December 29, the same section announced, "L'Ambigu vient de donner sa revue de l'année, dont on a eu le bon esprit de changer le titre (*Le Feuilleton* au lieu du *Mariage du Critique*)" (The Ambigu gave its annual revue, for which they were good-natured enough to change the title [to *The Feuilleton* instead of *The Critic's Marriage*].)[26] The persistent inaccuracy of *La Presse*'s information on the title suggests that journalists might have been intentionally multiplying their references to its former title (and therefore to the flap over Janin's article) for as long as they possibly could, even as the censor tried to erase such traces in the play itself. Given that Nerval himself wrote regularly for *La Presse* and had finished his convalescence after his second bout of mental illness the month before these articles appeared, it seems likely that he or colleagues of his were interested in prolonging the scandal surrounding the vaudeville, and thus getting a bit of revenge against Janin.

In *Le Feuilleton et la raison*, La Raison, considering union with Le Feuilleton, says that she always wants to be in agreement (*d'accord*) with him. Le Feuilleton says that he wants that, too, and that he will call up all the year's dramatic productions so that La Raison can evaluate for herself whether he has judged them correctly or not. La Raison is impressed: "Comment, vous auriez ce pouvoir ?" (Really, you can do that?) she asks. "Certainement," says Le Feuilleton, "les chefs d'œuvre pour lesquels nous ne nous dérangeons pas, se dérangent pour nous ; et viennent en secret nous confier leurs merveilles. Que de pièces dont nous faisons l'analyse la veille de la représentation, que de romans dont les comptes rendus sont achevés avant leur impression, eh ! tenez, vous allez en juger" (Masterpieces we don't trouble ourselves over take the trouble to come see us, and secretly tell us about their marvels. Oh, the plays we analyze the night before they open! Oh the novels whose reviews are finished before they are printed. Look, you can judge for yourself).[27] Making the *feuilleton* a vaudeville narrator, whose role was to present artistic productions to reason, and by extension, to the audience, was a neat way of taking account of its mediating role while refusing it ultimate authority.[28] The *feuilleton* character upholds his reputation for basing his judgments of plays on favors granted by their supporters, for critics were not supposed to finish their articles before having seen or read the works they were reviewing. Such habits are, however, useful for Le Feuilleton in his role as the master of ceremonies who organizes a vaudeville revue, in that they allow for rapid display of a great number of literary productions. It is far more efficient to hold court as novels and actresses ask for favors than to be obliged to read and to attend all the novels and plays one is supposed to cover.

Reintroducing the difficulties of finding a wife after one's reputation has been tarnished, as Nerval did by republishing Janin's premature obituary of him, was, then, a reminder of the scandal that had surrounded Janin's own published struggle to court his wife. In addition to his wedding article that inspired a vaudeville, Janin had caused a stir after his marriage by initiating a trial for *diffamation* (libel) against Lepoitevin Saint-Alme, the editor of the *Corsaire Satan*, which had published a rumor about his wife dallying with a baritone. Not only did the lawsuit renew sarcastic talk about Janin and his wife, but it also turned out to be the first of two *diffamation* trials that Janin initiated in the 1840s. When Janin, who was so vocally unconcerned about authors' rights, took such an aggressive approach to enforcing their responsibilities, he looked especially opportunistic and self-interested, attacking at will and shielding himself behind the law when attacked.

When he found himself in the midst of a different fight with Félix Pyat, who had taken him to task for his negative review of a play by Marie-Joseph Chénier, in 1844, Janin tried a supposedly conciliatory response. Janin's defender, Georges Dairnvaell, writing in Janin's voice, proposed that a serious and principled writer like Pyat couldn't possibly have attacked him so violently, and he screened himself behind the ostentatious pleasures of married life, writing, "sais-je seulement si j'écris et ne donnerais-je pas toute la gloire littéraire pour un regard de cette femme que j'aime et qui porte mon nom, pour une heure de douce causerie avec elle" (am I even aware of what I am writing, wouldn't I give up all literary glory for a look from this woman who I love, and who bears my name . . . for an hour of pleasant conversation with her?).[29] When Pyat responded with more vitriol, Janin did have him jailed for six months, so his willingness to say that Pyat must not really be the author of the attacks was limited. Jail and exile were part and parcel of Pyat's political career, but having to face the former for libel charges against a serial slanderer was a particularly galling situation.

The offenses leading up to Pyat and Janin's dispute, which came to a head when Janin successfully sued Pyat for *diffamation* in 1844, had been accumulating for years. Though the two started as friends and fellow republicans under the Restoration, Janin changed political allegiances, moving from *Le Figaro* to *La Quotidienne* in 1828. He also plagiarized Pyat's work at least once and promised a positive review for Pyat's play *Ango*, which he then took down in the *Journal des débats*. What set off the 1844 dispute, though, was an article that Janin wrote critiquing Marie-Joseph Chénier's play *Tibère*.

Chénier, who was dead by then, was a foundational figure for leftist writers, so Pyat took up the banner of his defense, beginning the pamphlet he published to attack Janin with "Il manquait à la gloire de Chénier d'etre insulté par un certain critique. Ce complément d'ovation, ce comble, cet excès de'honneur etaient dus au poète de la Révolution" (The only thing missing from Chénier's glory was to have been insulted by a certain critic. This extra ovation, this summit, this excess of honor, was due to the poet of the Revolution).[30] Pyat concluded by comparing Janin to a beggar throwing mud from the ditch at the side of the road—you're angry with him for the mess until you see that he has no legs, at which point compassion prevails. Janin is just like the beggar, says Pyat, except that what he lacks is more serious; the last line of the pamphlet is "Il lui manque le Cœur" (He has no heart).[31] After a round or two of jousting in the press, Janin brought Pyat to court for libel.

Pyat's legal defense in the trial that Janin intitiated was a collection of clippings from Janin's articles, which juxtaposed them with those he had copied, or which placed two of Janin's columns in which he had said opposite things next to each other, thus showing the critic's inconsistency. The morally questionable positions he had taken were also covered. Because *diffamation* cases were not allowed to be decided on the factuality of the accusations put forward by the person accused of libel, such samples of Janin's writings were not admitted as evidence. When the judge made this ruling, Pyat's lawyers and, following them, Pyat himself, renounced his right to a defense, saying that defense was impossible if a critic's published work could not be used as evidence against him. Their argument was that Pyat had attacked Janin as a writer, not as a person.

Both Pyat and Janin were adept at blurring the distinction between personal and professional accusations. In the interest of his polemic, Pyat's comments about lacking *Cœur* certainly stray from the factual and enter into a discourse of honor (or lack thereof) that William Reddy has shown was still very current in the 1840s.[32] Janin, however, was arguably the inventor—certainly the most visible practitioner—of a highly personal anecdotal style of critique, which significantly confused questions of where the personal ended and the professional began. An anonymous account of Pyat's trial framed the question as follows:

> Le procès en diffamation de M. Janin contre M. Pyat, a donné lieu à un incident grave, jugé par le tribunal dans un sens qui, selon nous, est contraire à la liberté de l'écrivain et à la liberté du défenseur. . . . Que disait M. Marie pour M. Pyat ? Qu'il respecterait M. Janin dans sa vie privée, mais que s'agissant d'un critique littéraire, qu'il croyait pouvoir le suivre dans sa vie littéraire. C'est là la distinction que le tribunal n'a voulu admettre qu'avec des restrictions qui la rendait illusoire ; distinction qui ressortait cependant de la nature même du procès. . . . l'esprit de cette loi, c'est le respect, le respect peut être

exagéré pour le repos de la vie privée ; aller plus loin, c'est énerver les mœurs publiques et rendre impossible, non la diffamation, mais la critique.[33]

The libel trial of Mr. Janin against Mr. Pyat brought about a serious incident which was judged by the tribunal in a way that is, to our mind, contrary to the liberty of the writer and to the liberty of the defender . . . What did Mr. Marie say for Mr. Pyat? That he respected Mr. Janin in his private life, but that since he is a literary critic, that he thought that he could pursue him in his literary life. The distinction was admitted with so many restrictions that it became illusory. . . . a distinction that grew out of the very nature of the trial . . . the spirit of this law is respect. Respect for private life can be exaggerated; to go too far is to irritate public opinion and to make criticism, rather than libel, impossible.

The same author of this account of the trial complains that the law as it is currently structured provided no way of knowing whether the defendant was an upstanding citizen or a crazy person. Though Pyat's attempt to defend himself by citing Janin's articles failed, the evidence was published. Whether or not its performance in court was admitted, the accusatory collage of Janin's journalistic inconsistencies and betrayals entered the written record.

In retrospect, Pyat's collection of incriminating texts by Janin seems like a sort of precursor to the most famous scene in his most famous play. In Pyat's 1847 *Le Chiffonnier de Paris*, Père Jean, the eponymous hero, sifts through the detritus that he has gathered in his basket, commenting on its uses and speculating on how it got there. Quite a lot of that detritus is made up of scraps of newspaper, upon which Père Jean comments. After the revolution of 1848, Père Jean brought down the house by fishing a crown from his basket as part of the night's collection of refuse. The socially charged scraps the *chiffonnier* (ragpicker) gathers serve him primarily as material from which new paper will eventually be made, but for the audience they are the stuff of theater.

Pyat's play opens with a villain who is talked out of suicide by Père Jean. The villain's first act as a saved man is to murder a bank cashier who is returning from work with the day's earnings. Père Jean, too drunk to be of much use in preventing the situation, promises the dying cashier that he will look after his infant daughter. The villain becomes a baron, and Marie, the daughter, Père Jean's ward. Twenty years later, the baron's daughter gives birth to an illegitimate child, which is abandoned at Marie's door by the midwife charged with disposing of the baby. She returns to kill the baby, though, and when its corpse is discovered, Marie is accused of infanticide. To clear her name and allow her marriage with a certain Henri, Père Jean, having gone clean after the initial scene, obtains the truth of what happened by burning bank notes before the eyes of the evil midwife until she reveals that the infant was the illegitimate grandchild of the villain-turned-baron.

Le Chiffonnier de Paris refuses newspapers any ability to influence people. To dissuade the play's villain from committing suicide in the opening scene, Père Jean first points out that if he does, his body will be displayed at the morgue and his name may be in the newspapers, and then gives him a newspaper article that moralizes about the cowardice of suicide. The villain is saved from drowning himself by this combination of press-related reasoning, but he immediately turns to murder. The newspaper's message has been effective, but not at all in the way it was meant to be. Pyat's critique of the press works on several levels. In addition to staging its unforeseen effects, the play discredits newspaper content by looking at it through the eyes of a *chiffonnier*, for whom its primary value is as paper to be recycled, rather than as a vehicle for any particular idea. Père Jean is a literate and philosophical *chiffonnier*, though, and he sorts out the lives of other characters as he sorts out the paper traces of Parisian social life. For Pyat did more than just choose a lowly figure as a hero, he also created a drama in which people and paper are cast off by society, and he who can find the value in the leavings they represent is a heroic figure. After all, the villain (who in the first scene is also masquerading as a *chiffonnier*) spears a virtuous man instead of refuse. Years later he ensures that his daughter's illegitimate child will be disposed of on a trash heap, despite the efforts of Père Jean and his protégée (the murdered man's daughter, Marie) to keep the baby alive. When Père Jean drinks, or smokes, or sleeps, the wealthy villain gets the upper hand and makes garbage of people. As long as the *chiffonnier* works at recuperating what is cast off, virtue prevails. Pyat's message, then, is not simply that those living in poverty can be heroic, but also that this profit-driven society reserves the same treatment for people and for documents that are no longer of use, including bits of newspaper.

The daughter of the murdered cashier nearly commits suicide herself, in the most famous scene of the play, one which takes place on a split stage, with the *chiffonnier* downstairs sorting the contents of his *hotte* (basket) and Marie upstairs preparing to gas herself for financial reasons. Her attempt is interrupted by the discovery of the abandoned baby, for whom she chooses to live. Thrown-away lives are explicitly paralleled with thrown-away print matter as Père Jean goes through his *hotte*. In it he finds deeds and love letters, posters and newspapers. One bit of newsprint mentions that it is time to renew subscriptions, an injunction that the *chiffonnier* points out does not apply to him, for a ragpicker's newspaper is always free. With the depoliticization of the press, it matters little which paper this is—in any case, it puts Père Jean to sleep while Marie is still in danger upstairs. The press's disengagement from matters of substance is, then, part of the problem in Pyat's condemnation of July Monarchy social relations.

In 1848, once theaters reopened after the revolution, *Le Chiffonnier de*

Paris made a triumphant return to the stage, bringing down the house by including a crown among the rubbish that Père Jean fishes out of his *hotte*. There is some debate as to whether this bit of royal refuse was, as Pyat contended, a part taken out by the pre-1848 censors and reestablished, or another addition dreamed up by Fréderick Lemaître, who played the *chiffonnier*. Lemaître, who had launched his career by dressing Robert Macaire in rags during the Restoration, had famously played in its last performance before its censorship made up as Louis Philippe, and he repeated his Louis Philippe disguise for the first and only staging of Balzac's play *Vautrin*. His return to rags in the *Chiffonnier de Paris* may have recalled his first reinvention of a character, though Père Jean was the anti-Macaire, at one point burning money in exchange for truth. Lemaître's performance was, by most accounts, an excellent one. Charles de Matharel, *Le Siècle*'s theater critic and a friend of Pyat's, declared himself at a loss for words faced with such virtuosity but nonetheless managed to say that Lemaître's performance had made him forget all of the actor's former roles, including Robert Macaire and Kean.[34]

Charles de Matharel's mention of the roles that *Le Chiffonnier* supplanted suggests that whereas Robert Macaire had used the press to spread false information, and Kean (Alexandre Dumas's actor character) declaimed against press venality, Père Jean was taking his critique of the press in a new direction by confounding the materiality of words and that of bodies in order to critique the effects of poverty. Suicide was one of the topics likely to draw attention from the censors, though, as Odile Krakovitch puts it, "Ce ne fut pas tant le péché de suicide qui choquait ces bourgeois que la misère physique et morale dont il était l'aboutissement . . . Incapables de faire face aux problèmes de leur époque, les censeurs restèrent à la surface des choses" (It was less the sin of suicide which shocked these bourgeois types than the physical and moral misery that led to it. . . . Incapable of facing the problems of their era, the censors stayed on the surface of things).[35] By the time *Le Chiffonnier* was staged in 1847, with the surface-level cuts required by the censors, the urban misery it portrayed had a name: *la question sociale*, a question of class inequality, which was understood by the censors and the government itself to be a politically volatile one. *Les Mystères de Paris* had given one highly episodic and eventful account of the *question sociale* while nonetheless maintaining social hierarchies and respect for property. Pyat called both into question with *Le Chiffonnier de Paris*. His repeated inclusion of newspapers among the scraps used on stage suggests that the press innovations of 1836, which promised to substitute social questions for political ones in the move to increase newspaper circulation, had succeeded all too well. There were more newspapers than there had been, and they did less than they might have done to address the widening income gap. Their moralizing could push a bad man to crime, and their standardization could lull the virtuous poor, whose engagement was necessary for right to be maintained in society, into a dangerous sleep. Abandoning political argument in favor of social questions had just accelerated the July Monarchy's movement toward the Social Question of what to do about massive poverty.

Recent scholarship, often following Walter Benjamin, has seen in the figure of the *chiffonnier* an image of the Marxist historian, the Romantic artist, or the enterprising editor composing with the social reality of his world.[36] While these are surely useful metaphors, it is worth remembering that Pyat's chiffonnier is both a reality of the Parisian nightscape (leaving the theater, audiences might come across one on the way home) and a consolidator of the material from which new paper would be made. Père Jean saves people as he recycles scraps. As is fitting for a socialist politician and journalist, Pyat creates a "realistic" chiffonnier whose gatherings will found the new medium, not give access to ignored elements of the bad old reality. As *La Muette de Portici* sparked the revolution of Belgian independence in 1830, *Le Chiffonnier de Paris* was credited with fanning the flames of 1848. If so, it was not because of its treatment of offscourings but rather because of the full humanity accorded to one who spent his life gathering them. When Pyat returned to France from political exile in 1880, he rewrote *Le Chiffonier de Paris* as a novel, which he published serially and then in two volumes. In the process, he took on a collaborator to help with the structure of the serial novel, and he combined his original play with material from another of his dramatic works, *L'homme de peine*.

Much of the novel reads like a pamphlet. The first half is a reasonably straightforward transposition of *Le Chiffonnier de Paris*, though polemics about social institutions are abundant, and an antisemitism that was not obvious in the play becomes all too present in the novel. In the novel version, Père Jean, the *chiffonnier*, dies on the barricades in 1848, having successfully married off his ward, Marie. The second half of the book, however, follows the fate that could have befallen Marie had Père Jean not taken her in. Marianne Chaumette, abandoned at the *enfants trouvés* (foundling hospital) because her mother had died and her republican father did not have the means to support her, has challenges as she grows which are similar to Marie's, except that unlike her counterpart, Marianne is abandoned by her fiancé, who leaves her in favor of a rich marriage. The novel ends with Marianne launching a bomb into the salon where her aristocratic onetime lover is about to be properly engaged. She blows up the seat of the prejudices that prevent her from having access to such a consecration of her relationship. The sacrosanct salon, where vaudevilles are set and where marriages are negotiated, is done away with. In the novel version of the *Chiffonnier de Paris*, Père Jean, the moral *chiffonnier* who shed light on the relation between the media and the *question social*, is only half the story. The next generation takes down the very structure perpetuating inequalities. Though Pyat explained in his introduction to the novel form of *Le Chiffonnier de Paris* that an advantage of the novel genre was that there were "pas de coulisses"—that is, nothing stayed in the wings; all could be shown and told—his attention to the exploded remained. Unlike

Père Jean, who assembles the stuff on which a new story might be printed, the allegorically named Marianne surveys the damage of the failure of 1848.

Nerval and Pyat, whose sanity and liberty had suffered from their contact with Jules Janin, put their faith in book-format accounts of paper and printing when it came time to correct the record about their own practices as playwrights and authors. To continue their arguments with Janin, they finally turned to the page to rectify the distortions that had been imposed in the press, in court, and on the stage.

This return to paper and books in the face of damage done by the ephemeral press and its theatrical manifestations located the long game of overcoming press corruption in bound volumes. Not only did literature define itself in opposition to newspaper publication in the middle of the century, as Richard Terdiman and many others have shown, but literary texts, like the ones considered here, left durable traces of their attempts to engage with the stage and the press in their permanent volume form.[37] Maurice Samuels has traced the formal implications of Balzac and Stendhal's reactions to spectacularized history.[38] Here, even some of the most accomplished playwrights who dealt with the press turned away from the theater and the press's spectacularity, focusing instead on the materiality of the book to frame their efforts.

If Balzac both thematized and used publication in volume form as a way of preserving even his theatricalized discussions of journalism for the historical record, Nerval and Pyat tried similar strategies for their own work after media skirmishes with Janin. Like Balzac, whose long-term solution relied on new paper technology, invented by David Séchard, Nerval contextualized his definitive version of *Léo Burckart* by enclosing it in a volume that attended to the history of the printing press, while Pyat made his *chiffonnier* another source of the stuff that paper was made of. The insistence on materiality in each of these works grounds reflections on the volatile nature of the commercial press, and it preserves those reflections—sometimes those samples—quite materially, for a time when that press will no longer be the arbiter of influence for the readership of these works. Having reached that time, it is worth remembering not only that period newspapers provide a useful context for literary works we continue to read but that plays, too, informed the debates in which they were caught up—often much more than individual newspapers did.

CONCLUSION

Newspapers remained on stage well into the 1860s, and even beyond, but the end of the July Monarchy marked a certain dedramatization of their status. When Théophile Gautier wrote a preface to Delphine de Girardin's *Œuvres complètes* in 1861, he praised *L'École des journalistes*' formal innovation but said:

> Cette pièce, très-vraie à cette époque (1839) où le journalisme usait et abusait d'une liberté presque illimitée dans une société trop habituée, malgré son scepticisme, à le croire sur parole, semblerait peut-être exagérée aujourd'hui. Elle n'en peint pas moins d'une façon fidèle et frappante une phase de mœurs disparue.[1]

> This play, which was very true in its time (1839), when journalism used and abused nearly unlimited liberty in a society which, despite its skepticism, was too much in the habit of believing it at its word, may seem exaggerated today. Nonetheless, it is a striking and faithful portrait of the ways of a bygone period.

As we have seen, the *mœurs disparues* (bygone ways) of the July Monarchy press and theater had given rise to plays and criticism that both educated audiences about the habits of the press and encouraged skepticism as to the transparency of information it presented.

In 1848, outright cynicism about press behavior was considered passé, but using advertisement to finance the press was taken as a given. *Le Charivari* itself discouraged the directors of the Porte Saint-Martin theater from staging *Robert Macaire* in March 1848, and the paper expressed relief when, after two performances, the public seemed bored.[2] The fact that a newfound idealism about the role of the press could suddenly be reconciled with its persistent commercialism suggests a fading of concern about newspapers' use of advertisement blocking their role as instruments of civic publicity.

In a vaudeville revue that opened on December 19, 1848, the night before presidential election results were announced, a chorus of personifications of *nouveaux journaux* (new newspapers) sang, "À la liberté / nous devons d'être / Et de paraître / Par nous vont renaître / Égalité / Fraternité ! . . . Nous sommes tous nés / Pour la défense / de la France : / Nous sommes tous nés / Pour avoir beaucoup d'abonnés" (Thanks to liberty we exist and appear.

Through us Equality and Fraternity will be born again. . . . We were all born for the defense of France, we were all born to have many subscribers).[3] However much the *quarante-huitards* (those involved in the February Revolution of 1848) tried to institute a new relationship between the people and their government, including through the use of newspapers, marketing had become an established part of press production. The theater would continue to question the press's claims, but with less performative zeal, and newspapers would gradually become more neatly integrated into the plots of plays during the Second Empire.

From 1836 to 1848, newspapers could still be imagined as bodies and impersonated. The very irony usually employed when playwrights staged the press was a mark of concern about the disintegration of civic publicity—and a gesture toward correcting it. What plays about the press, critical *feuilletons*, and Balzac, Nerval, and Pyat's books about press and publicity had in common was a skeptical citational humor that raised questions about calumny and collective authorship, advertising and the social and political effects of elicited desire. To reach a broader audience, papers tried to diversify their appeal, but personal scandal and attention-grabbing allusions turned out to be some of the easiest techniques for doing so. Other media (sometimes cooperating, sometimes competing) gloried in pointing out that such strategies were far more likely to exacerbate social divisions than to diminish them. For example, an 1848 caricature of Émile de Girardin portrays him as a *chiffonnier* (ragpicker) gathering bits of paper marked "calumny," "filth," "bitterness," and "trash"—presumably to compose his newspaper from such dregs of human relations (see figure 6, the title of which says, "A Well-Known Journalist Looks for Material to Fill Up His Rag").

A key critique of press expansion, which is reflected in this caricature, was that it simply gathered and disseminated what would otherwise be the detritus of social relations. This image suggests that the commercial press reaches the masses not as enlightenment but as an assemblage of useless scraps of divisive information. Whereas real *chiffonniers* had lamps to allow them to see what they were doing as they gathered the garbage put out at night (the standard iconography of the *chiffonnier* included basket, spike, and lamp) the image of Girardin includes no lantern—it deprives him of the light he so frequently claimed to be bringing to his readers.

It also keeps press corruption solidly in the realm of the material world: a newspaper can be qualified as a news rag because it is made up of rags and will eventually be recycled in that same form. Send-ups of newspapers that relied on their materiality were commonplace in the theater, and critical responses to such scenes often presented their accounts to readers as if they, the readers, were the ultimate judges of the play in question. In many cases, they were. Maurice Descotes points out that the public who attended any given play changed during the course of its run, with only spectators at the first performance seeing it without being influenced by the opinions of other

Figure 6. Émile de Girardin as *chiffonnier*. Rigobert, *Un journaliste très connu cherchant des matériaux pour remplir sa feuille* (Paris: Imp. Vial, 1848). Courtesy of Bibliothèque nationale de France.

audiences or *feuilletonistes*.[4] In novels, on stage, and in the press, reliance on techniques associated with the vaudeville (pastiche, *actualité* [topicality], interpellation of the audience) kept heterogeneous and relatively popular audiences from taking the commercial press at face value. By presenting the expectation of press transparency as one of the illusions audiences needed to lose, the works considered here practiced civic publicity. Their efforts meant that the beginning of the era of mass media did not necessarily coincide with the advent of passive consumerism.

Hegel's dictum about the morning newspaper having taken on the role of morning prayer[5] links newspaper reading to other, older daily routines of connection with the world beyond oneself. While July Monarchy newspapers dreamed of gathering a diverse readership and leading them as a preacher might, though, their solution for doing so—the use of commercial publicity and the relative depoliticization of content—was widely seen as an abdication of the very role that might have made leaders of them.

Meanwhile, another participatory routine, that of attending the theater, encouraged audiences to think about how new media practices were shaping society. Plays had the advantage of being able to perform alternate ways of spreading information, as they criticized the nascent mass press and educated audiences about its claims and practices. They were effective enough at doing so that *feuilletonistes* and novelists borrowed vaudeville techniques in their own efforts to weigh in on the dangers of scandal and the virtues of debate. Journalists and novelists sought to capture vaudeville's critical but engaged popular verve, often while distancing themselves from its ephemeral and spectacular nature. Honoré de Balzac's innovative publishing practices, developed as the *Comédie humaine* evolved, Eugène Scribe's well-wrought comedies, which dominated European theaters for the first half of the nineteenth century, and the genre-defining criticism practiced by Théophile Gautier and Jules Janin were all integrally engaged with the development of the forty-franc press and of the vaudevilles that sent it up, promoted it, and both advertised and questioned its claims. Émile de Girardin pioneered the commercial strategies of the forty-franc press, while Delphine de Girardin explained the promise and dangers of its operations in her plays and her journalism. Vaudevilles cited from the plays and events of each year, and citation became a mark of superior judgment for journalists, and of historical documentation for novelists. Jules Janin came up with an inimitable style for his *feuilleton* and was pastiched and pilloried by Balzac, Gérard de Nerval, Félix Pyat, and Dennery and Clairville for his abuses of his power as a critic.

While journalism itself was not, at the time, a profession for which one could study, a sort of deontology was already being projected by those who questioned the actions of critics and journalists. This code of conduct, shimmery and nebulous as it may have been in the early days of the commercial press, has continued to inform our understanding of the role of the press as a source of transparency in political life.[6] Its abuses, in addition to providing material for any number of jokes on the Parisian stage, contributed to a literary focus on paper-based documentation of publicity practices which prefigured modernist self-consciousness about media of communication. The bodily metaphor that held that newspapers were organs of political opinion gave way, with the commercialization of the press, to embodiments of newspapers on stage, which, in turn, inspired journalists and novelists to situate their own authority on the printed page, rather than in the space of oratory and action that was the theater.

Appendix 1

Plays about the Press (1836–1848)

The table on the following pages shows plays dealing with the press in July
Monarchy France, which I identified in my survey of roughly a thousand
plays from the period 1836–1848. It includes plays that were performed but
not published as well as some published plays that provided no information
about where (or whether) they were performed. When that information was
unavailable, no theater is listed in the table. Titles in parentheses refer to plays
I was unable to consult, but which were referred to by newspaper articles as
treating journalism. Below is a key to the identities of the authors who used
pseudonyms; the table of plays gives the pseudonym only (in italics).

Pseudonym	Name
Angel	Eustache, A.-J.-R
Adolphe (collective pseduonym)	D'Ennery, Adolphe-Philippe, and D'Artois, Achille
Alzay	Sauzay, Charles-Antoine-Alexis
Barthélemy	Thouin, Mathieu-Barthélemy
Clairville	Nicolaïe, Louis François
Cordier, Jules	Vaulabelle, Eléonore Tenaille de
Delatour	Gay de La Tour de Lajonchére, Auguste
Dennery	D'Ennery, Adolphe Philippe
Desvergers	Chapeau, Armand
Dubourg, Félix	Cavelier, J.-F. et Neuville, A.
Dumanoir	Pinel, Philippe-François
Eugène (1)	Cormon, P.-E. Piestre
Eugène (2)	Grangé, E.P. Basté

Pseudonym	Name
Eugène (3)	La Merlière, Hugues-Marie-Humbert Bocon de
Honoré	Rémy, Charles-Honoré
Laurencin	Chapelle, P.-A
Léonce	Laurençot, Charles-Henri-Ladislas
Lubize	Martin, Pierre-Henri
Marc-Michel	Michel, Marc Antoine Amédée
Nadar	Tournachon, Félix
Toreinx, F.-R. de	Ronteix, Eugène
Valory	Mourier, Charles
Varin	Voirin, Charles

Date of first performance	Theater	Authors	Title	Genre
Jan. 20, 1836	Variétés	Mennechet, Edouard Dupin, Henri	*Mila, ou l'esclave*	anecdote from 1827
Mar. 5, 1836	Palais-Royal	Foucher, Paul-Henri Duport, Paul	*Coliche ou un pamphlet sous M. de Maurepas*	comedy-vaudeville in 1 act
May 24, 1836	Théâtre Français	Rosier, Joseph-Bernard	*Un procès criminel ou les femmes impressionnables*	comedy in 3 acts, in prose
June 6, 1836	Palais-Royal	Roche, Eugène-Germain Dumanoir, Antonin	*Une spéculation*	vaudeville in 1 act
June 30, 1836	Variétés	Rochefort, Edmond Artois, Achille d'	*Le Comédien de salon*	comedy-vaudeville in 1 act
Aug. 20, 1836	Ambigu-Comique	Desnoyer, Charles Rimbaut, François et Hippolyte	*Vaugelas ou le Ménage d'un savant*	comedy-vaudeville in 1 act
Aug. 31, 1836	Variétés	Dumas, Alexandre Théaulon, Emmanuel Courcy, Frédéric de	*Kean*	comedy in 5 acts, with songs
Sept. 22, 1836	Jeunes Artistes	Ronteix, Eugène Lubize	*Le Bon et le mauvais chemin*	comedy-vaudeville in 1 act
Oct. 9, 1836	Gaîté	Dumersan, Théophile Marion	*Le Pensionnaire ou Cent francs par mois*	comedy in 1 act, with rhymes
Dec. 31, 1836	Ambigu-Comique	Delatour Clairville	*Revue-1836 dans la lune*	revue with rhymes

Date of first performance	Theater	Authors	Title	Genre
Printed in 1837		Jouhaud, Auguste	L'Anti-camaraderie, ou la France au XXe Siècle	comedy in 5 acts and in prose
Printed in 1837, restaged 1848	Porte Saint-Martin	Cogniard, Théodore	La Fin du monde	fantasy revue in 3 acts and 9 tableaux
First perf. Feb. 6, 1834, restaged 1837	Gymnase	Bayard, Jean-François-Alfred Varner, Antoine-François	Le Mari d'une muse	comedy-vaudeville in 1 act
Jan. 1, 1837	Palais-Royal	Courcy, Frédéric de Bayard, Jean-François-Alfred	L'Année sur la sellette	revue with rhymes
Jan. 6, 1837	Théâtre du Gymnase, Lyon	Labie, Charles Augier, Joanny	Le Cauchemar Revue Lyonnaise de 1836	episodic vaudeville in 1 act
Jan. 19, 1837	Théâtre Français	Scribe, Eugène	La Camaraderie	comedy in 5 acts and in prose
Mar. 31, 1837	Théâtre du Gymnase, Lyon et Paris	Eugène (3) Labie, Charles Augier, Joanny	Les Giboulées de mars	April Fool's in 11 pieces
Apr. 9, 1837	Ambigu-Comique	Desnoyer, Charles Chasseriau	Paul et Julien	comedy-vaudeville in 2 acts

Date	Theater	Author	Title	Description
May 6, 1837	Ambigu-Comique	Vanderburch, Émile Simonnin, Antoine-Jean-Baptiste	*Le Marchand des chansons*	vaudeville in 1 act
July 22, 1837	Gymnase	Théaulon, Emmanuel Desnoyers, C. H. Edmond	*Sans nom ! Drames et Romans*	mystery-folly-vaudeville in 1 act
Sept. 9, 1837	Gaîté	Desnoyer, Charles Labie, Charles	*L'Ombre de Nicolet ou de plus fort en plus fort !*	episodic vaudeville in 1 act
Sept. 23, 1837	Porte Saint-Antoine	Salvat, Adolphe Henri, Charles	*Le Chemin de fer de Saint Germain*	occasional vaudeville in 1 act
Oct. 28, 1837	Variétés	Bayard, Jean-François-Alfred Théaulon, Emmanuel	*Le Père de la débutante*	vaudeville in 5 acts
Nov. 11, 1837	Vaudeville	Dupeuty, Charles Arago, Étienne Alhoy, Maurice	*Coucous et wagons*	revue in 1 act
Nov. 20, 1837	Théâtre Français puis Odéon	Scribe, Eugène	*Les Indépendants*	comedy in 3 acts and in prose
Nov. 20, 1837	Variétés	*Dumanoir*	*Un système*	vaudeville in 1 act
Nov. 26, 1837	Gaîté	Tournemine, Pierre	*La Révolte des coucous*	critico-comic-fantastic vaudeville
Dec. 27, 1837	Ambigu-Comique	*Clairville*	*Mathieu Laensberg est un menteur*	revue in 1 act, with rhymes

Date of first performance	Theater	Authors	Title	Genre
Dec. 20, 1837	Gymnase	Vanderburch, Émile	Le Sauté-ruisseau	office tableau in 1 act with rhymes
Dec. 30, 1837	Luxembourg	Delatour Clairville	1837 aux enfers	fantasy revue with rhymes
Jan. 1, 1838	Palais-Royal	Cogniard frères	Île de la folie	revue in 1 act, with rhymes
May 16, 1838	Variétés	Bayard, Jean-François-Alfred	M. Gogo à la bourse	vaudeville in 1 act and 1 tableau
June 13, 1838	Vaudeville	Lauzanne de Vauroussel, Augustin Théodore de Saintine, X. B. Duvert, Félix-Auguste	Impressions de voyage	vaudeville in 2 acts
July 1, 1838	Port-Royal	Dupin (and maybe Soulié, see Wicks)	(Un drame)	vaudeville-folly in 1 act
July 8, 1838	Gymnase	Auger, Hippolyte	Mlle Bernard ou l'autorité paternelle	vaudeville in 1 act
Oct. 11, 1838	Théâtre Français	Desnoyer, Charles Labat, Eugène	Richard Savage	drama in 5 acts
Dec. 1, 1838	Théâtre Français	Delavigne, Casimir	La Popularité	comedy in 5 acts in verse

Date	Theater	Author(s)	Title	Description
Dec. 24, 1838	Folies Dramatiques	Mourier, Charles Kock, Paul de	*Concierge du théâtre*	vaudeville in 1 act
Dec. 31, 1838	Variétés	Carmouche, Pierre-Frédéric-Adolphe *Varin* Huart, Louis	*Le Puff*	revue in 3 tableaux with *Ruy-Blag*, a rhyming prose parody of *Ruy-Blas*
Dec. 31, 1838	Ambigu-Comique	Gay de la Tour de Lajonchère, Auguste *Clairville*	*Les Mines de blagues*	spectacular fantasy revue, with rhymes
Jan. 1, 1839	Palais-Royal	Cogniard frères	*Rothomago*	revue in 1 act
Mar. 21, 1839	Ambigu-comique	Ménissier, Constant	*Une heure d'exposition*	revue in 1 act
Apr. 16, 1839	Porte Saint-Martin	Nerval, Gérard de Dumas, Alexandre	*Léo Burckart*	drama in 5 acts
May 22, 1839	Théâtre Français	Beauplan, Amédée de	*Le Susceptible*	comedy in 1 act, in verse
June 1, 1839	Gymnase	*Desvergers* *Dubourg* *Laurencin*	*Industriels et industrieux*	revue of the Exposition of 1839, in 3 tableaux
June 3, 1839	Porte Saint-Antoine	Tournemine, Pierre Guénée, Adolphe	*La France et l'industrie*	allegorical vaudeville in 1 act, about the products of the Exposition of 1839

Date of first performance	Theater	Authors	Title	Genre
June 20, 1839	Renaissance	Colet-Révoil, Louise	*La Jeunesse de Goethe*	comedy in 1 act and in verse
July 6, 1839	Renaissance	Sauvage, Thomas Maurice-Saint-Aguet, Louis-Charles	*Un vaudevilliste*	comedy in 1 act, in prose
July 14, 1839	Vaudeville	*Varin* *Desvergers* Alhoy, Maurice	*Les Belles femmes de Paris*	vaudeville in 3 tableaux
July 17, 1839	Variétés	Lauzanne de Vauroussel, Augustin Théodore de Duvert, Félix-Auguste Dumersan, Théophile Marion	*Les Belles femmes de Paris*	comedy-vaudeville in 2 acts
July 20, 1839	Porte Saint-Antoine	*Angel* Vanel, Eugène	*Les Belles femmes de Paris*	vaudeville in 1 act
July 20, 1839	Théâtre du Panthéon	Jouhaud, Auguste	*Les Beaux hommes de Paris*	vaudeville in 1 act
July 14, 1839	Porte Saint-Martin	*Honoré*	*(L'Épicier-journaliste)*	vaudeville in 1 act
Aug. 29, 1839	Folies Dramatiques	Labie, Charles Augier, Joanny	*Les Femmes laides de Paris*	comedy-vaudeville in 1 act

Date	Theater	Author	Title	Description
Oct./Nov. 1839	[contracted by Théâtre Français but not staged]	Girardin, Delphine de	L'École des Journalistes	comedy in 5 acts, and in verse
Oct. 12, 1839	Vaudeville	Laloue, Ferdinand Carmouche, Pierre-Frédéric-Adolphe	Belisario, ou l'Opéra impossible	vaudeville in 2 acts
Oct. 24, 1839	Porte Saint-Antoine	Jouhaud, Auguste	La Popularité	village tableau in 1 act, with rhymes
Nov. 18, 1839	Théâtre Français	Vaulabelle, Eléonore Tenaille de	L'Ami de la maison	comedy in 1 act
Dec. 8, 1839	Gaîté	Labie, Charles Augier, Joanny	La Maupin ou une vengeance d'actrice	comedy-vaudeville in 1 act
Dec. 28, 1839	Ambigu-comique	Clairville	Les Iroquois	fantasy revue in 1 act
Dec. 29, 1839	Gaîté	Grangé, Eugène Bourget, Ernest Ennery, Adolphe d'	1840 ou la guerre des saisons	revue-vaudeville in 1 act
Dec. 29, 1839	Palais-Royal	Muret, Théodore Cogniard frères	Les Bamboches de l'année	revue with rhymes
Feb. 20, 1840	Théâtre Français	Scribe, Eugène	La Calomnie	comedy in 5 acts
Aug. 15, 1840	Théâtre Saint-Marcel	Jouhaud, Auguste	Les Belles femmes de la rue Mouffetard	vaudeville 1 act

Date of first performance	Theater	Authors	Title	Genre
Nov. 3, 1840	Gymnase	Fournier, Louis-Pierre-Narcisse	*Un roman intime*	comedy in 1 act
Nov. 17, 1840	Théâtre Français	Scribe, Eugène	*Le verre d'eau, ou Les effets et les causes*	comedy in 5 acts and in prose
Nov. 30, 1840	Palais-Royal	*Dumanoir* Bayard, Jean-François-Alfred	*Les Guêpes*	revue with rhymes
Dec. 9, 1840	Folies Dramatiques	Cogniard frères Delaporte, Michel	*Job, l'afficheur*	vaudeville in 2 acts
Jan. 1, 1841	Porte Saint-Antoine	*Clairville*	*Les Français peints par eux-mêmes*	fantasy revue in 1 act
Mar. 5, 1841	Folies Dramatiques	Laya, Léon Carmouche, Pierre-Frédéric-Adolphe	*L'Esclave à Paris*	anecdotal comedy in 1 act, with rhymes
June 8, 1841	Folies Dramatiques	Veyrat, Xavier *Alzay*	*Le Boulevard du crime*	popular vaudeville in 2 acts
Sept. 18, 1841	Gaîté	Desnoyer, Charles	*La Mère de la débutante*	comedy in 2 acts, with rhymes

Date	Theater	Author	Title	Description
Oct. 28, 1841	Odéon	Dupin, Henri Dumersan, Théophile Marion	*L'Actionnaire*	comedy in 1 act and in verse
Nov. 27, 1841	Porte Saint-Martin	Bourgeois, Eugène Dumas, Alexandre	*Jeannic le Breton, ou le Gérant responsable*	drama in 5 acts and in prose
Dec. 3, 1841	Gymnase	Bayard, Jean-François-Alfred	*Les Fées de Paris*	comedy-vaudeville in 2 acts
Dec. 11, 1841	Ambigu-Comique	*Clairville Dennery*	*Le Feuilleton et la Raison*	vaudeville-revue in 1 act
Dec. 29, 1841	Porte Saint-Martin	Cogniard Muret, Théodore	*1841 et 1941, ou Aujourd'hui et dans cent ans*	fantasy revue in 2 acts
Oct. 1, 1842	Folies Dramatiques	*Léonce* Delaporte, Michel	*Un Ménage de garçon*	comedy-vaudeville in 1 act
Oct. 15, 1842	Odéon	Barrière, M. A.	*Le Poète, ou les Droits de l'auteur*	comedy in 1 act and in verse
Dec. 18, 1842	Variétés	Dumersan, Théophile Marion Fontaine, Émile	*Abd-el Kadr à Paris*	episodic vaudeville in 1 act
Feb. 18, 1843	Panthéon	Roger, Victor	*Thomas, l'imprimeur*	drama (with songs) in 3 acts
Mar. 9, 1843	Odéon	Harel, François-Antoine	*Le Succès*	comedy in 2 acts, in prose

Date of first performance	Theater	Authors	Title	Genre
Mar. 28, 1843	Palais-Royal	Bayard, Jean-François-Alfred	Mlle Déjazet au sérail	vaudeville in 1 act
Apr. 19, 1843	Théâtre Français	Veyrat, Xavier Masselin, Victor	L'Art et le métier	comedy in 1 act and in verse
June 3, 1843	Gymnase	Lécosse	L'Assassin de Boyvin ou l'Avocat stagiaire	comedy-vaudeville in 1 act
June 25, 1843	Variétés	Clairville Salvat, Adolphe	La Jeune et la vielle garde	episode from 1814, in 1 act
Sept. 27, 1843	Ambigu-Comique	Ennery, Adolphe d' Grangé, E.P. Basté	Les Bohémiens de Paris	drama in 5 acts and 8 tableaux
Nov. 9, 1843	Odéon	Guillard, Léon	Les Moyens dangereux	comedy in 5 acts and in verse
Dec. 9, 1843	Porte Saint-Martin	Cogniard frères Muret, Théodore	Les Îles marquises revue de 1843	revue of 1843, in 2 acts
Dec. 14, 1843	Folies Dramatiques	de Kock, Paul	Le Théâtre et la cuisine	vaudeville-drama buffoonery, larded with rhymes, with swordplay, with stage business, etc. in 2 acts

Date	Theater	Author	Title	Description
Dec. 22, 1843	Variétés	Dumanoir Clairville Dennery, Adolphe	*Paris dans la comète*	revue in 3 acts
Dec. 31, 1843	Théâtre du Luxembourg	Tournemine, Pierre Augier, Joanny	*Paris aux îles marquises*	revue of 1843
Sometime in 1843, published in *Le Corsaire*		Jouhaud, Auguste	*Tigresse*	parody in 1 act
Probably 1843 or 1844		Boulois, F. C. de	*Ôte-toi de là que je m'y mette ou l'installation d'un préfet en 1830*	dramatic proverb
Jan. 17, 1844 (Wicks gives date as Jan. 31)	Délassements Comiques	Clairville Hostein, Hippolyte	*Le Monument de Molière*	revue in 2 acts and 4 tableaux
Jan. 18, 1844	Odéon	feu Camille Bernay	*Le Pseudonyme*	comedy in 1 act and in verse
Feb. 18, 1844	Gymnase	Lardenois	*La Tante Bazu*	comedy-vaudeville in 2 acts
Apr. 18, 1844	Vaudeville	Laurencin Marc-Michel	*La Gazette des tribunaux*	comedy-vaudeville in 1 act

Date of first performance	Theater	Authors	Title	Genre
May 10, 1844	Folies Dramatiques	*Léonce* Delaporte, Michel	*Un Tribunal des femmes*	vaudeville in 1 act
May 15, 1844	Beaumarchais	Prémaray, Jules Regnault de	*Part à deux*	comedy in 1 act, with songs
June 6, 1844	Folies Dramatiques	*Lubize* Dugard, Louis	*Les Petits métiers*	vaudeville in 3 acts
July 11, 1844	Variétés	Leuven, Adolphe de Dumersan, Théophile Marion	*Les Bédouines de Paris*	comedy in 1 act, with rhymes
July 23, 1844	Vaudeville	*Clairville* Damarin, Edouard	*Satan ou le diable à Paris*	comedy vaudeville in 4 acts
July 31, 1844	Beaumarchais	Simonnin, Antoine Jean-Baptiste Llaunet, François	*Le Diable à Paris*	vaudeville in 1 act
Dec. 24, 1844	Vaudeville	*Clairville*	*Paris à tous les diables*	spectacular revue in 5 tableaux
Jan. 25, 1845	Vaudeville	*Clairville* Hostein, Hippolyte	*Les Trois loges*	comedy-vaudeville in 3 acts
Mar. 16, 1845	Gymnase	Fournier, Narcisse	*Amina, ou le Turc moderne*	comedy-vaudeville in 1 act

July 26, 1845	Gymnase	Carmouche, Pierre Frédéric Adolphe Varin	Les Sept merveilles du monde	spectacular revue in 5 tableaux, with rhymes
Sept. 30, 1845	Gymnase	Léonce Demolière, H.-J.	Entre l'arbre et l'écorce	comedy-vaudeville in 1 act
Dec. 20, 1845	Palais-Royal	Clairville Dumanoir	Les Pommes de terre malades	revue of the year 1845, in 3 acts
Dec. 30, 1845	Vaudeville	Dennery Clairville	V'là c'qui vient d' paraître, bulletin de la grande année 1845	revue-vaudeville
Dec. 31, 1845	Cirque Olympique	Carmouche, Pierre Frédéric Adolphe Vermond, Paul	Paris à cheval	horseback revue in 5 relays
Feb. 26, 1846	Vaudeville	Cordier, Jules Clairville	Les Dieux de l'Olympe à Paris	comedy-vaudeville in 5 tableaux
Mar. 8, 1846	Variétés	Souvestre, Émile	Les Deux Camusot	comedy-vaudeville in 1 act
Apr. 9, 1846	Délassements Comiques	Barthélemy Jouhaud, Auguste	La Faute du mari	comedy-vaudeville in 2 acts

Date of first performance	Theater	Authors	Title	Genre
Apr. 4, 1846	Vaudeville	*Dennery* Cormon, P.-E. Piestre Romain	*Le Roman comique*	vaudeville in 3 acts adapted from Scarron's *Roman comique*
Apr. 9, 1846	Palais-Royal	Lefranc, Auguste Labiche, Eugène	*Mademoiselle ma femme*	comedy-vaudeville in 1 act
Apr. 30, 1846	Gymnase	Henriot, J.-B.-A. Fournier, Narcisse Alphonse	*Les Ennemis*	comedy-vaudeville in 1 act
June 9, 1846	Gymnase	Duchatelard, Auguste	*Babolard ou le dramaturge dans son ménage*	comedy-vaudeville in 1 act
June 25, 1846	Folies Dramatiques	Masson, Michel Thomas, Frédéric	*La Fée du bord de l'eau*	comedy-vaudeville in 3 acts
July 2, 1846	Vaudeville	*Laurencin* Muret, Théodore	*Si j'étais homme ! ou les Canotiers de Paris*	comedy-vaudeville in 2 acts
July 25, 1846	Délassement Comiques	Jouhaud, Auguste Bricet	*Par les femmes*	comedy-vaudeville in 1 act
Dec. 11, 1846	Palais-Royal	*Dumanoir* Clairville	*La Poudre-coton*	revue of the year 1846 in 4 acts and 1 interlude with rhymes

Date	Theater	Author	Title	Description
Dec. 12, 1846	Vaudeville	Depeuty, J. Gabriel Duvert, Félix Auguste	*La Planète à Paris*	revue of 1848, in 3 acts and 4 tableaux
Jan. 7, 1847	Folies Dramatiques	Cormon, P.-E. Piestre Grangé, E.P. Basté	*La Planète ******	revue in 2 acts
Jan. 15, 1847	Théâtre Français	Barbier, Paul-Jules	*L'Ombre de Molière*	interlude
Jan. 18, 1847	Variétés	Leuven, Adolphe de Brunswick, Léon Lévy Jaime, Ernest	*L'Illustration*	vaudeville with magic lantern and colored glass
Mar. 2, 1847	Vaudeville	Jousserandot, Louis	*Les Collaborateurs*	comedy in 1 act, in verse
May 11, 1847	Porte Saint-Martin	Pyat, Félix	*Le Chiffonnier de Paris*	drama in 5 acts and 1 prologue
May 18, 1847	Folies Dramatiques	Lefranc, Auguste Labiche, Eugène	*La Chasse aux jobards*	vaudeville in 1 act
May 20, 1847	Rouen Théâtre des arts puis Odéon	Coquatrix, Émile	*Il ne faut pas jouer avec le feu*	comedy in 1 act, in verse
Dec. 10, 1847	Odéon	Bechard, Frédéric	*Les Tribulations d'un grand homme*	comedy in three acts, in prose
Dec. 21, 1847	Palais-Royal	*Dumanoir Clairville*	*Un Banc d'huîtres*	revue of the year 1847, in 4 acts and 7 tableaux, with rhymes

Date of first performance	Theater	Authors	Title	Genre
Dec. 30, 1847	Odéon	Doucet, Camille	*Le Dernier banquet de 1847*	comedy-revue in 3 tableaux
Jan. 8, 1848	Folies Dramatiques	Cormon, P.-E. Piestre Grangé, Eugène-Pierre Basté	*Les Canards de l'année*	revue in 3 acts
Jan. 22, 1848	Théâtre Francais	Scribe, Eugène	*Le Puff*	comedy in 5 acts and in prose
Jan. 20, 1848	Porte Saint-Martin	Cogniard frères	*La Fin du monde*	fantastic revue in 3 acts and 9 tableaux
Mar. 2, 1848	Funambules	*Nadar* (see BnF catalogue) Champfleury (see Wicks)	*Pierrot Ministre*	republican pantomime in 8 tableaux by an out-of-work peer of France
Mar. 3, 1848	Montansier	*Laurencin Marc-Michel*	*— 34 francs ! ou Simon ! . . .*	comedy-vaudeville in 1 act
Apr. 20, 1848	Vaudeville	*Clairville Cordier, Jules Dumoustier, Léon*	*Ah ! Enfin !*	opening play in 3 acts and 2 interludes

Date	Theater	Authors	Title	Description
June 8, 1848	Montansier	Lefranc, Auguste Labiche, Eugène	*Le Club Champenois*	occasional play in 1 act, with rhymes
Sept. 30, 1848	Vaudeville	*Clairville* Cordier, Jules	*L'Avenir dans le passé, ou les Succès au paradis*	occasional vaudeville in 1 act
Oct. 31, 1848	Porte Saint-Martin	Cogniard frères	*L'Île de Tohu-Bohu*	gibberish in 3 acts
Dec. 19, 1848	Montansier	*Dumanoir* *Clairville*	*Les Lampions de la veille et les lanternes du lendemain*	revue of the year 1848, in 5 tableaux
Dec. 27, 1848	Porte Saint-Martin	Cogniard frères Muret, Théodore	*Les Marrons d'Inde, ou les Grotesques de l'année*	fantastic revue in 3 acts and 8 tableaux

ASSOCIATION

DE LA LIBRAIRIE

ET DE

LA PRESSE QUOTIDIENNE.

En souscrivant pour un abonnement soit de trois mois (20 francs) au FIGARO, soit de 6 mois (38 francs) à ESTAFETTE, on reçoit immédiatement, à titre de prime gratuite, le nouveau roman de M. de BALZAC : *Histoire de la grandeur et de la décadence de* CÉSAR BIROTTEAU, *parfumeur, chevalier de la Légion-d'Honneur, adjoint au maire du deuxième arrondissement de la ville de Paris*. 2 vol. in-8°.

C'était une idée heureuse que d'associer la Librairie à la Presse Quotidienne ; que d'augmenter la circulation des Livres au moyen des Journaux ; que de soumettre les productions intermittentes de la Librairie à la précision, à la régularité des mouvemens de la Presse Périodique. Cette idée neuve, quoique simple, quoique bien naturelle, n'avait eu aucun précédent avant l'essai qu'en ont fait les Éditeurs du FIGARO. Comme toutes les idées justes, le public l'a comprise, et le succès l'a sanctionnée.

Ainsi, le LIVRE et le JOURNAL vont désormais marcher réunis et se servir réciproquement.

Le Journal, acceptant les sujets à mesure qu'ils se présentent ; écrivant pour être utile aujourd'hui, pour être oublié demain, pour recommencer toujours, fraiera les voies à la Pensée, qui se recueille dans les livres, dont les effets sont plus durables, mais qui pour se produire a besoin de laborieuses études, de longues méditations. Ces rapports intimes des deux expressions de l'intelligence humaine, cette combinaison d'efforts simultanés, dirigés vers un même but, doivent avoir nécessairement pour résultat définitif l'agrandissement du domaine de la pensée : ce que le Journal ébauche, le Livre le finit ; ce qui n'é-

Appendix 2

Prospectus, *César Birotteau*

ASSOCIATION
OF BOOKSELLERS

AND OF

THE DAILY PRESS.

Subscribe to either the FIGARO for three months (20 francs) or to ESTAFETTE for six months (38 francs) to receive M. de Balzac's new novel, *History of the Grandeur and Decadence of CÉSAR BIROTTEAU, perfumer, knight of the Legion of Honor, adjunct to the mayor of the second arrondissement of Paris* as a free gift. 2 volumes, in-octavo.

It was a fine idea to associate Booksellers with the Daily Press, to increase the circulation of Books by means of Newspapers, to submit the intermittent productions of book editors to the regularity of the periodical press. This new idea, however simple and natural it was, was without precedent before the editors of the FIGARO tried it. Like all good ideas, it was understood by the public, and met with success.

And so it is that the BOOK and the NEWSPAPER will, from now on, work together and benefit each other.

The Newspaper, accepting material as it presents itself, writing to be useful today, forgotten tomorrow, to perpetually begin again, breaks the trail for Thought, which gathers itself in long reflection. These deep connections between two expressions of human intelligence, this combination of simultaneous efforts toward a common goal, will necessarily result in the expansion of thought's domain: what is sketched by the Newspaper is finished by the Book, what

tait qu'un aperçu devient plus tard une formule habilement déduite. Le lecteur achèvera ainsi de comprendre dans le Livre ce qu'il n'avait fait que saisir dans le Journal.

Il appartenait au FIGARO de prendre l'initiative dans ce nouveau développement de la Presse, lui qui d'un trait de plume vient d'en élargir la sphère; lui qui le premier a enfin brisé ces barrières étroites élevées par le fanatisme des partis et qui comprimaient l'essor de la pensée; lui qui a rompu tous les liens de la camaraderie politique ou littéraire, et qui, dans son vaste éclectisme, va chercher chaque jour ses objets d'étude, de critique d'éloge ou de blâme au milieu de tous les partis, au sein de toutes les classes, n'importe quel drapeau les protége.

Mais, pour que le succès fût certain, il devait y avoir accord entre tous les termes de cette combinaison; il fallait qu'il y eût entre le LIVRE et le JOURNAL une corrélation constante; il ne fallait pas surtout que des livres médiocres vinssent se faire traîner à la remorque par le journal, et que l'allure franche et décidée de celui-ci fût alourdie par l'impopularité des ouvrages. Il fallait que le Livre, comme le Journal, eût sa valeur propre, et qu'ils possédassent l'un et l'autre leur principe de vitalité. C'est la réunion difficile de toutes ces conditions, qui a fait le succès de l'entreprise.

FIGARO et BALZAC! quels noms plus heureusement *juxtà*-posés! où trouver une similitude plus intime d'esprit, de pensées, de sentimens, d'individualisme, que celle qui existe entre Beaumarchais et M. de Balzac? Tous les deux, pleins de verve et d'originalité, ils ont tour à tour attaqué, blâmé, défendu les mœurs de leur époque, et leurs personnifications sont restées comme des types à jamais populaires.

Les *Études Philosophiques* de M. de Balzac devinrent la première assise de cette opération. A peine le public en fut-il instruit, à peine les premiers numéros du FIGARO furent-ils mis en circulation avec cette annonce, que mille souscripteurs se présentèrent pour avoir leur BALZAC et leur FIGARO; pour rire le matin avec leur journal des ridicules d'ici-bas; et pour en étudier le soir, avec le livre, les causes et les résultats. En moins de quinze jours *deux mille exemplaires* étaient enlevés.

Mais, pendant que le livre s'épuisait; pendant que l'auteur mettait la dernière main à un nouveau travail, les éditeurs du FIGARO offraient à l'empres-

was an outline becomes a carefully deduced formula. The reader will be able to understand in the Book what he has merely glimpsed in the Newspaper.

It was fitting that the FIGARO would take the initiative in this new development of the Press. It has just enlarged the sphere of the media with a pen stroke, has been the first to break the narrow partisan barriers that limited the extension of thought. It has done away with all bonds of political or literary nepotism and, in its vast eclecticism, goes looking every day for material to study, to critique, or to praise, across parties and classes, regardless of which flag protects them.

But for success to be assured, there had to be agreement about the terms of this cooperation: there had to be an equivalency of quality between the BOOK and the NEWSPAPER: mediocre books could not be allowed to drag along behind newspapers; their unpopularity mustn't weigh down the frank, decisive allure of the press. The Book, like the Newspaper, needed to have its own value. Each must posess its own principle of vitality. It is the difficult fulfillment of all of these conditions that has led to the success of this enterprise.

FIGARO and BALZAC! what names could go better together? Where to find a deeper similarity of wit, of thought, of sentiment and individualism than that which exists between Beaumarchais and Balzac? Both of them, full of verve and originality, have attacked, blamed, defended the ways of their era, and their personifications have become perpetually popular types.

M. de Balzac's *Philosophical Studies* became the first stage of this operation. No sooner had the public learned of it, the moment that the first numbers of the FIGARO with this advertisement appeared, a thousand subscribers presented themselves, looking for their BALZAC and their FIGARO, to laugh in the morning with their newspaper about the ridiculous ways of this earth, and to study the causes and results of them carefully in the evening, with the book. In less than two weeks, *two thousand books* had been seized.

As the books ran out, while the author put the finshing touches on a new project, the editors of the FIGARO offered other, equally interesting (if differently titled) works to the public. For every three-month subscription, they offered one of the three books whose titles appear below:

sement du public d'autres ouvrages non moins dignes d'intérêt, mais à des titres différens. A chaque abonnement de trois mois, ils offraient l'un des trois ouvrages dont nous reproduisons ici les titres :

OEUVRES COMPLÈTES
DE
CASIMIR DELAVIGNE,
DE L'ACADÉMIE FRANÇAISE;

SEULE ÉDITION AVOUÉE PAR L'AUTEUR ET PUBLIÉE SOUS SA DIRECTION,

Ornée d'un beau portrait de l'auteur, par Montvoisin,

ET DE DOUZE BELLES GRAVURES SUR ACIER, PAR JOHANNOT.

CINQ-MARS,
OU
UNE CONJURATION SOUS LOUIS XIII;
PAR M. LE COMTE ALFRED DE VIGNY,

NOUVELLE ÉDITION DE LUXE,

Entièrement revue par l'auteur, ornée d'un *fac simile*, et d'autographes de CINQ-MARS et du cardinal RICHELIEU.

MÉMOIRES SUR LA RESTAURATION,
OU
SOUVENIRS HISTORIQUES
Sur cette époque, la révolution de 1830 et les premières années du règne de Louis-Philippe,

PAR MADAME LA DUCHESSE D'ABRANTÈS.

6 volumes in-8°, publiés au prix de 45 fr.

Casimir Delavigne, Alfred de Vigny, madame d'Abrantès, ont aussi eu leur

THE COMPLETE WORKS

OF

CASIMIR DELAVIGNE,

OF L'ACADÉMIE FRANÇAISE;

THE ONLY OFFICIAL EDITION EDITED BY THE AUTHOR,

Including a portrait of the author by Montvoisin,

AND TWELVE FINE STEEL-PLATE ENGRAVINGS BY JOHANNOT.

CINQ-MARS,

OR

A CONSPIRACY UNDER LOUIS XIII;

BY COUNT ALFRED DE VIGNY,

NEW LUXURY EDITION,

Entirely revised by the author, embellished with a facsimile of the signatures of CINQ-MARS and of cardinal RICHELIEU.

MEMOIRS OF THE RESTORATION,

OR

HISTORICAL RECOLLECTIONS

Of this era, the Revolution of 1830, and the first years of the reign of Louis-Philippe,

BY MADAME LA DUCHESSE D'ABRANTÈS.

6 volumes in-8°, available at a price of 45 fr.

Casimir Delavigne, Alfred de Vigny, madame d'Abrantès, are also

part d'influence et de succès. Aujourd'hui le FIGARO compte *cinq mille abonnés*, qui tous possèdent un ou plusieurs des ouvrages dont nous venons d'indiquer le titre. Le nouveau Roman de M. de Balzac va bientôt en augmenter le nombre. Il ne nous appartient pas d'en faire l'éloge ; mais tous ceux qui ont lu le PÈRE GORIOT, cette admirable épopée de famille, qui réunit tous les genres, où tant de caractères divers ont été esquissés d'une manière si vraie, ne pourront s'empêcher de lire ces nouvelles annales qui ont encore une plus grande portée. Ce n'est pas ici la biographie d'une existence obscure, isolée, exceptionnelle, mais bien l'histoire de tout un peuple qui, à Paris comme à Londres, comme à Berlin, partage les mêmes joies, les mêmes douleurs, les mêmes espérances, les mêmes déceptions. Aussi, ne devra-t-on pas trouver trop ambitieux le titre que nous inscrivons ici :

HISTOIRE DE LA GRANDEUR ET DE LA DÉCADENCE

DE

CÉSAR BIROTTEAU,

Parfumeur, chevalier de la Légion-d'Honneur, adjoint au maire du deuxième arrondissement de la ville de Paris,

NOUVELLES SCÈNES DE LA VIE PARISIENNE ;

PAR M. DE BALZAC.

L'ESTAFETTE qui, dans sa spécialité, n'est pas moins éclectique que le FIGARO ; l'ESTAFETTE, qui chaque jour s'adresse à toutes les opinions en les reproduisant toutes, accordera à tous ceux de ses abonnés qui souscriront pour six mois (38 FRANCS) le CÉSAR BIROTTEAU de M. de Balzac.

successsful, influential authors. The FIGARO currently has *five thousand subscribers*, all of whom own one or several of the works whose titles we have listed. M. de Balzac's new Novel will soon increase that number. It is not our role to praise it, but anyone who has read OLD GORIOT, that admirable family epic, which unites all genres, which sketches such a diversity of characters so truly, will feel compelled to read these new chronicles, whose scope is even larger.

This is no biography of an obscure, isolated, exceptional existence, but rather the history of a whole people who, in Paris as in London and in Berlin, share the same joys, the same pains, the same hope and the same disappointments. Given this, the following title is hardly too ambitious:

HISTORY OF THE GRANDEUR AND DECADENCE

OF

CÉSAR BIROTTEAU

Perfumer, Knight of the Legion of Honor, Adjunct to the mayor of the second arrondissement of Paris.

NEW SCENES OF PARISIAN LIFE

BY M. DE BALZAC.

L'ESTAFETTE which, in its own realm, is no less eclectic than the FIGARO; L'ESTAFETTE, which, each day adresses itself to all opinions by reproducing all of them, will give M. de Balzac's CÉSAR BIROTTEAU to any of its subscribers who renew for six months (38 FRANCS).

All translations from the French are my own. Nineteenth-century spellings have been modernized, so that *méchans* now reads *méchants*, for example. Obvious typographical errors have been corrected.

Introduction

1. Given the shifting meaning of "publicity" at the time, her youth and versatility made Mlle St-Albe a particularly appropriate actress for the role. She had debuted two years earlier, at Mme Saqui's theater in a vaudeville written specifically for her with a variety of roles that allowed her to show off her skills. "Bulletin des théâtres, des arts et de la littérature," *Le Figaro*, April 8, 1835, 3.

2. *Coucous* were horse-drawn hackney carriages often used to go between Paris and neighboring towns. Élise Fau, "Le Cheval dans le transport public au XIXe siècle, à travers les collections du musée national de la Voiture et du Tourisme, Compiègne" *In Situ* 27 (2015), accessed January 26, 2019. URL : http://journals.openedition.org/insitu/12124.

3. Pierre Tournemine, *La Révolte des coucous, comédie-vaudeville en un acte* (Paris: Michaud Pilout Barba, 1838), 15.

4. For a wonderful analysis of the press' role in this historical period, see Jeremy Popkin, *Press, Revolution, and Social Identitites in France, 1830–1835* (University Park: Pennsylvania State University Press, 2002).

5. Marc Martin, *Trois siècles de publicité en France* (Paris: Odile Jacob, 1992), 13–14, 54. A good nineteenth-century account is provided under the entry "publicité" in Pierre Larousse, *Grand dictionnaire universel du XIXe siècle français, historique, géographique, mythologique, bibliographique* (Paris: Slatkine, 1982), 390.

6. For Mme de Staël, writing before 1820, *publicité* had meant something like what we would now call "political transparency." In an essay praising the effects of education on the British nobility, she wrote, "Rien de factice ne peut réussir dans un pays où tout est soumis à la publicité" (Nothing false can succeed in a country where everything is subject to publicity). Germaine de Staël, *Considérations sur la Révolution française*, ed. Jacques Godechot (Paris: Tallandier, 1983), 546.

7. Marie-Ève Thérenty and Alain Vaillant, *1836 L'An I de l'ère médiatique: Analyse littéraire et historique de La Presse de Girardin* (Paris: Nouveau monde, 2001).

8. In the 1780s, Bonneville's prospectus for *La Bouche de Fer* identified the press as what Marcel Gauchet calls a necessary "pouvoir censorial," whose role was to make government activities known so that citizens could ensure that no one branch was overstepping its mandates and that individual liberties were being

respected. See "Censure, surveillance, tribunat," in Marcel Gauchet, *La Révolution des pouvoirs* (Paris: Gallimard, 1995), 83.

9. Lucien Jaume, *L'Individu effacé ou le paradoxe du libéralisme français* (Paris: Fayard, 1997), 436, n. 115. For the liberal response from Laboulaye, see the following page, 437, note 117.

10. The phrase *les Trois Glorieuses* refers to the three "glorious" days of fighting, July 27–29, and is also used in reference to the revolution that began the July Monarchy.

11. Elizabeth Eisenstein credits this as the most famous source of the term "fourth estate" but points out that it is relatively undocumented compared to a similar comment, "by Macaulay in the 1820's." See Elizabeth Eisenstein, "The Tribune of the People," in *The Press in the French Revolution*, ed. Harvey Chisick (Oxford: Oxford University Press, 1991), 155.

12. Elizabeth Eisenstein cites J. A. W. Gunn for an account of variations in its meaning in the British context: J. A. W. Gunn, *Beyond Liberty and Property: The Process of Self-Recognition in Eighteenth-Century Political Thought* (Montreal: McGill-Queen's University Press, 1983), 89–94.

13. The text of the law is reproduced in "Annexe 2. Loi du 9 septembre 1835," with commentary by Barbara T. Cooper, Médias 19, June 5, 2015, http://www.medias19.org/index.php?id=22079.

14. For an account of this conflict, see Maurice Reclus, *Émile de Girardin, le créateur de la presse moderne* (Paris: Hachette, 1934), 83.

15. "Prospectus," *La Presse*, June 15, 1836.

16. Book 5 of *L'Histoire de dix ans* cited in Jean-Noël Jeanneney, *Une histoire des médias des origines à nos jours* (Paris: Ed. du Seuil, 1996), 95. Louis Blanc was put in charge of *Le Bon Sens* when the September Laws took effect.

17. Madeleine Lassère, *Delphine de Girardin, journaliste et femme de lettres au temps du romantisme* (Paris: Perrin, 2003), 146. Also see Roger Bautier and Élisabeth Cazenave, *Les Origines d'une conception moderne de la communication: Gouverner l'opinion au XIXe siècle*, La communication en plus (Grenoble, Fr.: Presses universitaires de Grenoble, 2000), 60. Chapter 1 explains how *La Presse* and *Le Siècle* aimed to educate the newly enlarged electorate.

18. Émile de Girardin, "De la liberté de la presse et du journalisme," *La Presse*, December 5, 1839, 2.

19. In this view, he was like the thinkers whom Alan Kahan has called "aristocratic liberals." Alan S. Kahan, *Aristocratic Liberalism the Social and Political Thought of Jacob Burckhardt, John Stuart Mill, and Alexis de Tocqueville* (New York: Oxford University Press, 1992), 427. Lucien Jaume and Pierre Rosanvallon are also interesting on *publicité* in liberalism. See Jaume, *L'Individu effacé*, 427–29; Pierre Rosanvallon, *Le Moment Guizot* (Paris: Gallimard, 1985).

20. Madeleine Fargeaud, in an article about publicity in *César Birotteau*, points out that "le mot apparaît d'ailleurs dans *César Birotteau*, avec son sens moderne dont le *Dictionnaire de l'Académie* ne reconnaîtra l'existence qu'en 1878, et Balzac est l'un des premiers à l'employer, après Girardin" (the word appeared in *César Birotteau* with its modern meaning, which the Academy's dictionary would not include until 1878, and Balzac was one of the first to use it, after Girardin). Madeleine Fargeaud, "Balzac, Le commerce et la publicité," *L'Année balzacienne* (1974): 188. *L'Année balzacienne* has been published in three series since its

creation, always at a rate of one issue a year. Years are cited here, but not volume and issue numbers which are mostly superfluous for this publication.

The Larousse dictionary of 1872 said that "la publicité d'affaires . . . prit pour levier de sa puissance le journal politique, dans lequel elle a fini par s'incarner au point que, pendant longtemps, il ne put rien sans elle" (business publicity used the political press as its instrument of power and became so incarnated by the newspaper that for a long time the press could do nothing without [business publicity]). Larousse, *Grand dictionnaire*, 390.

A word search in the Frantext database reveals no uses with the commercial meaning before 1836. Véronique Bui, too, notes Balzac's use of the word in 1837 in *César Birotteau*. Véronique Bui, "Comment l'huile céphalique vint à Balzac," in *Presse et plumes*, ed. Alan Vaillant and Marie-Ève Thérenty (Paris: Nouveau monde, 2004), 465.

21. For a good account of this situation, see the introduction to Lise Dumasy, ed., *La Querelle du roman-feuilleton: Littérature, presse et politique, un débat précurseur (1836–1848)* (Grenoble, Fr.: ELLUG, 1999). Jann Matlock's pathbreaking work on how regulation of prostitution and of literature echoed each other is informative in this context. See Jann Matlock, *Scenes of Seduction: Prostitution, Hysteria, and Reading Difference in Nineteenth-Century France* (New York: Columbia University Press, 1994.) Éléonore Reverzy has recently revisted the prostitution-journalism metaphor in *Portrait de l'artiste en fille de joie* (Paris: CNRS éditions, 2016).

22. Paul Bénichou, *Le Sacre de l'écrivain 1750–1830, essai sur l'avénement d'un pouvoir spirituel laïque dans la France moderne* (Paris: J. Corti, 1973).

23. Sainte-Beuve quoted in Dumasy, *La Querelle du roman-feuilleton*, 32.

24. Sainte-Beuve quoted in Dumasy, *La Querelle du roman-feuilleton*, 43.

25. Olivier Bara and Jean-Claude Yon, *Eugène Scribe: Un Maître de la scène théâtrale et lyrique du Xixe siècle* (Rennes: Presses universitaires de Rennes, 2016). See also Guillaume Pinson, "Présentation du dossier," in *Presse, prostitution, basfonds (1830–1930)*, Médias 19, June 9, 2013, http://www.medias19.org/index .php?id=13457.

26. For lively discussion of Darnton's uses of the term "Grub Street" with regard to print culture and the Enlightenment, see Charles Walton, ed., *The Darnton Debate: Books and Revolution in the Eighteenth Century* (Oxford: Voltaire Foundation, 1999).

27. Harold Mah, *Enlightenment Phantasies: Cultural Identity in France and Germany, 1750–1914* (Ithaca, N.Y: Cornell University Press, 2004).

28. Pierre Bourdieu, *Les Règles de l'art* (Paris: Seuil, 1998), 176.

29. Amelie Calderone, "Au croisement du Vaudeville anecdotique et de la féerie: Codification du genre de la revue de fin d'annee sous la Monarchie de Juillet," in "En revenant à la revue," ed. Olivier Bara, Romain Piana, and Jean-Claude Yon, special issue, *Revue d'histoire du Théâtre* 2, no. 266 (April–June 2015): 215.

30. Geraldine Muhlman, *Du journalisme en démocratie* (Paris: Payot et Rivages, 2004).

31. Rosanvallon, *Le Moment Guizot*, 68. See also Corinne Pelta, *Le Romantisme Liberale 1815–1830: La représentation souveraine* (Paris: L'Harmattan, 2001); and Sheryl Kroen, *Politics and Theater: The Crisis of Legitimacy in Restoration France, 1815–1830* (London: University of California Press, 2000).

32. See the introduction to Bara, Piana, and Yon, "En revenant à la revue," 197.

33. Odile Krakovitch, *Censure des répertoires des grands théâtres parisiens (1835–1906)* (Paris: Centre Historique des Archives Nationales, 2003), 15–16.

34. Berthier, *Le Théâtre au xixe siècle* (Paris: PUF, 1986), 4. See also Jean-Yves Mollier et al., *La Production de l'immatériel: Théories, représentations et pratiques de la culture au Xixe siècle* (Saint-Étienne, Fr.: Publications de l'Université de Saint-Étienne, 2008).

35. Wicks and Schweitzer, *The Parisian Stage: III (1831–1850)* (Tuscaloosa: University of Alabama Press, 1961).

36. Krakovitch, *Censure des répertoires des grands théâtres parisiens (1835–1906)* (Paris: Centre Historique des Archives Nationales, 2003).

37. See Olivier Bara, "Éléments pour une poétique du feuilleton théâtral," in *Le Miel et le fiel: La critique théâtrale en france au XIXe siècle*, ed. Mariane Bury and Hélène Laplace-Claverie (Paris: PUPS, 2008), 21–30.

38. In French, *glaces déformantes*. Robert Abirached uses this term to characterize Eugène Labiche's technique. Robert Abirached, *La Crise du personnage dans le théâtre moderne* (Paris: Gallimard, 1994), 167.

39. Juli Léal has shown that Eugène Labiche, whose caustic approach to social issues of his day has recently piqued scholars' interest, staged newspapers extensively to just such ends. Juli Léal, "Le Discours du fait divers et des petites annonces dans le théâtre de Labiche," in *Les Genres insérés dans le théâtre*, ed. Anne Sancier and Pierre Servet (Lyon: C.E.D.E.C., 1997), 109–23.

Innovations in dramaturgy and set design are the only lasting contributions Robert Abirached sees between Romanticism and Naturalism in the theater, but, as we will see, newspapers often played new and socially relevant roles in both domains. Abirached, *La Crise du personnage*, 163.

For an excellent collection of essays on spectacle and dramaturgy, see Isabelle Moindrot, Olivier Goetz, and Sylvie Humbert-Mougin, *Le Spectaculaire dans les arts de la scène du romantisme à la Belle époque* (Paris: CNRS éd., 2006). John McCormick has also argued that innovations in set design and the role of the *metteur en scène* made the July Monarchy a great period for studying the interaction between the public and the "theater event." John McCormick, *Popular Theatres of Nineteenth-Century France* (New York: Routledge, 1993), 227.

40. Philippe Hamon has described literary irony's double function as to: "mettre à distance les naifs" and to "communier avec l'autre partie du public transformée en complice" (hold the naïfs at arm's length and connect with the other part of the audience, which has been transformed into accomplices). Philippe Hamon, *L'Ironie littéraire: Essai sur les formes de l'écriture oblique* (Paris: Hachette supérieur, 1996), 125.

41. Berthier calls Lemaître's transformation of his character in *L'Auberge des Adrets* in 1823, "un tournant décisif. Tirant parti d'un texte fort ordinaire, l'acteur, par son costume et sa mimique, détourna le rôle du bandit, Robert Macaire, de façon à lui rendre drôle et sympathique. Dès lors il y eut peu à peu inversion ou subversion des valeurs morales du mélodrame ; il peignit le vice avec moins d'horreur, et concurrença le drame dans sa description des passions. L'idéologie d'opposition prit l'habit du mélodrame pour exprimer à l'aise républicanisme, bonapartisme, esprit antireligieux" (a decisive change. Starting from an ordinary text, the actor used his costume and his gestures to change the bandit's role,

making him funny and likable. From then on, the moral values of melodrama were subverted bit by bit; vice was portrayed with less horror, and the description of passions started to rival that of the drama. Opposition ideology dressed itself in the costume of melodrama to promote republicanism, Bonapartism, and antireligious sentiment.) Berthier, *Le Théâtre au xixe siècle*, 69–70. Also see Olivier Bara, "Le Rire subversif de Frédérick-Lemaître/Robert Macaire, ou la force comique d'un théâtre d'acteur," *Revue en ligne Insignis*, no. 1, http://s2.e-monsite .com/2010/05/15/82924582le-rire-subversif-olivier-bara-pdf.pdf.

42. Odile Krakovitch, who insists on the entirely negative approach of Macaire's permanent critique, says that by 1848 he had lost some of his appeal, for, "Robert Macaire n'apporte pas de solution, pas de valeur positive. Symbole d'une révolution détournée, il représente également l'échec de l'idéologie du siècle des lumières" (Robert Macaire offers no solution, no positive value. Symbol of a revolution redirected, he also represents the failure of enlightenment ideology). Odile Krakovitch, "Robert Macaire ou la grande peur des censeurs," *europe: Revue littéraire mensuelle*, no. 703–4 (1987): 53. For a thoughtful examination of the ways in which Frédérick Lemaître's performance contributed to making a social type of Macaire, see Marion Lemaire, "Robert Macaire, la construction d'un mythe: du personage théâtral au type social: 1823–1848," abstract (Ph.D. diss.,Université de Paris 8 St. Denis, 2015), http://www.theses.fr/2015PA080079.

43. That is, "n'a affaire qu'à un spectateur à la fois" (only deals with one spectator at a time). Stendhal [Marie-Henri Beyle], *Œuvres complètes*, ed. Victor Del Litto and Ernest Abravanel (Geneva: Cercle du bibliophile, 1972), 265.

44. This is no accident. Both Schiller and Guizot were inspired by Immanuel Kant's ideas about public use of reason, as was Jürgen Habermas. Jürgen Habermas, *The Structural Transformation of the Public Sphere*, trans. Thomas Burger and Frederick Lawrence (Cambridge, Mass.: Polity, 1989).

45. Olivier Bara, *Le Théâtre de l'Opéra-comique sous la restauration: Enquête autour d'un genre moyen*, ed. Herbert Schneider (Zurich: Musikwissenschaftliche Publikationen Verlag, 2001), 382.

46. Jacques Rancière, *The Emancipated Spectator*, trans. Gregory Elliott (London: Verso, 2009).

47. Steven Mullaney, *The Reformation of Emotions in the Age of Shakespeare*. (University of Chicago Press, 2015), 45.

48. Violaine Heyraud and Adrienne Martinez, eds., *Le Vaudeville à la scène*, (Grenoble, Fr.: UGA Éditions, 2015), Collection la fabrique de l'œuvre, 15.

49. In eighteenth-century historiography, Carla Hesse has suggested that the *how* of the Enlightenment has come to take precedence over questions of what the Enlightenment itself was. Carla Hesse, "Towards a New Topography of Enlightenment," *European Review of History: Revue européenne d'histoire* 13, no. 3 (2006), 499–508.

50. Honoré de Balzac, *La Comédie humaine*, ed. Pierre-Georges Castex, vol. 5 (Paris: Gallimard, 1977), 112–13.

51. Alexis Lévrier and Adeline Wrona, eds. *Matière et esprit du journal: Du "Mercure Galant" à Twitter* (Paris: Presses de l'université Paris-Sorbonne, 2013).

52. Olivier Bara and Marie-Ève Thérenty, eds., *Presse et scène au XIXe siècle*, Médias 19, October 19, 2012, http://www.medias19.org/index.php?id=1569; Olivier Bara and Marie-Ève Thérenty, eds., *Presse et opéra aux XVIIIe et*

XIXe siècles, Médias 19, March 25, 2018, http://www.medias19.org/index
.php?id=24195.

53. See especially Roxane Martin's and Jean-Marie Thomasseau's contributions
to Bury and Laplace-Claverie, *Le Miel et le fiel.*

54. Bara, Piana, and Yon, "En revenant à la revue"; Stéphanie Loncle, *Théâtre
et libéralisme (Paris, 1830–1848)* (Paris: Classiques Garnier, 2017), 514–21.

55. Dominique Kalifa, et al., eds. *La Civilisation du journal: Histoire culturelle
et littéraire de la presse française au xixe siècle* (Paris: Nouveau Monde éditions,
2012); Bara and Yon, *Eugène Scribe.* According to Patrick Berthier, of 2,802
new plays produced between 1836 and 1845, 1,924 of them were vaudevilles
(Berthier, *Le Théâtre au xixe siècle*, 4). While other genres of popular theater have
received recent critical attention, vaudeville has largely been left by the wayside.
Jennifer Terni's dissertation and her article of 2006 rely on vaudevilles, as do the
articles in a special issue of *europe* devoted to the genre in 1994, but much work
remains to be done. See Jennifer Terni, "A Genre for Early Mass Culture: French
Vaudeville and the City, 1830–1848," *Theatre Journal* 58, no. 2 (2006), 221–48;
"Le Vaudeville," special issue, *europe* 72, no. 786 (1994). For graphs representing
vaudeville's relative popularity, see Lothar Matthes, *Vaudeville Untersuchungen
zu Geschichte und literatursystematischem Ort einer Erfolgsgattung* (Heidelberg:
C. Winter, 1983).

Another popular genre gets its due in Roxane Martin, *La Féerie romantique
sur les scènes parisiennes 1791–1864* (Paris: H. Champion, 2007). See also Henry
Gidel, *Le Vaudeville* (Paris: Presses universitaires de France, 1986), 3.

56. Rita Felski, *Rethinking Tragedy* (Baltimore: Johns Hopkins University Press,
2008); Peter Brooks, *The Melodramatic Imagination: Balzac, Henry James, Melodrama and the Mode of Excess* (New Haven, Conn.: Yale University Press, 1996).

57. April Alliston, "Transnational Sympathies, Imaginary Communities," in *The
Literary Channel: The Inter-National Invention of the Novel*, ed. Margaret Cohen
and Carolyn Dever (Princeton, N.J.: Princeton University Press, 2002), 133–48.

58. Guillaume Pinson, *L'Imaginaire mediatique: Histoire et fiction du journal
au XIX'siecle* (Paris: Classiques Garnier, 2013).

59. Jacques Boncompain, *De Scribe à Hugo: La condition de l'auteur (1815–
1870)* (Paris: Honoré Champion, 2014); Odile Krakovitch, *La Censure théâtrale
(1835–1848): Édition des procès-verbaux* (Paris: Classiques Garnier, 2016);
Amélie Calderone, "Entre la scène et le livre: Formes dramatiques publiées dans
la presse à l'époque romantique (1829–1851)" (Ph.D. diss., Université de Lyon
2, 2015), http://www.theses.fr/2015LYO20101; Agathe Novak-Lechevalier, "La
Théâtralité dans le roman: Stendhal, Balzac" (Ph.D. diss., Université de Paris 3,
2007), http://www.theses.fr/2007PA030131

60. Thomasseau calls this "un frottement d'idées auquel le burlesque n'enleve
rien d'une pertinence qu'au contraire il souligne" (a rubbing together of ideas
whose burlesque form in no way diminishes—in fact, it underlines—its pertinence). Jean-Marie Thomasseau, "Le Théâtre critique de lui-même dans les
vaudevilles de l'époque romantique," in Bury and Laplace-Claverie, *Le Miel et
le fiel*, 90. For a look at crossed influence between theatrical and press reviews
over the nineteenth century, see Romain Piana, "L'Imaginaire de la presse dans la
revue théâtrale," in Bara and Thérenty, *Presse et scène au XIXe siècle*, Médias 19,
October 19, 2012, http://www.medias19.org/index.php?id=3005.

Chapter 1

1. Rancière argues that "le spectateur aussi agit . . . Il observe, il sélectionne, il compare, il interprète. Il lie ce qu'il voit à bien d'autres choses qu'il a vues sur d'autres scènes, en d'autres sortes de lieux" (the spectator, too, takes action . . . He observes, he selects, he compares, he interprets. He relates what he sees to many other things he has seen, on other stages and in other kinds of places). Jacques Rancière, *Le spectateur émancipé* (Paris: La Fabrique éditions, 2008), 23.

2. Martine de Rougemont, *La Vie théâtrale en France au XVIIIe siècle* (Paris: H. Champion, 2001), 266.

3. Eighteenth-century vaudevilles as they existed at the *foires* often integrated characters and plots from the Commedia dell'Arte, while also specializing in mocking revues of theatrical performances being staged at the other, privileged, theaters of Paris. Aside from Martine de Rougemont's excellent study, cited in note 2, Jeffrey Ravel's book on the parterre has also informed my description of eighteenth-century audiences: Jeffrey Ravel, *The Contested Parterre: Public Theater and French Political Culture, 1680–1791* (Ithaca, N.Y.: Cornell University Press, 1999).

For the history of the vaudeville itself, Henry Gidel's book, and the special issue of *europe* devoted to the vaudeville are good overviews, while Lothar Matthes's study provides much helpful information (see intro., n. 51). Robert Dreyfus, too, did an introduction to the genre over a century ago: Robert Dreyfus, *Petite histoire de la revue de fin d'année* (Paris: Charpentier et Fasquelle, 1909).

4. Michel Corvin, ed., *Dictionnaire encyclopédique du théâtre à travers le monde* (Paris: Bordas, 2008); Dreyfus, *Petite histoire*, 1909. Specific information about year-end revues can be found in Dreyfus and in Corvin. Such annual revues were more prone than any other sort of July Monarchy vaudeville to stage the press. The only other category of vaudevilles as likely to do so consisted of occasional plays written in response to media events. There were regular vaudeville revues at Mardi Gras as well, but they almost never mentioned the press. As recently as 2015, the issue of the *Revue d'histoire du théâtre* devoted to the year-end vaudeville revue said that "la revue de fin d'année n'a pas encore suscité tous les travaux que son extraordinaire richesse semblerait autoriser" (the year-end revue has not yet been the subject of all the research that its extraordinary richness seems to justify). Bara, Olivier, Romain Piana, and Jean-Claude Yon, eds. "En revenant à la revue: La revue de fin d'annee au XIXe siècle." Special issue, *Revue d'histoire du théâtre* 2, no. 266 (April–June 2015), 195.

5. Jennifer Terni's work on consumerism in vaudevilles reminds us that vaudevilles could be both full participants in a consumer economy and—as is argued here—spurs to critical thought. See Terni, "Genre for Early Mass Culture" (see intro., n. 51).

6. "VAUDEVILLE–PALAIS ROYAL–AMBIGU." *Le Charivari*, January 2 and 3, 1837, 2. *Le Charivari* appears to have made a printing error, producing two newspapers dated December 30, and none that were dated December 31, in 1836. The Bibliothèque nationale's copy of the second December 30 paper is hand annotated as December 31, and given that the very same newspaper refers to the article in question as appearing in a December 31 issue, I will refer to the later of the two issues as December 31, though that is not what the dateline says. As it happens, the first December 30 issue prominently featured an editorial attacking Émile de

Girardin's behavior, and published his response letter a few columns later in the space reserved for jokes. "M. de Girardin" and "Charade," *Le Charivari*, December 30, 1836, 1, 3.

7. "Adieux à l'année 1836." *Le Charivari*, December 31, 1836, 1.

8. "Adieux à l'année 1836," 2.

9. Courcy, Bayard, and Théaulon, *L'Année sur la sellette* (Paris: Marchant, 1837), 2.

10. *Le Charivari* was a small but influential center-left satirical newspaper which replaced *La Caricature* when the former was obliged to close for political infractions. Honoré Daumier was its best-known artist. A number of its journalists and administrators also worked at *Le Siècle*, the forty-franc paper with the largest circulation. See Gilles Feyel, *La Presse en France des origines à 1944* (Paris: Ellipses, 1999), 104.

11. "La Presse est représentée par une jeune fille ayant sur la tête un bonnet de papier comme les imprimeurs: Le Siècle est joué par un enfant dont tout le costume est en argent" (La Presse is played by a girl wearing a paper printer's hat, and Le Siècle is played by a child whose entire costume is silver). For a pre–September Laws example of the iconography of the printer's hat, see Ségolène Le Men, *Daumier et la caricature* (Paris: Citadelles et Mazenod, 2008), 214.

12. Clairville and Delatour, *1836 dans la lune* (Paris: Morain, 1837), 16. All quotations from the production come from this source. Clairville and Delatour are both pseudonyms, use of which was a practice employed by a number of playwrights of the period. A list of these playwrights' pseudonymns and real names appears in a table at the beginning of appendix 1.

13. For a parallel process in Grandville's human-animal caricatures, see Judith L. Goldstein, "Realism without a Human Face," in *Spectacles of Realism*, ed. Margaret Cohen and Christopher Prendergast (London: University of Minnesota Press, 1995), 78.

14. For more on this, see Cary Hollinshead-Strick, "La Mise en page et le passage à la postérité dans *Les Belles femmes de Paris* et *Les Guêpes* d'Alphonse Karr," in *L'Écrit à l'épreuve des médias*, ed. Greta Komur-Thilloy and Anne Réach-Ngo (Paris: Classiques Garnier, 2012), 277–95.

15. Bara, *Le Théâtre de l'Opéra-comique sous la restauration*, 385 (see intro., n. 41).

16. For this overlap, see Sandrine Berthelot, "La Bohème: avec ou sans style," in *Bohème sans frontière*, cd. Pascal Brissette and Anthony Glinoer (Rennes: Presses universitaires de Rennes, 2010). For a succinct, helpful characterization of *petits journaux*, see Jean-Didier Wagneur, "La Place de la littérature dans l'univers des journaux," in *Les Écrivains et la presse*, Le Blog Gallica, January 22, 2018, https://gallica.bnf.fr/blog/22012018/la-place-de-la-litterature-dans-lunivers-des-journaux.

17. Théophile Gautier, "Feuilleton de la Presse," *La Presse*, December 11, 1842.

18. About two years earlier, Gautier had called a vaudeville he was reviewing, "une espèce de feuilleton en action, et qui a le tort de venir un an ou six mois après les feuilletons des journaux" (a sort of *feuilleton* in action, which has the disadvantage of arriving a year or six months after the newspapers' *feuilletons*). Théophile Gautier, "Feuilleton de la Presse," *La Presse*, January 6, 1842, 1. Another earlier year, in a similar context, he wrote, "Vous voyez défiler des suites d'articles pris dans les petits journaux, et dans les feuilletons, sur la pommade de

lion et celle du chameau" (You watch as series of articles on lion or camel pomade, all taken from the minor newspapers and *feuilletons*, parade past). Théophile Gautier, "Feuilleton de la Presse," *La Presse*, January 7, 1839, 2.

19. Eugène Guinot (Pierre Durand), "Revue de Paris," *Le Siècle*, January 1, 1848, 3.

20. Charles de Matharel, "Revue des théâtres," *Le Siècle*, July 6, 1846, 2. In this piece, Matharel also says, "Trois lignes d'une revue signée par Charles de Boigne ont servi à faire la pièce nouvelle. L'histoire de notre confrère était spirituellement racontée, la pièce est heureusement faite" (Three lines from a review signed by Charles de Boigne were used to make the new play. Our colleague's story was wittily told, the play is nicely made).

21. Eugène Guinot (Pierre Durand), "Revue de Paris," *Le Siècle*, June 5, 1847, 1. In one vaudeville, one character accused another of stealing a joke from *Le Charivari*. Eugène Grangé, Ernest Bourget, and Adolphe d'Ennery, *1840, ou la Guerre des saisons* (Paris: Mifliez, 1839), 4. In another play, a young man put off a prospective father-in-law by saying the he was the model for a *Charivari* cartoon that showed a young man eating his way through an inheritance at a fancy restaurant. Ménissier, *Une heure d'exposition, revue un acte* (Paris: Archives Nationales, 1839).

22. Charles de Matharel, "Théâtres," *Le Siècle*, December 29, 1847, 3. See the discussion of *Le Charivari*'s focus on news and the vaudeville's more structural critique above. When Jules Janin wrote, of a vaudeville revue, "quand j'assiste à ces sortes de choses, il me semble que je m'amuse à lire les feuilletons ou l'almanach de l'an passé" (when I attend this sort of thing, it seems like I am amusing myself by reading almanacs from the past year), he, too, called vaudevilles derivative of the press and drew attention to their comparatively infrequent periodicity. Jules Janin, "La Semaine dramatique," *Le Journal des débats*, December 25, 1843, 2.

23. Charles de Matharel, "Revue des théâtres," *Le Siècle*, December 27, 1844.

24. For a throrough analysis of how objectivity became an ideal for critics in the period just preceding the one considered here, and how pace limited critical perspective, see Patrick Berthier, *La Presse littéraire et dramatique au début de la Monarchie de Juillet (1830–1836)* (Villeneuve-d'Ascq, Fr.: Presses universitaires du septentrion, 2001), 508–12, 1067. Chapter 5 of Maurice Descotes, *Histoire de la critique dramatique en France* (Paris: J.-M. Place, 1980), also gives an account of this process. For essays on the nature of criticism in this period, see Bury and Laplace-Claverie, *Le Miel et le fiel* (see intro., n. 49).

25. Y., "Théâtres," *Le Constitutionnel*, January 2, 1837, 1.

26. Jules Janin, "La Semaine dramatique," *Le Journal des débats*, January 2, 1837, 3. This comparison to magic lanterns was not reserved exclusively for revues—it was said of *La Camaraderie* when it was being treated as a series of veiled portraits, and of *Les Mystères de Paris* because of the necessarily episodic structure of its theatrical adaptation. Charles de Matharel, "Feuilleton," *Le Siècle*, February 17, 1844, 3. Other reviews of revues: At the end of 1845, *La Quotidienne* said, of a vaudeville called *Les Pommes de terre malades* (Rotten Potatoes), "Cette burlesque lanterne magique offre quelques silhouettes assez amusantes" (this burlesque magic lantern offers relatively amusing shadows), while in August of the same year, *Le Siècle* noted of another revue that "La Smala a passé dans leur lanterne magique" (the Smala has passed through their magic lantern). J.T. "Revue

dramatique," *La Quotidienne*, December 29, 1845; Hippolyte Lucas, "Feuilleton," *Le Siècle*, August 4, 1845. In 1847, Lucas confounded the dramatic revue he was announcing with the publication from which it took its name. He wrote of "la première représentation de *l'Illustration*, lanterne magique en douze verres de couleurs peints par le spiritual dessinateur Cham" (the opening night of *l'Illustration*, magic lantern with twelve scenes painted by the clever illustrator Cham). Hippolyte Lucas, "Théâtres," *Le Siècle*, January 18, 1847.

27. Charles de Matharel, "Revue des théâtres." *Le Siècle*, May 25, 1844, 2.

28. Joseph-Marc Bailbé, "La Lanterne magique au service de l'évocation litté-raire dans le texte de Janin et Banville," *Cahiers d'histoire culturelle: La lanterne magique, pratiques et mise en écriture* 2 (1997): 93.

29. For an interesting discussion of the various roles of the magic lantern and its operator with good bibliography, see Helen Weston, "The Light of Wisdom: Magic Lanternists as Truth-Tellers in Post-Revolutionary France," in *The Efflorescence of Caricature, 1759–1838*, ed. Todd Porterfield (Burlington, Vt.: Ashgate, 2011), 97–104.

30. From Le Men, *Daumier et la caricature*, 210.

31. Lise Dumasy has noted a similar process by which critics were less tolerant than authors of the popular appeal of *romans-feuilletons*. Dumasy, *La Querelle du roman-feuilleton*, 20 (see intro., n. 19).

32. Eléonore Tenaille de Vaulabelle et al., *Ah ! enfin !* (Paris: Beck, 1848), act 2, scene 3, line 10.

33. For a good chronology of theater openings and closings, especially when, as in 1848, they were due to political uprisings or decrees, see F. W. J. Hemmings, *The Theatre Industry in Nineteenth-Century France* (Cambridge: Cambridge University Press), 1993, viii–xiii.

34. Stéphanie Loncle, *Théâtre et libéralisme* (see intro., n. 50).

Chapter 2

1. Tili Boon Cuillé, *Narrative Interludes: Musical Tableaux in Eighteenth-Century French Texts* (Toronto: University of Toronto Press, 2006), 51–61, 89.

2. For an account of the trend toward staging journalism at these more respect-able theaters, see Barbara T. Cooper, introduction to Eugène Bourgeois and Alexandre Dumas, *Jeannic le Breton* (1841), Médias 19, June 19, 2016, http://www.medias19.org/index.php?id=17675.

3. Barbara Cooper points out that the press played a minor role in contributing to Chatterton's suicide, too, in her excellent introduction to her annotated edi-tion of *Richard Savage*. See introduction to Desnoyer and Labat, *Richard Savage* (1838), Médias 19, June 7, 2015, http://www.medias19.org/index.php?id=22070. Cooper's earlier reading of the play itself as an embodiment of economic forces is also important here. Barbara Cooper, "Exploitation of the Body in Vigny's *Chatterton*: The Economy of Drama and the Drama of Economics," *Theatre Journal* 34, no. 1 (1982): 20–26. See also Loncle, *Théâtre et libéralisme*, 554–606 (see intro., n. 50).

4. For this background, see: Marie-Ève Thérenty, *Mosaïques être écrivain entre presse et roman, 1829–1836* (Paris: H. Champion, 2003); Bénichou, *Le Sacre de l'écrivain* (see intro., n. 20). For how Balzac and Vigny defended

authors' rights, see Philippe Delorme, "Le Thème du paria chez Alfred de Vigny: *Chatterton, Servitude, et grandeur militaire* et 'La Flûte' (*Les Destinées*)" (master's thesis, Université de Pau et des Pays de l'Adour, April 15, 2015), 25, HAL archives-ouvertes, https://dumas.ccsd.cnrs.fr/dumas-01142450/document.

5. Jean Jourdheuil, "L'Escalier de Chatterton," *Romantisme* no. 38 (1982): 106–16, https://doi.org/10.3406/roman.1982.4581.

6. Mce d'A——, *Considérations sur quelques-unes des causes qui ont perdu la restauration et qui menacent le trône de juillet; en réponse à la brochure de M. Duvergier de Hauranne* (Paris: Impr. de Béthune et Plon, 1838).

7. Robert Howell Griffiths, "Cross-Channel Enlightenments," in *The Routledge Companion to the French Revolution in World History*, ed. Alan I. Forrest and Matthias Middell (London: Routledge, 2016), 142.

8. Jacques-Charles Bailleul, *Dictionnaire critique du langage politique, gouvernemental, civil, administratif et judiciaire de notre époque* (Paris: Renard, 1842), 612.

9. Michel Masson's 1836 novel *Une Couronne d'épines.* See Cooper, introduction to *Richard Savage.*

10. Corinne Saminadayar-Perrin, *Les Discours du journal: Rhétorique et médias au XIXe siècle (1836–1885)* (Saint-Etienne, Fr.: Publications de l'Université de Saint-Etienne, 2007).

11. A topical touch, in that 1838 saw the introduction of a law governing the conditions under which people could be committed to asylums in France. *Le Siècle* and *Le Courrier français* in April 1837 fretted over whether new Bastilles were being made for people with opposition views. One concern that opponents raised was that the new law might be used to opportunistically remove political opponents from activity. See Jan Ellen Goldstein, *Console and Classify: The French Psychiatric Profession in the Nineteenth Century* (Chicago: University of Chicago Press, 1987), 281.

12. Note 24 in Cooper, Introduction to *Richard Savage.* The 1831 play followed Girardin's autobiographical novel, also called *Émile*, by four years.

13. Desnoyer and Labat, *Richard Savage* (Paris: Barba Delloye Bezou, 1838), 511.

14. Jules Janin, "La Semaine dramatique," *Le Journal des débats*, October 15, 1838, 2.

15. Janin, "La Semaine dramatique," October 15, 1838, 2.

16. Saminadayar-Perrin, *Les Discours du journal.*

17. Delphine de Girardin, "Courrier de Paris," *La Presse*, December 8, 1838, 1.

18. D. de Girardin, "Courrier de Paris," 1.

19. Casimir Delavigne, *La Popularité* (Paris: H. Delloy, 1839), 103.

20. Claudine Grossir, "Scribe: L'histoire en scene," in Bara and Yon, *Eugène Scribe*, 232 (see intro., n.23).

21. Krakovitch, *La Censure théâtrale*, 318, 340 (see intro., n. 55).

22. Olivier Bara, "Scribe, un homme sans style ?" in Bara and Yon, *Eugène Scribe*, 159–78.

23. Jules Janin, "La Semaine dramatique," *Le Journal des débats*, November 22, 1837, 3.

24. Daniel Lindenberg gives an account of Scribe's politicized audiences in "La Tentation du vaudeville," in *Le Théâtre en France 2 de la Révolution à nos jours*, ed. Jacqueline de Jomaron-Leyvastre (Paris: A. Colin, 1989), 167.

25. J.T., "Revue dramatique," *La Quotidienne*, January 22–23, 1837, 1–2.

26. Jules Janin, "Feuilleton du Journal des débats" *Le Journal des débats*, January 24, 1848, 2.

27. *La Quotidienne* said that Scribe plays were invariably *ministeriel*, and this one was written quickly to keep people from turning independent before elections. J.T., "Revue dramatique," January 22–23, 1837.

28. The anonymous *feuilletoniste* mentioned the fact that the play was being considered for production at the Théâtre français and called it an "ouvrage de moeurs qui met en scène les bizarreries littéraires de nos jours" (a comedy of manners that stages the literary peculiarities of our day). "Théâtre français," *Le Constitutionnel*, October 17, 1836. Once it was performed, it was reviewed tepidly. O. "Théâtre français," *Le Constitutionnel*, January 22, 1837.

29. O, "Théâtre français," *Le Constitutionnel*, November 22, 1837, 1.

30. Auguste Jouhaud, *L'Anti-camaraderie, ou la France au XXe siècle* (Brussels: J. A. Lelong, 1837), 50.

31. Jouhaud, *L'Anti-camaraderie*, 29.

32. Other July Monarchy comedies share Jouhaud's evaluation of the motivations of journalists. In *Part à deux* of 1844, a playwright reads a newspaper review of his recently opened play aloud: "Nous sommes dans le siècle des problèmes introuvables . . . témoin le succès fait par on ne sait quel public à *La Réputation d'une femme*, pièce représentée hier. L'ouvrage est au-dessous de la critique" (We live in the century of irresolvable problems, as the success of *The Reputation of a Woman*, thanks to who knows what public, proves. The work is below criticism). The author, hurt, says, "Tiens, pourquoi le critique-t-elle alors" (So why is he criticizing it?), only to conclude that he and his collaborator must visit each of the journalists who has reviewed their play, but that it will be even more important to curry favor with the ones who have written negative reviews than with those who approved of it. Jules Regnault de Prémaray, *Part à deux* (Paris: Gallet, 1844), 6.

33. Scribe also integrated some of his story "Judith," which had been printed in *La Presse*, into his opera. This information, along with the relationship of Jouhaud's work to Scribe's, is described in Victor Moulin, *Scribe et son théâtre, études sur la comédie au XIXe siècle* (Paris: Tresse, 1862), 117–18.

34. Barbara T. Cooper, "Les Publics Du Magasin Théâtral." *Revue d'Histoire Du Théâtre* 1–2, no. 245–46 (2010).

35. Cogniard frères, *Rothomago* (Paris: Marchant, 1839). See also Jean-Claude Yon, "La Féerie ou le royaume du spectaculaire: L'Exemple de *Rothomago*," in *Le Spectaculaire dans les arts de la scène du romantisme à la belle époque*, ed. Isabelle Moindrot (Paris: CNRS éditions, 2006).

36. Cogniard frères, *Rothomago*, 9. See Susan Hiner's chapter on parasols as standing for women who carry them and Michelle Hanoosh on Grandville. Susan Hiner, *Accessories to Modernity* (Philadelphia: University of Pennsylvania Press, 2010); Michelle Hanoosh, "The Allegorical Artist and the Crises of History: Benjamin, Grandville, Baudelaire," *Word and Image* 10, no. 1 (1994): 38–54.

37. The *juste-milieu* was the name of the center-right governing party at the time.

38. Cogniard frères, *Rothomago*, 9.

39. Roxane Martin points out, "La presence de la Popularité permet de reveler que classiques et romantiques sont égaux dans leur volonté de séduire le public"

(The presence of Popularity reveals that Classics and Romantics are equal in their desire to appeal to the public). Roxane Martin, "Les Parodies 'intra-dramatiques,' ou Les voix d'une critique en mouvement," in Bury and Laplace-Claverie, *Le Miel et le Fiel*, 105 (see intro., n. 49).

40. Delphine de Girardin, *L'École des journalistes* 2nd ed. (Paris: Dumont, 1839), vii.

41. D. Girardin, *L'École des journalistes*, 3. See Amélie Calderone, introduction to *L'École des journalistes* by Delphine de Girardin (1839), Médias 19, March 27, 2014, http://www.medias19.org/index.php?id=17674.

42. Fragmentation was entirely characteristic of the new press's imagined identity, as Guillaume Pinson and Marie-Ève Thérenty have demonstrated (in *L'Imaginaire médiatique*, and *Mosaïques*, respectively), but theatrical approaches to the new press took a different approach to the evolving media sphere. See Pinson, *L'Imaginaire médiatique* (see intro., n. 54); Thérenty, *Mosaïques*. Audience points of view might differ, but they could still be brought to bear on a common dramatic work. Or, as Victor Hugo put it in his preface to *Ruy Blas* (also from 1838), Mont Blanc looks different depending which city you see it from, but it remains the same mountain nonetheless. He concludes, "Tous ces aspects sont justes et vrais, mais aucun d'eux n'est complet. La vérité n'est que dans l'ensemble de l'oeuvre." (All of these aspects are correct and true, but none of them are complete. The truth is only in the work as a whole). Victor Hugo, *Théâtre complet*, vol. 1, ed. Josette Mélèze and Jean-Jacques Thierry (Paris: NRF / Gallimard, 1964), 1494.

43. "Théâtre français: L'École des journalistes," in *Commission d'examen, Ministère de l'intérieur, Division des beaux arts* (Paris: Archives Nationales, 1839).

44. In *Jeannic Le Breton*, another 1838 calumny play that Barbara Cooper has annotated for Media19's collection of theater about the press, as for Scribe's *La Calomnie* and Delavigne's *La Popularité*, the honor of the retired father (or father figure) is also threatened by press calumnies.

45. See Calderone, introduction to *L'École des journalistes*, 29.

46. Reproduced in Adolphe Jullien, *Le Romantisme et l'éditeur Renduel: Souvenirs et documents sur les écrivains de l'école romantique, avec lettres inédites adressées par eux à Renduel* (Paris: E. Fasquelle, 189), 7, 27.

47. References to Balzac, Karr, and Sainte-Beuve's impressions are cited in Henri Malo, *La Gloire du vicomte de Launay: Delphine Gay de Girardin* (Paris: Émile-Paul frères, 1925), 64.

48. Calderone has also examined how Émile de Girardin used this situation as an occasion to shore up his position against censorship. Amélie Calderone, "Petits arrangements entre époux: De la scène théâtrale à la scène médiatique; l'exemple de la publication de *L'École des journalistes* dans *La Presse* (1839)," Médias 19, October 19, 2012, http://www.medias19.org/index.php?id=1295.

49. Delphine de Girardin, *Lettres parisiennes du vicomte de Launay par Madame de Girardin*, vol. 1,(Paris: Mercure de France, 1986), 442.

50. D. de Girardin, *Lettres parisiennes*, vol. 1, 442–43.

51. "Théâtre français: L'École des journalistes," 1–2. Janin also warned Mme Girardin that Delavigne's *La Popularité* had already failed becase of overreliance on allusion, saying, "On pourrait même vous citer des comédies bien faites, écrites par des poètes aimés, et qui sont mortes, uniquement parce qu'elles avaient

employé l'allusion. Je ne veux pas d'autre preuve que la comédie de M. Casimir Delavigne,—la Popularité. Dans cette comédie, il y avait des allusions pour et contre tout le monde, carlistes, juste-milieu, républicains ; il (sic) y étaient tous" (we could even cite well-made comedies written by beloved playwrights that flopped simply because of their allusions. I need no more proof than the fate of M. Casimir Delavigne's play, *La Popularité*. In this comedy there are allusions for and against everyone, Carlists, *juste-milieu*, republicans; they were all there). Jules Janin, "La Semaine dramatique," *Le Journal des débats*, August 12, 1839, 3.

52. D. de Girardin, *L'École des journalistes*, 44.

53. D. de Girardin, *L'École des journalistes*, xiii.

54. Saint Victor's remarks are cited in Théophile Gautier, introduction to *Œuvres complètes de Madame Émile de Girardin née Delphine Gay* (Paris: Plon, 1861), i–xx.

55. See Mullaney, *Reformation of Emotions* (see intro., n. 43).

Chapter 3

1. Théodore Muret, "Un grand homme de province à Paris par M. de Balzac," *La Quotidienne*, December 10, 1839.

2. Jules Janin, "L'École des journalistes, Lettre à Madame Émile de Girardin," *L'Artiste*, 1839. Théophile Gautier, "Lettre 173: Théophile Gautier to Gérard de Nerval (around December 5, 1839)," in *Correspondance générale*, ed. Claudine Lacoste-Veysseyre (Geneva: Droz, 1985), 164.

3. See appendix 1.

4. Pierre Laubriet, Introduction to *César Birotteau* by Honoré de Balzac (Paris: Garnier, 1964).

5. Honoré de Balzac, *César Birotteau*, ed. Pierre Laubriet (Paris: Garnier, 1964), 319 (hereafter cited in text as *CB*).

6. Nicole Mozet points out that Balzac also references Beaumarchais by making Suzanne's movements serve as the aesthetic and ideological motor of *La Vieille fille*. Nicole Mozet, *Balzac au pluriel* (Paris: Presses universitaires de France, 1990), 271–79.

7. Michel Lichtlé's article on Balzac's legal opinions points out that Balzac favored abolition of the dowry, both for its negative effects on sincerity of affection and for its tendency to divide inheritances. Michel Lichtlé, "Balzac, *Illusions Perdues*," *Information littéraire 55*, no. 3 (2003): 58–61. In the examples I give, the roles from *Figaro* are not fixed: at first Suzanne is the mother and then the daughter, but Balzac used Beaumarchais broadly as a referent. In *Illusions perdues* the fictional playwright Du Bruel has imitated Beaumarchais, and Lucien has sprinkled some character names from the Figaro trilogy across the article he writes about Du Bruel's play.

8. Roger Chartier, *Les Origines culturelles de la révolution française* (Paris: Seuil, 1990), 84.

9. Mozet points out that in *La Peau de chagrin* Finot had already served as an "homme-étiquette" (tag-man). Mozet, *Balzac au pluriel*, 15. Vautrin tells Lucien, "Si vous aviez cherché dans l'Histoire les causes humaines des événements, au lieu d'en apprendre par cœur les étiquettes" (If you had looked for the causes of human events in History instead of learning the tags by heart), you would have learned how to behave already. Balzac, *La Comédie humaine*, 696 (see intro., n. 46).

10. Shoshana Felman's chapter on *L'Illustre Gaudissart* is an interesting analysis of the *commis voyageur*'s uses of language. Shoshana Felman, *La Folie et la chose littéraire* (Paris: Seuil, 1978).

11. By 1839, Balzac was disenchanted with *L'Estafette*, which had reprinted part of the *Curé du village* without permission. He wrote a letter, which was published in *La Presse* on August 18, 1839, saying, "le journal à quatre-vingt fr. dépouille ici le journal à quarante fr. La parcimonie des journaux à quatre-vingt fr. envers la littérature est flagrante, ils se défendent de la nouvelle et du roman comme une maladie ; ils ont tant peur de venir en aide à quelques plumes souffrantes, qu'ils vivent des citations prises aux livres sous presse, afin de simuler une rédaction onéreuse" (the eighty-franc newspaper picks apart the forty-franc newspaper. The parsimony of eighty-franc papers toward literature is flagrant, they defend themselves against novels and stories like a sickness; they are so afraid of helping a few suffering pens that that they live off citations from books that are in press in order to simulate great efforts at writing). Honoré de Balzac, *Correspondance de Balzac*, ed. Roger Pierrot (Paris: Garnier Frères, 1960–69), 3: 674.

12. Fargeaud, "Balzac, Le commerce et la publicité" (see intro., n. 18).

13. Fargeaud and Greene have pointed out that Donnard has shown perfumers to have been early users of publicity, making Balzac's antedating of publicity techniques to the Restoration more accurate for a perfumer than it would have been for most other businesses. Fargeaud, "Balzac, Le commerce et la publicité"; J. P Greene, "Cosmetics and Conflicting Fictions in Balzac's *César Birotteau*," *Neophilologus* 83, no. 2 (1999): 197–208; Jean-Hervé Donnard, *Balzac: Les réalités économiques et sociales dans "La Comédie Humaine"* (Paris: A. Colin, 1961).

14. Laubriet's note calls it curious that *Le Figaro* ran articles against publicity as it was practiced by *La Presse* while *César Birotteau* was being published. I would go so far as to call it strategic. During *César Birotteau*'s distribution, articles about advertising entitled "Critique de la critique," and "La Littérature des annonces," as well as a spoof of a prospectus by a certain, "de Blaguanville" for *La Peau de chagrin* appeared in the pages of *Le Figaro*. Ibid.

15. Laubriet's introduction says that this vaudeville was published in the *Musée Dramatique* in 1837, though not performed until April 1838. Given that Balzac's corrections lasted from November to mid-December of 1837, it seems likely that he was aware of the adaptation. According to Laubriet, *Jerome Paturot* was also partly inspired by *César Birotteau*. Laubriet, introduction to *César Birotteau*, CLXIII–CLXV.

16. Pierre Laubriet, "L'Élaboration des personnages dans César Birotteau: Enseignement des épreuves corrigées," *L'Année balzacienne* (1964): 269.

17. I use "metadiscourse" here in the sense that Françoise van Rossum-Guyon assigns to it in her chapter 1, "Metadiscours et commentaire esthétique," in *Balzac: La littérature réfléchie*, ed. Stéphane Vachon (Montréal: Département d'études françaises, Université de Montréal, 2002), 3–20.

18. Édouard Ourliac, "Malheurs et aventures de *César Birotteau* avant sa naissance," *Le Figaro*, December 15, 1837.

19. When *César Birotteau* was promised to *Le Figaro*, it was supposed to appear serially. Just a year before it did appear, *Le Figaro* still published *romans-feuilletons* rather than bound novels. A large advertisement for *César Birotteau* on the fourth page of the December 16, 1836, paper read, "Le roman publié jour par

jour est un mode adopté. On se rappelle que *Clarisse Harlowe*, admirable ouvrage de Richardson, en 12 colonnes in-8, fut publié de cette manière et devint chaque jour pour l'Angleterre, pendant une année, l'occasion d'une fièvre d'impatience et de curiosité. Un essai récent prouve que la lecture des romans par fragmens doit avoir la même vogue en France" (The novel published day by day is a fashion that has been adopted. Just remember *Clarissa Harlowe*, the admirable work by Richardson, 12 columns of in-octavo published in this manner which brought impatience and curiosity to a fever pitch every day in England for a whole year. A recent test has shown that reading novels in fragments will have the same success in France). "César Birotteau (annonce)," *Le Figaro*, December 16, 1836, 4.

20. Because such publicity material was not considered part of the literary work itself, few first editions still include the prospectus. The Bibliothèque nationale de France, for example, has two first editions of *César Birotteau*, neither of which includes advertising material. Luckily, the Maison de Balzac in Paris owns two first editions that have retained the advertisements with which they were originally published, as well as three first editions that do not include it. Appendix 2 is a transcription of the prospectus for *César Birotteau* included in the Maison de Balzac's books.

21. Laubriet, introduction to *César Birotteau*, LI.

22. Véronique Bui cites Vachon and Wurmser and points out that Wurmser relies on the Laubriet preface to which we have referred for his argument. Bui, "Comment l'huile céphalique vint à Balzac" (see intro., n. 18). Given the ephemeral and anonymous nature of most publicity, Balzac could well have written much more advertisement than we are aware of.

23. Honoré de Balzac, *Illusions perdues* (Paris: Gallimard "Pléiade," 1977), 403 (hereafter cited in text as *IP*).

24. Roland Chollet, "Notes et variantes" to *Illusions perdues*, by Honoré de Balzac (Paris: Gallimard "Pléiade," 1977), 1299. Chollet also points out similarities between Balzac's critiques and Girardin's prospectus for *Le Journal des connaissances utiles*, while warning about the perils of both looking for direct models and of attributing the (sometimes contradictory) opinions of characters to Balzac himself.

25. For a fine articulation of ways that Balzac's Romantic irony involved composing with the real, see Marie de Gandt, "Ironies romantiques dans les années 1830," in *Ironies balzaciennes*, ed. Éric Bordas (Saint-Cyr-sur-Loire, Fr.): Christian Pirot, 2003), 17–30.

26. Gilles Feyel, "La Querelle de l'anonymat des journalistes, entre 1836 et 1850," in *Figures de l'anonymat, médias et société*, ed. Frédéric Lambert (Paris: L'Harmattan, 2001), 27–56.

27. This article was published in a volume of Girardin's collected essays in 1842. It also appeared in *La Presse* on December 5, 1839, two days before extracts from Delphine de Girardin's censored play, *L'École des journalistes*, was published there. Émile de Girardin, *Questions de Presse* (Paris: Béthune et Plon, 1842); Émile de Girardin, "De la liberté de la presse et du journalisme," *La Presse*, December 5, 1839, 2.

28. É. de Girardin, "De la liberté de la presse et du journalisme," 2.

29. Balzac, *La Comédie humaine*, 1295.

30. M. de Salvandy, "Une fête au Palais-Royal," in *Paris, ou Le livre des cent et un*, ed. Ladvocat (Paris: 1831–1834), 398. Cited in Charles Rozan, *Petites ignorances de la conversation* (Paris: Lacroix-Comon, 1857).

31. Letter 1542 in Balzac, *Correspondance de Balzac*, 640. Delphine de Girardin had written poems for Balzac to serve as samples from Lucien's first collection of poems—a splendid irony, given her own meditations on transitioning from poetry to journalism (see chapter 2). "Le Grand Homme" refers to the second section of *Illusions perdues*, which, as mentioned earlier, was published under the title *Un grand homme de province à Paris*.

32. Cited in José-Luis Diaz, *Illusions perdues d'Honoré de Balzac* (Paris: Gallimard, 2001), 185–86.

33. Cited in Diaz, *Illusions perdues d'Honoré de Balzac*, 396.

34. Joseph-Marc Bailbé, *Jules Janin, une sensibilité littéraire et artisitique* (Paris: Lettres modernes Minard, 1974), 13.

35. Balzac, *La Comédie humaine*, 112–13.

36. His appearance was not unlike Balzac's description of Gautier, who "est entré, fouet en main . . . en plein cœur du journalisme" (entered, whip in hand, into the heart of journalism; Balzac, *La Comédie humaine*, 113) with his preface to *Mlle de Maupin*, which Balzac praises in his own preface. Romain Piana, "Du dramaturge au feuilletoniste: Aristophane hors de la scène française au XIXe siècle," *Lieux Littéraires* 4 (2001): 185–203.

37. Agathe Novak-Lechevalier has explored Balzac's relationship to Scribe more broadly in "De la construction stratégique d'un cliché: Scribe vu par les romanciers." in *Eugène Scribe, Un Maître de la scene théâtrale et lyrique au XIXe siècle*, Olivier Bara and Jean-Claude Yon eds. (Rennes: Presses universitaires de Rennes, 2016). See also Agathe Novak-Lechevalier, "La Théâtralité Dans Le Roman: Stendhal, Balzac" (Ph.D. diss., Université de Paris 3, 2007), http://www .theses.fr/2007PA030131.

38. Jean-Claude Yon, "Balzac et Scribe: 'Scènes de la vie théâtrale,'" *L'Année balzacienne* (1999): 445.

39. See appendix 2.

40. In her study of *Les Souffrances de l'inventeur*, the third part of *Illusions perdues*, Isabelle Tournier draws attention to the jokey, ironic appeal of the chapter titles, which, like the prefaces, would disappear when the work was integrated into the *Comédie humaine*. Isabelle Tournier, "Portrait de Balzac en Shéhérazade," in *Balzac, œuvres complètes, le moment de "La comédie humaine,"* ed. Claude Duchet and Isabelle Tournier (Saint-Denis, Fr.: Presses Universitaires de Vincennes, 1993), 77–109.

41. Balzac, *La Comédie humaine*, 399.

42. Balzac, *La Comédie humaine*, 1295, for the successive versions.

43. Chollet, "Introduction," 105. For some alternate readings of this scene, see van Rossum-Guyon, *Balzac: La littérature réfléchie*, 136; Marie-Ève Thérenty, "Quand le roman [se] fait l'article: Palimpseste du journal dans *Illusions perdues*," in *Illusions perdues, actes du colloque des 1er et 2 décembre 2003*, ed. José-Luis Diaz and André Guyaux (Paris: Presses de l'Université de Paris-Sorbonne, 2004), 233–45; Christopher Prendergast, *The Order of Mimesis: Balzac, Stendhal, Nerval, Flaubert* (New York: Cambridge University Press, 1986), 112–13.

44. Honoré de Balzac, *Splendeurs et misères des courtisanes*, ed. Pierre Barbéris (Paris: Folio/Gallimard, 1973), 124.

45. Vautrin was hardly alone in this interpretation. Rosanvallon points out, however, that "Enrichissez-vous" was part of a speech meant to encourage social mobility and the improvement of everyone's lot through labor and industry. As for Guizot's theories about the theater, Lucien had failed to create the *éléctricité de la salle* (to electrify the audience), an ability that Guizot praised in his preface to the works of Shakespeare, when he read his poems aloud at Mme de Bargeton's: "Pour être traduite par la voix, comme pour être saisie, la poésie exige une sainte attention. Il doit se faire entre le lecteur et l'auditoire une alliance intime, sans laquelle les électriques communications des sentiments n'ont plus lieu. Cette cohésion des âmes manque-t-elle, le poète se trouve alors comme un ange essayant de chanter un hymne céleste au milieu des ricanements de l'enfer" (To be translated by the voice, as to be written, poetry requires a sacred attentiveness. An intimate alliance must be established between the the reader and the audience, without which the electric communication of feelings cannot take place. When this fusing of souls fails, the poet finds himself like an angel trying to sing a celestial hymn in the midst of the snickerings of hell). Balzac, *La Comédie humaine*, 199. When Lucien recalls Shakespeare later, it is just such *ricanements* (snickerings) that come to his mind: "Au bout d'une heure le poète quitta le Cénacle, maltraité par sa conscience qui lui criait : tu seras journaliste ! comme la sorcière crie à Macbeth : tu seras roi" (After an hour, the poet left the cenacle, bothered by his conscience which cried to him: you will be a journalist! as the witch cries to Macbeth, you will be king). Balzac, *La Comédie humaine*, 421–22.

46. Balzac, *Splendeurs et misères des courtisanes*, 468.

47. Philippe Ortel, "Le Stade de l'écran: Écriture et projection au dix-neuvième siècle," in *L'Écran de la représentation*, ed. S. Lojkine (Paris: L'Harmattan, 2001), 115–20.

48. Roland Chollet, *Balzac journaliste: Le tournant de 1830* (Paris: Klincksieck, 1983), 534.

49. For a concise treatment of the historiography surrounding the difference between medium and mode, see Carla Hesse, "Books in Time," in *The Future of the Book*, ed. Geoffrey Nunberg (Berkeley: University of California Press, 1997).

50. Isabelle Michelot has written about theatricality in Balzac's *Scènes de la vie parisienne*, Anne-Marie Baron and Christopher Prendergast have considered how Balzac's fiction exploited and overturned melodrama's conventions, while André Vanoncini shows that Balzac's theater also refuses totalizing systems. Olivier Bara has shown how vaudeville adaptations of Balzac's works undid all the subversion of dramatic convention written into the original novels by adding conventional moralizing endings. For a concise bibliography on Balzac and the theater, see "Le Théâtre de Balzac," *fabula*, January 15, 2013, http://www.fabula.org/actualites /le-theatre-de-balzac_52913.php. Isabelle Michelot, "Récit romanesque et théâtralité dans les Scènes de la vie parisienne et le 'cycle de Vautrin' d'Honoré de Balzac" (Ph.D. diss., Université Paris: 4 La Sorbonne, 2002); Anne-Marie Baron, "Mélodrame et feuilleton," in Duchet and Tournier, *Balzac, œuvres complètes: Le moment de "La comédie humaine,"* 243–56; Christopher Prendergast, *Balzac Fiction and Melodrama* (London: E. Arnold, 1978); André Vanoncini, "Le Théâtre de

Balzac: Triomphe et crise d'une esthétique d'identification," *Œuvres et Critiques* 11, no. 3 (1986): 297–311.

51. Quoted in van Rossum-Guyon, *Balzac: La littérature réfléchie*, 184.

52. Thérenty applies Lucien Dallenbach's theory of mosaic writing to the compostion of the *Comédie humaine* in Thérenty, *Mosaïques*, 495.

Chapter 4

1. Frédéric de Courcy, Jean-François-Alfred Bayard, and Théaulon, *L'Année sur la sellette* (Paris: Marchant, 1837), 7.

2. Dumanoir and Clairville, *La Poudre-coton: Revue de l'année 1846* (Paris: Michel Lévy frères, 1847), act 3, scene 1, line 32. *Le Chemin de traverse* was also the title of an 1836 book by Jules Janin, so its inclusion in the stage-curtain advertising poster suggests that Janin's journalistic esprit was a selling point for the paper that employed him. The published version of the play in which it appeared provided an extra page with the exact layout and typography for the advertising poster for *La Plaine Saint-Denis* that was to be reproduced on the curtain.

3. Feyel, *La Presse en France*, 67 (see intro., n. 10).

4. Éléonore Reverzy cites Charles Monselet's description of this in *Portrait de l'artiste en fille de joie*, 138 (see intro., n.19).

5. Théophile Marion Dumersan and Gabriel de Lurieu, *Le Pensionnaire, ou Cent francs par mois* (Paris: Nobis, 1836), 13.

6. Dumanoir, *Un Système* (Paris: Archives Nationales 1837), 2.

7. Dumanoir, *Un Système*, 2.

8. See Amélie Chabrier, "Des drames du Palais aux tribunaux comiques: La théâtralité de la chronique judiciaire en question, in Bara and Thérenty, *Presse et scène au XIXe siècle*, Médias 19, October 19, 2012, http://www.medias19.org /index.php?id=2970 (see intro., n. 48); Cary Hollinshead-Strick, "Le Boulevard du crime sélectionne son jury: La presse judiciaire sur scène sous la Monarchie de Juillet," in *European Drama and Performance Studies: Spectacles, commerce et culture matérielle (1715–1860)*, ed. Sabine Chaouche and Roxane Martin (Paris: Classiques Garnier, 2013), 167–76.

9. Hippolyte Auger, *Mlle Bernard ou l'autorité paternelle* (Brussels: Lelong et Gambier, 1838), 779. Text references are to act, scene, and line number of the play in this source.

10. See Susan McCready's analysis of *Antony* in part 2 of *The Limits of Performance in the French Romantic Theater* (Durham, N.C.: Durham University Press, 2007), 36–42.

11. Draner's name is marked directly on the print as its illustrator, but he would have been twelve years old when *Les Pommes de terre malades* was first performed, and not yet living in Paris. It is hard to know whether he was unusually precocious or whether there is an error in attribution or date.

12. According to Marc Martin, "C'est, après la création de la presse à 40 francs, le second grand épisode de la constitution d'un marché national de la publicité au profit de la presse parisienne. En 1846, la SGA gère la publicité de dix-huit titres, tous les plus importants, et contrôle, pour l'essentiel, ce marché" (After the creation of the forty-franc press, this is the second great step toward the constitution of a national market for publicity via the Parisian press. By 1846, the

SGA managed advertising for the eighteen most important papers, and basically controlled the market). M. Martin, *Trois siècles de publicité*, 74 (see intro., n. 3).

13. Like Grandville's images, which, "illustrate and enact the processes they critique," this play obscures sightlines with posters for *L'Époque*. See also Daniel Grojnowski, Préface to *Un Autre Monde*, by Jean-Jacques Grandville (Paris: Classiques Garnier, 2010), xix.

In a sense Grandville did visually what vaudevilles did physically for the newspapers and plays they reviewed—made them obviously strange as a way of revealing their motives and priorities.

14. Dumanoir and Clairville, *Les Pommes de terre malades, revue de l'année 1845* (Paris: Beck, 1846), 6. For how George Sand used this materiality to her own advantage when she published *Le Péché de Monsieur Antoine* in *L'Époque*, see Cary Hollinshead-Strick, "La Campagne publicitaire de *L'Époque* en 1845 vue par le vaudeville,"in Bara and Thérenty, *Presse et scène au XIXe siècle*, Médias 19, October 19, 2012, http://www.medias19.org/index.php?id=2884.

15. Other plays showed *Le Soleil* as a large newspaper, rather than personifying it. Auguste Jouhaud, Barthélemy, *La Faute du mari* (Paris: Beck, 1846), act 1, scene 1, line 1. Or they referred to it as one: Pierre-Frédéric-Adolphe Carmouche and Eugène Guinot, *Paris à cheval* (Paris: Tresse, 1845), act 3, scene 2, line14; Adolphe Dennery and Clairville, *V'la c'qui vient d' paraître, bulletin de la grande année 1845* (Paris: Beck, 1846), act 2, scene 1, line 5.

16. Dumanoir and Clairville, *Les Pommes de terre malades*, 8.

17. "Nez fourré dans un journal" was an expression common enough to be used by the maid in *La Gazette des tribunaux*, an 1844 vaudeville: "Dire que Monsieur a lu tout ça depuis une semaine ! Il a toujours le nez fourré là-dedans" (To think that Monsieur has read all that in one week! He's always got his nose in there). Laurencin and Marc-Michel, *La Gazette des tribunaux* (Paris: Marchant, 1844), act 1, scene 1, line 2.

18. See Sylvie Vielledent, "Dumas Parodié," *Revue de l'Histoire littéraire de la France* 4, no. 104 (2004): 126, who cites Barbara Cooper, "Parodie et pastiche: La réception théâtrale d'Antony," *Œuvres et critiques* 21, no. 1 (1996). See also Sylvie Vielledent, 1830 aux théâtres (Paris: Honoré Champion, 2009), 112–31.

19. J.T., "Revue dramatique," December 29, 1845, 2.

20. Information about how many times a play was performed and the amount of revenue it generated for the theater (and therefore its author) can be gleaned from the archives of the Société des Auteurs et Compositeurs Dramatiques (SACD), which has registers from several of the most popular theaters. These records indicate the amount due to playwrights based on each day's earnings. Most reasonably successful year-end revues ran for around thirty performances, so *Les Pommes de terre malades* was exceptional at eighty-two.

In his excellent article on *Le Chevalier de la Maison Rouge*, which he, with Thomasseau, identifies as one of the essential dramatic moments of the revolutionary July Monarchy, Vincent Robert estimates attendance at a successful play at two-thirds of a theater's capacity over the run of the play. This formula would give more than fifty-two thousand spectators for *Les Pommes de terre malades*. Given that the Théâtre du Palais-Royal, where it played, had fewer than a thousand seats, and that it was a vaudeville revue, this was an impressive run. Christophe Charle contends that by midcentury the greatest successes could reach one hundred thousand spectators. Vincent Robert, "Theater and Revolution on the Eve of 1848: Le Chevalier de Maison Rouge," *Actes de la recherche en sciences sociales*, nos. 186–87 (2011); Nicole Wild, *Dictionnaire des théâtres parisiens au XIXe siècle* (Paris: Aux Amateurs de livres, 1989), 351; Jean-Marie Thomasseau, "Le Théâtre et les révolutions," *Comédie française les cahiers* 13 (1994): 40–51; Christophe Charle, *Théâtres en capitales: Naissance de la société du spectacle à Paris, Berlin, Londres et Vienne, 1860–1914* (Paris: A. Michel, 2008).

21. J.T., "Revue dramatique," December 29, 1845, 2.

22. The most famous one was between Émile de Girardin and Armand Carrel in 1836 (see introduction and chapter 1.) William Reddy's work on honor and journalism sheds light on this practice. William M. Reddy, "Condotteiri of the Pen: Journalists and the Public Sphere in Postrevolutionary France (1815–1850)," *American Historical Review* 99, no. 5 (1994): 1546–70; William M. Reddy, *The Invisible Code: Honor and Sentiment in Postrevolutionary France, 1814–1848* (London: University of California Press, 1997).

23. George Sand, *Le Péché de Monsieur Antoine* (Paris: Hetzel, 1859), 2.

24. Clairville, one of the authors of *Les Pommes de terre malades*, also collaborated on a concurrent revue that commented on Sand's pseudonym: Dennery and Clairville, *V'la c'qui vient d' paraître,* 10. For Sand's reaction to such teasing, see George Sand, "Lettre 3257 à Anténor Joly [Nohant, October 14 or 15, 1845]," *Correspondance*, vol. 7, ed. Georges Lubin (Paris: Garnier, 1970), 328.

25. Charles Desnoyer and Charles Labie, *L'Ombre de Nicolet ou de plus fort en plus fort ! vaudeville épisodique en un acte*, 23.

26. In *Le Siècle* of September 11, 1837, the journalist (who is also discussing the recent unionization of playwrights under the Société des auteurs et compositeurs dramatiques) adapts this formula when arguing that a greater number of theaters means more opportunity for authors: "Refusé par un directeur qui se trompe (cela s'est vu quelquefois) il peut aller frapper à une porte voisine" (Refused by a director who is making a mistake [it has been known to happen] he can go knock on the neighbor's door). Ed. L. "Feuilleton," *Le Siècle,* September 11, 1837, 2.

27. Manuel Charpy points out that such a combination of parody and publicity was common in vaudeville theater and caught on quickly in the press. See Manuel Charpy, "La Ronde des produits: Revue de fin d'annee, produits industriels et publicité à Paris au XIXe siècle," in Bara, Piana, and Yon, "En revenant à la revue," 267 (see intro., n. 27).

28. "Théâtre de la Gaîté," *Le Constitutionnel*, September 11, 1837, 1.

29. "Théâtre de la Gaîté," *Le Constitutionnel*, September 11, 1837, 1.

30. Barbara Cooper has called attention to another tour de force of this sort of materially self-conscious discussion of the roles of newspapers and theaters with regard to each other in note 11 to her introduction to *Jeannic le Breton* (see ch. 2, n. 3).

31. J.T., "Chronique des théâtres," *La Quotidienne*, July 11, 1836, 2.

32. Jules Janin, "Feuilleton du Journal des débats," *Le Journal des débats*, September 5, 1836, 2.

33. J.T., "Revue dramatique," *La Quotidienne*, September 5, 1836, 2.

34. J.T., "Revue dramatique," *La Quotidienne*, July 1, 1839, 2.

35. Y., "Théâtres," *Le Constitutionnel*, December 13, 1841, 1.

36. Y., "Théâtres."

37. Panurge's sheep, in Rabelais' *Quart livre*, blindly follow one another off the deck of a ship. Sarcey's parallel between them and critics was published in *L'Opinion nationale*, July 16 and 23, 1860, reprinted in *Quarante ans de théâtre* (Paris, Bibliothèque des annales politiques et littéraires, 1900–1902), vol. 1, p. 54. Cited by Marianne Bouchardon, "Introduction" in *Francisque Sarcey: un critique dramatique à contre-courant de l'histoire du théâtre?* (Rouen: Publications numériques du CÉRÉdI, no. 12, 2015).

38. "Théâtre du Gymnase," *Le Charivari*, February 25, 1844, 2.

39. J.T., "Revue dramatique," *La Quotidienne*, February 26, 1844, 2.

40. Dumanoir, Clairville, and Adolphe Dennery, *Paris dans la comète* (Paris: Detroux, 1843), act 2, scene 5, line 9.

41. Hippolyte Lucas, "Revue des théâtres," *Le Siècle*, January 24, 1848.

42. R., "Théâtres," *Le Constitutionnel*, January 24, 1848, 1–2.

43. "Théâtre français," *Le Charivari*, January 24, 1848, 2.

44. R., "Théâtres," January 24, 1848, 1–2.

45. Auguste Lefranc and Eugène Labiche, *Le Club champenois* (Paris: Beck, 1848), 16.

46. See Hemmings, *Theatre Industry in Nineteenth-Century France* (see ch. 1, n. 33). For a good discussion of Labiche's verbal virtuosity, see Léal, "Le Discours du fait divers," 109–23 (see intro., n.35).

47. Tournemine, *La Révolte des coucous*, 8 (see intro., n. 2).

48. Recent work on dramatic parodies of *Hernani* from just before this period and on a Labiche play from just after it wrestle with the ambiguous social positioning of vaudeville. In his edition of *L'Affaire de la rue Lourcine*, Olivier Bara, having remarked that vaudeville songs participate more in collective festivity than in critical reflection, continues, "cependant le vaudeville goûté sur les boulevards parisiens nourrit l'intelligence critique et parodique" (and yet the vaudeville of the Parisian boulevards fosters critical and parodic thought). Olivier Bara, introduction to *L'Affaire de la rue de Lourcine*, by Eugène Labiche (Paris: Gallimard, 2011), 83. Likewise, Sylvie Vielledent, discussing parodies of *Hernani* from 1830, says that "les textes considérés sont ambivalents : ils colportent le discours dominant, et s'en démarquent ; ils sont normatifs et émancipés ; ils vilipendent le drame hugolien et l'exhaussent . . . Reste que leur irrévérence, la relative license qui leur est concédée . . . les rendent moins négligeables qu'on veut bien le dire" (the texts considered are ambivalent; they spread the dominant discourse and differentiate themselves from it; they are normative and emancipated; they make fun of Hugolian drama and raise it up. . . . In the end their irreverence, and the relative liberty conceded them . . . make them less negligible than people have supposed). Vielledent, *1830 aux théâtres*, 37.

Chapter 5

1. Antoine Compagnon's study of the *chiffonnier* (ragpicker) gives a good account of Pyat's encounters with the stage and with the government in *Les Chiffonniers de Paris* (Paris: Gallimard, 2017), 209–43.

2. Charles Nodier to Charles Weiss, November 6, 1838, in Charles Nodier, *Feuilletons du Temps*, vol. 1, ed. Jacques-Rémi Dahan (Paris: Classiques Garnier, 2010), 22–23.

3. Margaret Miner, "Devouring Streets: Jules Janin and the Abjection of

Paris," *MLN* 113, no. 4 (September 1998): 780–811, http://www.jstor.org/stable /3251403.

4. Félix Pyat, *Le Chiffonnier de Paris grand Roman dramatique* (Paris: A. Fayard, 1892).

5. Gérard de Nerval, *Léo Burckart, scènes de la vie allemande* (Coeuvres-et-Valsery, Fr.: Ed. Ressouvenances, 1995), 22.

6. Nerval, *Léo Burckart*, 19.

7. Nerval, *Léo Burckart*, 70.

8. Nerval, *Léo Burckart*, 27.

9. Ross Chambers, "Duplicité du pouvoir, pouvoir de la duplicité dans *Léo Burckart*," in *Nerval, une poétique du rêve*, ed. Jacques Huré, Joseph Jurt, and Robert Kropp (Paris: Champion, 1989), 98.

10. Nerval translated the first part of Goethe's *Faust* before he was twenty and translated much of the second part later. The work was a leitmotif in much of his writing as well as a significant contribution to his reputation. He mentioned *Léo Burckart*'s debt to *Faust* in a letter to Jules Janin, cited in Gérard de Nerval, *Œuvres complémentaires*, vol. 4, *Théâtre 2*, ed. Jean Richer (Paris: Minard, 1981), viii.

11. Janin wrote, "Jusqu'à présent la censure a été bénigne, elle a fait peu parler d'elle, ou bien quand par hasard elle a voulu faire des coups d'état, les auteurs mutilés en ont appelé au ministre ; alors il s'est trouvé que le ministre avait plus d'intelligence et de courage que ses gardiens, Par exemple, lorsqu'il fut question de jouer *Léo Burckart*, la censure arrêta la représentation de ce drame, dans lequel étaient racontées tout au long les conspirations politiques de l'Allemagne. Dans cette occurrence que fit l'auteur ? Il en appela à M. de Montalivet, à lui-même, lui remontrant qu'aujourd'hui les furibonds compagnons de Sand étaient devenus de bons pères de familles très dévouées a la Sainte-Alliance, des conseilleurs intimes, des conseilleurs auliques, des colonels de régimens, des gardes de l'empereur Fran-çois, et qu'ainsi une conspiration qui se terminait par des uniformes de la cour de Berlin, n'était pas d'une imitation bien dangereuse" (Until now censorship has been benign, it didn't draw much attention to itself, and on the rare occasions when it tried coups d'état, the mutilated authors called upon the minister for sup-port, and so it was discovered that the minister was more intelligent and daring than his guardians. For example, when it was a question of staging *Léo Burckart*, the censor stopped performance of this drama in which the political conspiracies of Germany were recounted. What did the author do? He called upon M. de Mon-talivet himself, pointing out that today the furious companions of Sand had all become good heads of families, devoted to the Sacred Alliance, trusted counselors, colonels of regiments, guards of Emperor Franz-Joseph, and that a conspiracy that ends with uniforms at the court of Berlin is not particularly dangerous to imitate). Janin, "La Semaine dramatique," *Le Journal des débats*, August 12, 1839, 2.

12. Gérard de Nerval, *Œuvres complètes*, vol. 2 (Paris: Gallimard, 1993), 1306.

13. Jonathan Strauss, *Subjects of Terror* (Stanford, Calif.: Stanford University Press, 1998), 104.

14. For a fascinating discussion of this process in Nerval's work, see Patrick Bray, *The Novel Map: Space and Subjectivity in Nineteenth-Century French Fic-tion* (Evanston, Ill.: Northwestern University Press, 2013), 61–83.

15. Louise Colet, *La Jeunesse de Goethe* (Paris: Vve Dondey-Dupré, 1839), 16.

16. Colet, *La Jeunesse de Goethe*, 16.

17. This apology for his "act in bad taste" was reprinted in *Le Figaro*. See Alphonse Karr, "Acte de mauvais gout," *Le Figaro*, July 9, 1840, n. 141, 2.

18. Gérard de Nerval, *Lorely*, ed. Jacques Bony (Paris: José Corti, 1995), 59.

19. Nerval, *Lorely*, 65.

20. Patrick M. Bray, "Lost in the Fold: Space and Subjectivity in Gérard De Nerval's 'Généalogie' and *Sylvie*." *French Forum*, vol. 31, no. 2, 2006, 41, https://www.jstor.org/stable/40552430.

21. The difference between *le critique* and *un critique* is not merely the one between a definite and an indefinite article, in that in French (as sometimes in English as well), a definite article used this way can make a general category of a word. *Le lundi* becomes every Monday, *le bonheur*, happiness. *Le critique*, then is the critic as a role, while *la critique* is criticism itself.

22. Dennery and Clairville, *Le Feuilleton et la raison ou Le Mariage du feuilleton* (Paris: Les Archives nationales, 1841).

23. Newspapers and friends noted that Janin had invited a remarkable number of public figures to his wedding. When Le Feuilleton of the play makes a speech on marriage to prove that he can make an article out of anything, he manages to integrate the names of fifteen Parisian newspapers into his monologue.

24. "Théâtres, fêtes et concerts," *La Presse*, December 21, 1841, 3.

25. "Théâtres, fêtes et concerts," *La Presse*, December 25, 1841, 3.

26. "Théâtres, fêtes et concerts," *La Presse*, December 29, 1841, 3.

27. Dennery and Claireville, *Le Feuilleton et la raison*, scene 2.

28. This scenario feels as though one of the authors might be playing with Kantian terms, with representations being made to Reason, but the match is not close enough to constitute a direct reference. Associating theatrical judgment with Reason, though, and inviting the parterre to participate in its exercise was consistent with the ideas of Antony Beraud, the director of the Ambigu-Comique, who had written for liberal newspapers during the Restoration and was probably sympathetic to ideas which located reason in the parterre.

29. Georges Dairnvaell, *À M. Félix Pyat, réponse du prince des critiques* (Paris: au dépôt central, sous les galeries de l'Odéon), 9.

30. Félix Pyat, *Marie-Joseph Chénier et le prince des critiques* (Paris: Leriche, 1844), 3.

31. Pyat, *Marie-Joseph Chénier*, 15.

32. William M. Reddy, *The Invisible Code: Honor and Sentiment in Postrevolutionary France, 1814–1848* (London: University of California Press, 1997).

33. *Procès en diffamation de M. J. Janin contre M. F. Pyat, condamnation . . . réflexions de plusieurs avocats à ce sujet* (Paris: Gazel, 1844).

34. Charles de Matharel, "Théâtres," *Le Siècle*, May 17, 1847, 1–2.

35. Odile Krakovitch, *Hugo Censuré* (Paris: Calmann-Lévy, 1985), 175.

36. For interesting analyses of the *chiffonnier* as a double for writers, see chapters 2 and 6 in Catherine Nesci, *Le Flâneur et les flâneuses les femmes et la ville à l'époque romantique* (Grenoble, Fr.: ELLUG, Université Stendhal, 2007), 82–84; and Emma M. Bielicki, "'Un artiste en matière de chiffons': The Rag-Picker as a Figure for the Artist in Champfleury's *La Mascarade de la vie parisienne*," *Nineteenth-Century French Studies* 37, no. 3–4 (2009), 262–75. Antoine Compagnon's study of the figure links it interestingly to the politics and aesthetics of

the century. Antoine Compagnon *Les Chiffonniers de Paris* (Paris: Gallimard, 2017).

37. Richard Terdiman, *Discourse-Counter-Discourse: The Theory and Practice of Symbolic Resistance in Nineteenth-Century France* (London: Cornell University Press, 1985).

38. Maurice Samuels, *The Spectacular Past: Popular History and the Novel in Nineteenth-Century France* (Ithaca, N.Y.: Cornell University Press, 2004).

Conclusion

1. Théophile Gautier, preface to *Œuvres complètes*, xii (see ch. 2, n. 54).

2. "Aux Directeurs de la Porte-Saint-Martin à propos de Robert Macaire," *Le Charivari*, March 23, 1848, 1.

3. Dumanoir and Clairville, *Les Lampions de la veille et les lanternes du lendemain, revue de l'année 1848* (Paris: Dondey-Dupré, 1849).

4. There were, of course, many cases in which advance publicity had influenced opening night audiences, too. Maurice Descotes, *Le Public de théâtre et son histoire* (Paris: Presses universitaires de France Vendôme, Impr. des P.U.F., 1964), 5–7.

5. Karl Rosenkranz, *Georg Wilhelm Friedrich Hegels Leben* (Berlin: Duncker und Humblot, 1844), 543. Cited in Susan Buck-Morss, *Hegel, Haiti, and Universal History* (Pittsburgh: University of Pittsburgh Press, 2009), 49.

6. Fox News's defense of CNN when it was wrongly accused of publishing uncorroborated information is an indication that a certain respect for codes of journalistic integrity is still shared across the political spectrum, at least as an ideal. See "Fox News Host Defends CNN Reporter," CNN Politics, January 12, 2017, video, 1:42, http://edition.cnn.com/videos/politics/2017/01/12/fox-news-shephard-smith-defends-cnn-reporter-cnni.cnn.

BIBLIOGRAPHY

A——, Mce d'. *Considérations sur quelques-unes des causes qui ont perdu la restauration et qui menacent le trône de juillet; en réponse à la brochure de M. Duvergier de Hauranne*. Paris: Impr. de Béthune et Plon, 1838.

Abirached, Robert. *La Crise du personnage dans le théâtre moderne*. Collection Tel. Paris: Gallimard, 1994.

"Adieux à l'année 1836." *Le Charivari*, December 31, 1836.

A.F. "Théâtre-Français." *Le Constitutionnel*, December 2, 1838.

Aguet, Jean-Pierre. "Le Tirage des quotidiens de Paris sous la monarchie de juillet." *Schweizerische Zeitschrift für Geschichte* 10 (1960): 216–86.

Allen, James Smith. *In the Public Eye: A History of Reading in Modern France, 1800–1940*. Princeton, N.J.: Princeton University Press, 1991.

Alliston, April. "Transnational Sympathies, Imaginary Communities." In *The Literary Channel: The Inter-National Invention of the Novel*, edited by Carolyn Dever and Margaret Cohen, 133–48. Princeton, N.J.: Princeton University Press, 2002.

Anderson, Benedict. *Imagined Communities: Reflections on the Origin and Spread of Nationalism*. London: Verso, 1991.

"Annexe 2: Loi du 9 septembre 1835." With commentary by Barbara T. Cooper. In Desnoyer and Labat, *Richard Savage* (1838). Médias 19, June 5, 2015. http://www.medias19.org/index.php?id=22079

Auger, Hippolyte. *Mlle Bernard ou l'autorité paternelle, comédie-vaudeville en un acte*. Brussels: Lelong et Gambier, 1838.

"Aux Directeurs de la Porte-Saint-Martin à propos de Robert Macaire." *Le Charivari*, March 23, 1848, 1.

Bailbé, Joseph-Marc. *Jules Janin, une sensibilité littéraire et artisitique*. Vol. 33,. Paris: Situation / Lettres modernes Minard, 1974.

———. "La Lanterne magique au service de l'évocation littéraire dans le texte de Janin et Banville." *Cahiers d'histoire culturelle: La lanterne magique, pratiques et mise en écriture* 2 (1997): 89–93.

Bailleul, Jacques-Charles. *Dictionnaire critique du langage politique, gouvernemental, civil, administratif et judiciaire de notre époque: Rédigé selon la lettre et l'esprit de la charte constitutionnelle, ou mon dernier mot, devant Dieu et devant les hommes, sur la révolution française, sur ses résultats possibles et nécessaires, sur la situation de la France et de son gouvernement; publié dans ma quatre-vingtième année*. Paris: Renard, 1842.

Balzac, Honoré de. *César Birotteau*. Edited by Pierre Laubriet. Paris: Garnier, 1964.

———. *Correspondance de Balzac*. 5 vols. Edited by Roger Pierrot. Paris: Garnier Frères, 1960–69.

————. *Illusions perdues*. Paris: Folio / Gallimard, 1974.

————. *Illusions perdues*, edited and annotated by Roland Chollet, in *La Comédie humaine*, edited by Pierre-Georges Castex, vol. 5. Paris: NRF / Gallimard, 1977.

————. *Splendeurs et misères des courtisanes*. Edited by Pierre Barbéris. Paris: Folio / Gallimard, 1973.

Bara, Olivier. "Balzac en vaudeville: Manipulations et appropriations du roman par la scène parisienne (1830–1840)." In *La Scène Bâtarde entre Lumières et romantisme*, edited by Philippe Bourdin and Gérard Loubinoux, 93–112. Clermont-Ferrand: Service Universités Culture, Presses universitaires Blaise Pascal, 2004.

————. "Éléments pour une poétique du feuilleton théâtral." in Bury and Laplace-Claverie, *Le Miel et le fiel*, 21–30.

————. Introduction to *L'Affaire de la rue de Lourcine* by Eugène Labiche. Paris: Gallimard, 2011.

————. "Le Rire subversif de Frédérick-Lemaître/Robert Macaire, ou la force comique d'un théâtre d'acteur." *Revue en ligne Insignis*, no. 1, : http://s2.e-monsite .com/2010/05/15/82924582le-rire-subversif-olivier-bara-pdf.pdf.

————. *Le Théâtre de l'Opéra-comique sous la restauration: Enquête autour d'un genre moyen*. Edited by Herbert Schneider. Zurich: Musikwissenschaftliche Publikationen Verlag, 2001.

————. "Scribe, un homme sans style ?" In Bara and Yon, *Eugène Scribe*, 159–78.

Bara, Olivier, Romain Piana, and Jean-Claude Yon, eds. "En revenant à la revue: La revue de fin d'annee au XIXe siècle." Special issue, *Revue d'histoire du Theâtre* 2, no. 266 (April–June 2015).

Bara, Olivier, and Marie-Ève Thérenty, eds. *Presse et scène au XIXe siècle*. Médias 19. October 19, 2012. http://www.medias19.org/index.php?id=1569.

Bara, Olivier, and Marie-Ève Thérenty, eds. *Presse et opéra au XIXe siècle*. Médias 19. March 25, 2018. http://www.medias19.org/index.php?id=24195.

Bara, Olivier, and Jean-Claude Yon, eds. *Eugène Scribe: Un maître de la scène théâtrale et lyrique du Xixe siècle*. Rennes: Presses universitaires de Rennes, 2016.

Baron, Anne-Marie. "Artifices de mise-en scène et art de l'illusion chez Balzac." *L'Année balzacienne* (1996): 23–35.

————. "Mélodrame et feuilleton." In Duchet and Tournier, *Balzac, œuvres complètes: Le moment de "La comédie humaine*," 243–56.

Barthes, Roland. "L'Effet de réel." In *Roland Barthes: Œuvres complètes*, edited by Éric Marty. Paris: Seuil, 2002.

Bautier, Roger, and Élisabeth Cazenave. *Les Origines d'une conception moderne de la communication: Gouverner l'opinion au XIXe siècle*. La communication en plus. Grenoble, Fr.: Presses universitaires de Grenoble, 2000.

Bautier, Roger, Elisabeth Cazenave, and Michael Palmer. *La Presse selon le XIXe siècle*. Paris: Université Paris III, 1997.

Béchard, Frédéric. *Les Tribulations d'un grand homme*. Paris: Pommeret et Guénot, 1847.

Beizer, Janet. *Ventriloquized Bodies: Narratives of Hysteria in Nineteenth-Century France*. Ithaca, N.Y.: Cornell University Press, 1994.

Bellanger, Claude, Jacques Godechot, Pierre Guiral, and Fernand Terrou, eds. *Histoire Générale de la presse française*. Vol. 2, *De 1815 à 1871*. Paris: Presses Universitaires de France, 1969.

Bénichou, Paul. *Le Sacre de l'écrivain 1750–1830: Essai sur l'avénement d'un pouvoir spirituel laïque dans la France moderne*. Paris: J. Corti, 1973.

Bennett, Benjamin. *All Theater Is Revolutionary Theater*. London: Cornell University Press, 2005.

Bergson, Henri. *Le Rire*. Paris: PUF, 1993.

Berthelot, Sandrine. "La Bohème: Avec ou sans style." In *Bohème sans frontière*, edited by Pascal Brissette and Anthony Glinoer. Rennes: Presses universitaires de Rennes, 2010, 115–26.

Berthier, Patrick. *La Presse littéraire et dramatique au début de la Monarchie de Juillet (1830–1836)*. Villeneuve-d'Ascq, Fr.: Presses universitaires du septentrion, 2001.

———. *Le Théâtre au xixe siècle*. Que sais-je ? Paris: PUF, 1986.

Bielicki, Emma M. " 'Un artiste en matière de chiffons': The Rag-Picker as a Figure for the Artist in Champfleury's 'La Mascarade de la vie parisienne.' " *Nineteenth-Century French Studies* 37, nos. 3–4 (2009), 262–75.

Boncompain, Jacques. *De Scribe à Hugo: La condtion de l'auteur (1815–1870)*. Paris: Honoré Champion, 2014.

Bordas, Éric, ed. *Ironies balzaciennes*. Saint-Cyr-sur-Loire, Fr.: Christian Pirot, 2003.

Bouchardon, Marianne. Introduction to "Francisque Sarcey: un critique dramatique à contre-courant de l'histoire du théâtre?," Actes de la journée d'étude organisée à l'Université de Rouen en janvier 2014, Publications numériques du CÉRÉdI, "Actes de colloques et journées d'étude, " no. 12, 2015.

Bourdieu, Pierre. *Les Règles de l'art*. Paris: Seuil, 1998.

Bray, Patrick M. "Lost in the Fold: Space and Subjectivity in Gérard de Nerval's 'Généalogie' and *Sylvie*." *French Forum* 31, no. 2 (2006): 35–51. https://www.jstor.org/stable/40552430.

———. *The Novel Map: Space and Subjectivity in Nineteenth-Century French Fiction*. Evanston, Ill.: Northwestern University Press, 2013.

Briffault, Eugène. "Variétés." *Le Constitutionnel*, November 12, 1843, 3.

Brooks, Peter. *The Melodramatic Imagination: Balzac, Henry James, Melodrama and the Mode of Excess*. New York: Columbia University Press, 1985.

Buck-Morss, Susan. *Hegel, Haiti, and Universal History*. Pittsburgh: University of Pittsburgh Press, 2009.

Bui, Véronique. "Comment l'huile céphalique vint à Balzac." In *Presse et plumes*, edited by Alan Vaillant and Marie-Ève Thérenty, 457–66. Paris: Nouveau monde, 2004.

"Bulletin des théâtres, des arts et de la littérature," *Le Figaro*, April 8, 1835.

Bury, Mariane, and Hélène Laplace-Claverie, eds. *Le Miel et le fiel: La critique théâtrale en france au XIXe siècle*. Paris: PUPS, 2008.

Calderone, Amélie. "Au croisement du vaudeville anecdotique et de la féerie: codification du genre de la revue de fin d'annee sous la monarchie de Juillet." In "En revenant à la revue," ed. Olivier Bara, Romain Piana, and Jean-Claude Yon, special issue, *Revue d'histoire du Théâtre* 2, no. 266 (April–June 2015): 201–16.

———. "Entre la scène et le livre: Formes dramatiques publiées dans la presse à l'époque romantique (1829–1851)." Ph.D. diss., Université de Lyon 2, 2015. http://www.theses.fr/2015LYO20101.

———. Introduction to *L'École des journalistes* by Delphine de Girardin (1839). Médias 19. March 27, 2014. http://www.medias19.org/index.php?id=17674.

———. "Petits arrangements entre époux: De la scène théâtrale à la scène médiatique; l'exemple de la publication de *L'École des journalistes* dans *La Presse* (1839)." Médias 19. October 19, 2012. http://www.medias19.org/index.php?id=1295.

Carmouche, Pierre-Frédéric-Adolphe, and Eugène Guinot. *Paris à cheval, revue cavalière en 5 relais, par MM. Carmouche et Paul Vermond* . . . . Paris: Tresse, 1845.

Carpenter, Scott. *Acts of Fiction, Resistance and Resolution from Sade to Baudelaire.* University Park: Pennsylvania State University Press, 1996.

"César Birotteau (annonce)." *Le Figaro*, December 16, 1836, 4.

Chabrier, Amélie. "Des drames du Palais aux tribunaux comiques: La théâtralité de la chronique judiciaire en question." In Bara and Thérenty, *Presse et scène au XIXe siècle*. Médias 19. October 19, 2012. http://www.medias19.org/index.php?id=2970.

Chambers, Ross. "Duplicité du pouvoir, pouvoir de la duplicité dans *Léo Burckart*." In *Nerval, une poétique du rêve*, edited by Jacques Huré, Joseph Jurt, and Robert Kropp, 89–100. Paris: Champion, 1989.

"Charade." *Le Charivari*, December 30, 1836, 3.

Charle, Christophe. *Théâtres en capitales: Naissance de la société du spectacle à Paris, Berlin, Londres et Vienne, 1860–1914.* Paris: A. Michel, 2008.

Charpy, Manuel. "La Ronde des produits. Revue de fin d'annee, produits industriels et publicité à Paris au XIXe siècle." In "En revenant à la revue," ed. Olivier Bara, Romain Piana, and Jean-Claude Yon, special issue, *Revue d'histoire du Théâtre* 2, no. 266 (April–June 2015): 253–68.

Chartier, Roger. *Les Origines culturelles de la révolution française.* L'Univers historique. Paris: Seuil, 1990.

Chollet, Roland. *Balzac journaliste: Le tournant de 1830.* Paris: Klincksieck, 1983.

Chollet, Roland. "Notes et variantes" to *Illusions perdues*, by Honoré de Balzac. Paris: Gallimard "Pléiade," 1977.

Clairville [Louis François Nicolaïe]. *Mathieu Laensberg est un menteur, revue en 1 acte, mêlée de couplets.* Paris: Marchant, 1839.

Clairville [Louis François Nicolaïe] and Delatour [Auguste Gay de La Tour de Lajonchére]. *1836 dans la lune.* Paris: Morain, 1837.

Cogniard frères. *Rothomago, revue en 1 acte.* Paris: Marchant, 1839.

Cohen, Margaret, and Carolyn Dever, eds. *The Literary Channel: The International Invention of the Novel.* Princeton, N.J.: Princeton University Press, 2002.

Colet, Louise. *La Jeunesse de Goethe, comédie en 1 acte, en vers.* Paris: Vve Dondey-Dupré, 1839.

Compagnon, Antoine. *Les Chiffoniers de Paris.* Paris: Gallimard, 2017.

Cooper, Barbara. "Exploitation of the Body in Vigny's 'Chatterton': The Economy of Drama and the Drama of Economics." *Theatre Journal* 34, no. 1 (1982): 20–26.

———. Introduction to *Richard Savage*, by Desnoyer and Labat (1838). Médias 19. June 7, 2015. http://www.medias19.org/index.php?id=22070.

———. Introduction to *Jeannic le Breton*, by Eugène Bourgeois and Alexandre Dumas (1841). Médias 19. June 19, 2016. http://www.medias19.org/index.php?id=17675.

———. "Encore un mot sur les publics du *Magasin théâtral.*" *Revue d'Histoire Du Théâtre* IV no. 256 (2012).

———. "Playing it again: A study of vaudeville and the aesthetics of incorporation in restoration France." *Nineteenth Century Contexts,* 13:2, (1989): 197-210.

———. "Les Publics du *Magasin théâtral* (XIXe Siècle)." *Revue d'Histoire Du Théâtre* 1–2, 245–246 (2010).

———. "Parodie et pastiche: La réception théâtrale d'*Antony.*" *Œuvres et critiques* 21, no. 1 (1996): 112–31.

———. "Staging a Revolution: Political Upheaval in *Lorenzaccio* and *Léo Burckart.*" *Romance Notes* 24, no. 1 (1983): 23–29.

Coquatrix, Émile. *Il ne faut pas jouer avec le feu, comédie en 1 acte, en vers.* Paris: P. Masgana, 1847.

Corvin, Michel, ed. *Dictionnaire encyclopédique du théâtre à travers le monde.* Paris: Bordas, 2008.

Couailhac, Louis. Preface to *Duchesse et Poissarde, comédie-vaudeville en deux actes.* Edited by Joanny Augier and Adolphe Salvat. Paris: Bibliothèque théâtral, 1842.

Courcy, Frédéric de, Jean-François-Alfred Bayard, and Théaulon. *L'Année sur la sellette, revue mêlée de couplets.* Paris: Marchant, 1837.

Cuillé, Tili Boon. *Narrative Interludes: Musical Tableaux in Eighteenth-Century French Texts.* Toronto: University of Toronto Press, 2006.

Dairnvaell, Georges. *À M. Félix Pyat, réponse du prince des critiques.* Paris: au dépôt central, sous les galeries de l'Odéon, 1844.

Damarin, Edouard, and Clairville [Louis François Nicolaïe]. *Satan, ou le Diable à Paris, comédie-vaudeville en 4 actes, avec un prologue et un épilogue, par MM. Clairville et E. Damarin.* Brussels: J.-A. Lelong, 1844.

Delavigne, Casimir. *La Popularité.* Paris: H. Delloy, 1839.

———. "La Popularité." In *Théâtre de Casimir Delavigne,* 1–163. Paris: Didier, 1850.

Delorme, Philippe. "Le Thème du paria chez Alfred de Vigny: *Chatterton, Servitude, et grandeur militaire* et 'La Flûte' (*Les Destinées*)." Master's thesis, Université de Pau et des Pays de l'Adour, April 15, 2015. HAL archives-ouvertes, https://dumas.ccsd.cnrs.fr/dumas-01142450/document.

Dennery [Adolphe Philippe D'Ennery], Romain Chapelain, and Eugène Cormon. *Le Roman comique.* Paris: Michel Lévy frères, 1846.

Dennery [Adolphe Philiippe D'Ennery] and Clairville [Louis François Nicolaïe]. *Le Feuilleton et la raison ou Le Mariage du feuilleton.* Paris: Les Archives nationales, 1841.

———. *V'la c'qui vient d' paraître, bulletin de la grande année 1845, revue-vaudeville.* Paris: Beck, 1846.

Descotes, Maurice. *Histoire de la critique dramatique en France.* Études littéraires françaises. Paris: J.-M. Place, 1980.

———. *Le Public de théâtre et son histoire.* Paris: Presses universitaires de France; Vendôme: Impr. des P.U.F., 1964.

Desnoyer, Charles, and Charles Labie. *L'Ombre de Nicolet ou de plus fort en plus fort ! Vaudeville épisodique en un acte.* Paris: Michaud Pilout Barba, 1837.

Desnoyer and Labat. *Richard Savage.* Paris: Barba Delloye Bezou, 1838.

Diaz, José-Luis. *Illusions perdues d'Honoré de Balzac.* Paris: Folio / Gallimard, 2001.

Donnard, Jean-Hervé. *Balzac: Les réalités économiques et sociales dans La Comédie Humaine.* Paris: A. Colin, 1961.

Dreyfus, Robert. *Petite histoire de la revue de fin d'année.* Paris: Charpentier et Fasquelle, 1909.

Dubois, Philippe C. "Savarin/BalZac: Du goût des excitants sur l'écriture moderne." *Nineteenth-Century French Studies* 33, nos. 1–2 (2004–2005): 75–88.

Duchet, Claude, and Isabelle Tournier. "Avertissement quasi littéraire." In Duchet and Tournier, *Le moment de "La comédie humaine,"* 9–18.

Duchet, Claude, and Isabelle Tournier, eds. *Balzac, œuvres complètes: Le moment de "La comédie humaine."* Saint-Denis, Fr.: Presses Universitaires de Vincennes, 1993.

Dumanoir [Philippe-François Pinel]. *Un Système.* Paris: Archives Nationales, 1837.

Dumanoir [Philippe-François Pinel] and Clairville. *La Poudre-coton: Revue de l'année 1846, en 4 actes et 1 entr'acte, mêlée de couplets.* Paris: Michel Lévy frères, 1847.

———. *Les Lampions de la veille et les lanternes du lendemain, revue de l'année 1848, en 5 tableaux, mêlée de couplets.* Paris: Dondey-Dupré, 1849.

———. *Les Pommes de terre malades, revue de l'année 1845, en trois actes . . .* Paris: Beck, 1846.

Dumanoir [Philippe-François Pinel], Clairville [Louis François Nicolaïe], and Dennery [Adolphe Philippe D'Ennery]. *Paris dans la comète, revue en 3 actes.* Paris: Detroux, 1843.

———. *Paris voleur, comédie-vaudeville en 3 actes et 6 tableaux.* Paris: Marchant, 1844.

Dumasy, Lise, ed. *La Querelle du roman-feuilleton: Littérature, presse et politique, un débat précurseur (1836–1848).* Grenoble, Fr: ELLUG, 1999.

Dumersan, Théophile Marion, and Gabriel de Lurieu. *Le Pensionnaire, ou Cent francs par mois, comédie en 1 acte mêlée de couplets.* Paris: Nobis, 1836.

D.-Y. "Second-Théâtre-Français." *Le Constitutionnel,* March 13, 1843, 1.

Ed. L. ""Feuilleton." *Le Siècle.* September 11, 1837, 2,

Eisenstein, Elizabeth. "The Tribune of the People: A New Species of Demagogue." In *The Press in the French Revolution,* edited by Harvey Chisick, 145–60. Studies in Voltaire and the Eighteenth Century. Oxford: Oxford University Press, 1991.

Fargeaud, Madeleine. "Balzac, Le commerce et la publicité." *L'Année balzacienne* (1974): 187–200.

Fau, Élise. "Le Cheval dans le transport public au XIXe siècle, à travers les collections du musée national de la Voiture et du Tourisme, Compiègne." *In Situ* 27 (2015), accessed January 26, 2019. URL: http://journals.openedition.org /insitu/12124.

Felkay, Nicole. *Balzac et ses éditeurs, 1822–1837: Essai sur la librairie romantique.* Paris: Promodis-Ed. du Cercle de la Librairie, 1987.

Felman, Shoshana. *La Folie et la chose littéraire.* Paris: Seuil, 1978.

Felski, Rita. *Beyond Feminist Aesthetics: Feminist Literature and Social Change.* Cambridge, Mass.: Harvard University Press, 1989.

———, ed. *Rethinking Tragedy.* Baltimore: Johns Hopkins University Press, 2008.

"Feuilleton." *Le Constitutionnel*, February 12, 1844.

"Feuilleton." *Le Siècle*, October 30, 1837, 1.

"Feuilleton." *Le Siècle*, October 31, 1837.

Feyel, Gilles. *La Presse en France des origines à 1944, histoire politique et materielle.* Paris: Ellipses, 1999.

———. "La Querelle de l'anonymat des journalistes, entre 1836 et 1850." In *Figures de l'anonymat, médias et société*, edited by Frédéric Lambert, 27–56. Paris: L'Harmattan, 2001.

"Fox News Host Defends CNN Reporter." CNN Politics, January 12, 2017. Video, 1:42. http://edition.cnn.com/videos/politics/2017/01/12/fox-news-shephard -smith-defends-cnn-reporter-cnni.cnn.

F.T.C. "Théâtre-Français." *Le Charivari*, November 22, 1837, 1.

Furet, François, Jacques Ozouf, and Centre de recherches historiques. *Lire et écrire: l'alphabétisation des Français de Calvin à Jules Ferry.* Le Sens commun. Paris: Éditions de Minuit, 1977.

Gandt, Marie de. "Ironies romantiques dans les années 1830." In Bordas, *Ironies balzaciennes*, 17–30.

Gauchet, Marcel. *La Révolution des pouvoirs.* Paris: Gallimard, 1995.

Gautier, Robert-Alphonse, and Narcisse Fournier. *Les Ennemis, comédie-vaudeville en 1 acte.* Paris: Tresse, 1846.

Gautier, Théophile. "Feuilleton de la Presse." *La Presse*, January 7, 1839, 2.

———. "Feuilleton de la Presse." *La Presse*, October 30, 1841, 1.

———. "Feuilleton de la Presse." *La Presse*, October 30, 1841, 1.

———. "Feuilleton de la Presse." *La Presse*, January 6, 1842, 1.

———. "Feuilleton de la Presse." *La Presse*, April 26, 1843, 1.

———. "Feuilleton de la Presse." *La Presse*, May 2, 1843.

———. "Feuilleton de la Presse." *La Presse*, December 11, 1843, 2.

———. "Lettre 173: Théophile Gautier à Gérard de Nerval (around December 5, 1839)." In *Correspondance générale*, edited by Claudine Lacoste-Veysseyre, 164. Geneva: Droz, 1985.

———. Introduction to *Œuvres complètes de Madame Émile de Girardin née Delphine Gay.* Paris: Plon, 1861.

———. "Théâtres." *La Presse*, January 24, 1848, 1.

Gay de La Tour de Lajonchère, Auguste, and Clairville [Louis François Nicolaïe]. *1837 aux enfers, revue fantastique mêlée de couplets.* Paris: Morain, 1838.

George, Jocelyne. "De l'influence du vaudeville sur l'image du midi: Le cas de Carpentras." In *La France démocratique, combats, mentalités, symboles, mélanges offerts a Maurice Agulhon*, edited by Christophe Carle, 77–84. Paris: Publications de la Sorbonne, 1998.

Gidel, Henry. *Le Vaudeville.* Que sais-je ? Paris: Presses universitaires de France, 1986.

Girardin, Delphine de. "Courrier de Paris." *La Presse*, December 8, 1838.

———. *L'École des journalistes.* 2nd ed. Paris: Dumont, 1839.

———. *Lettres parisiennes du vicomte de Launay par Madame de Girardin.* 2 vols. Paris: Mercure de France, 1986.

Girardin, Émile de. "De la liberté de la presse et du journalisme." *La Presse*, December 5, 1839, 2–3.

———. *Questions de Presse.* Paris: Béthune et Plon, 1842.

Glinoer, Anthony. "Critique donné(e), critique prostitué(e) au XIXe siècle." *Études littéraires, Penser la littérature par la presse* 40, no. 3 (2009): 29–42.

———. "L'Orgie bohème." *ConTEXTES* 6 (September 2009). https://journals .openedition.org/contextes/4369.

Gluck, Mary. *Popular Bohemia: Modernism and Urban Culture in Nineteenth-Century Paris.*

Goldstein, Jan. *Console and Classify: The French Psychiatric Profession in the Nineteenth Century.* 1987. Reprint, Cambridge, MA: Harvard University Press, 2005.

Goldstein, Judith L. "Realism without a Human Face." In *Spectacles of Realism*, edited by Margaret Cohen and Christopher Prendergast, 66–89. London: University of Minnesota Press, 1995.

Goode, Mike. "The Public and the Limits of Persuasion in the Age of Caricature." In *The Efflorescence of Caricature, 1759–1838*, edited by Todd Porterfield, 117–36. Burlington, VT: Ashgate, 2011.

Grangé, Eugène, Ernest Bourget, and Adolphe d Ennery [Adolphe Philippe D'Ennery]. *1840, ou la Guerre des saisons, revue-vaudeville en 1 acte.* Paris: Mifliez, 1839.

Greene, J. P. "Cosmetics and Conflicting Fictions in Balzac's *César Birotteau.*" *Neophilologus* 83, no. 2 (1999): 197–208.

Griffiths, Robert Howell. "Cross-Channel Entanglements (1689–1789)." In *The Routledge Companion to the French Revolution in World History*, edited by Alan I. Forrest and Matthias Middell, 137–158. Oxford: Routledge, 2016.

Grojnowski, Daniel. "Grandville et l'Invention d'*Un Autre Monde*, preface to *Un Autre Monde*, by Jean-Jacques Grandville, vii–xxiv. Paris: Classiques Garnier, 2010.

Grossir, Claudine. "Scribe: L'histoire en scene." In Bara and Yon, *Eugène Scribe*, 131–44.

Guinot, Eugène (Pierre Durand). "Revue de Paris." *Le Siècle*, June 5, 1847, 1.

———. "Revue de Paris." *Le Siècle*, January 1, 1848, 3.

Guise, René. "Balzac et le roman-feuilleton." *L'Année balzacienne* (1964): 283–338.

Gunn, J. A. W. *Beyond Liberty and Property: The Process of Self-Recognition in Eighteenth-Century Political Thought.* Montreal: McGill-Queen's University Press, 1983.

Habermas, Jürgen. *The Structural Transformation of the Public Sphere.* Translated by Thomas Burger and Frederick Lawrence. Cambridge, MA: Polity, 1989.

Hamon, Philippe. *L'Ironie littéraire: Essai sur les formes de l'écriture oblique.* Paris: Hachette supérieur, 1996.

Hanoosh, Michelle. "The Allegorical Artist and the Crises of History: Benjamin, Grandville, Baudelaire." *Word and Image* 10, no. 1 (1994): 38–54.

Harel, François-Antoine. *Le Succès, comédie en 2 actes, en prose.* Paris: Marchant, [1843].

Hemmings, Frederick William John. *The Theatre Industry in Nineteenth-Century France.* Cambridge: Cambridge University Press, 1993.

Hesse, Carla. "Books in Time." In *The Future of the Book*, edited by Geoffrey Nunberg. Berkeley: University of California Press, 1997.

———. "Reading Signatures: Female Authorship and Revolutionary Law in France, 1750–1850." *Eighteenth-Century Studies* 22, no. 3 (1989): 469–87.

———. "Towards a New Topography of the Enlightenment" (Afterword)

European Review of History: Revue européenne d'histoire, Volume 13 (2006), no. 3: 499–508. http://dx.doi.org/10.1080/13507480600893171

Heyraud, Violaine, and Adrienne Martinez, eds. *Le Vaudeville à la scène*. Grenoble, Fr.: UGA Éditions, Collection la fabrique de l'oeuvre, 2015.

Hiner, Susan. *Accessories to Modernity*. Philadelphia: University of Pennsylvania Press, 2010.

Hollinshead-Strick, Cary. "Le Boulevard du crime sélectionne son jury: La presse judiciaire sur scène sous la Monarchie de Juillet." In *European Drama and Performance Studies: Spectacles, commerce et culture matérielle (1715–1860)*, edited by Sabine Chaouche and Roxane Martin, 167–76. Paris: Classiques Garnier, 2013.

———. "La Campagne publicitaire de *L'Époque* en 1845 vue par le vaudeville." In Bara and Thérenty, *Presse et scène au XIXe siècle*. Médias 19. October 19, 2012. http://www.medias19.org/index.php?id=2884.

———. "La Mise en page et le passage à la postérité dans *Les Belles femmes de Paris* et *Les Guêpes* d'Alphonse Karr." In *L'Écrit à l'épreuve des médias*, ed. Greta Komur-Thilloy and Anne Réach-Ngo, 277–295. Paris: Classiques Garnier, 2012.

———. "Using *La Presse* to stage *La Vérité* in Delphine de Girardin's *L'École des journalistes*." *Dix-Neuf* 7, no. 1 (2013): 140–50.

Hugo, Victor. *Théâtre complet*. Vol. 1. Edited by Josette Mélèze and Jean-Jacques Thierry. Paris: NRF / Gallimard, 1964.

Janin, Jules. "Feuilleton du Journal des débats." *Le Journal des débats*, September 5, 1836, 2.

———. "Feuilleton du Journal des débats." *Le Journal des débats*, November 6, 1837.

———. "Feuilleton du Journal des débats." *Le Journal des débats*, January 24, 1848, 2.

———. "L'École des journalistes, Lettre à Madame Émile de Girardin." *L'Artiste*, 1839, 181–91.

———. "La Semaine dramatique." *Le Journal des débats*, January 2, 1837.

———. "La Semaine dramatique." *Le Journal des débats*, November 22, 1837, 1–3.

———. "La Semaine dramatique." *Le Journal des débats*, October 15, 1838, 2.

———. "La Semaine dramatique." *Le Journal des débats*, August 12, 1839.

———. "La Semaine dramatique." *Le Journal des débats*, January 10, 1840.

———. "La Semaine dramatique." *Le Journal des débats*, May 1, 1843.

———. "La Semaine dramatique." *Le Journal des débats*, December 25, 1843, 2.

———. "Un Grand homme de province à Paris par M. de Balzac." *Revue de Paris*, July 1839, 145–78.

Jaume, Lucien. *L'Individu effacé ou Le paradoxe du libéralisme français*. Paris: Fayard, 1997.

Jeanneney, Jean-Noël. *Une histoire des médias des origines à nos jours*. Paris: Ed. du Seuil, 1996.

Johnson, Joyce. *Women Dramatists, Humor, and the French Stage 1802 to 1855*. New York: Springer, 2014.

Jouhaud, Auguste. *L'Anti-camaraderie, ou la France au XXe siècle, comédie en 5 actes et en prose*. Brussels: J. A. Lelong, 1837.

Jouhaud, Auguste, Barthélemy. *La Faute du mari, comédie-vaudeville en 2 actes, par MM. Barthélemy et Jouhaud.* Paris: Beck, 1846.

Jourdheuil, Jean. "L'Escalier de Chatterton." *Romantisme*, no. 38 (1982): 106–16. https://doi.org/10.3406/roman.1982.4581.

J.T. "Chronique des théâtres." *La Quotidienne*, July 11, 1836, 2.

———. "Revue dramatique." *La Quotidienne*, September 5, 1836.

———. "Revue dramatique." *La Quotidienne*, January 22–23, 1837.

———. "Revue dramatique." *La Quotidienne*, October 30, 1837, 2–3.

———. "Revue dramatique." *La Quotidienne*, July 1, 1839.

———. "Revue dramatique." *La Quotidienne*, February 26, 1844, 2.

———. "Revue dramatique." *La Quotidienne*, December 29, 1845, 2.

———. "Revue dramatique." *La Quotidienne*, March 23, 1846, 1.

Jullien, Adolphe. *Le Romantisme et l'éditeur Renduel: Souvenirs et documents sur les écrivains de l'école romantique, avec lettres inédites adressées par eux à Renduel.* Paris: E. Fasquelle, 1897.

Kahan, Alan S. *Aristocratic Liberalism the Social and Political Thought of Jacob Burckhardt, John Stuart Mill, and Alexis de Tocqueville.* New York: Oxford University Press, 1992.

Kalifa, Dominique, Philippe Régnier, Marie-Ève Thérenty, and Alain Vaillant, eds. *La Civilisation du journal: Histoire culturelle et littéraire de la presse française au xixe siècle.* Paris: Nouveau Monde éditions, 2012.

Karr, Alphonse. "Acte de mauvais gout." *Le Figaro*, July 9, 1840, 2.

Kerr, David. *Caricature and French Political Culture, 1830–1848.* New York: Oxford University Press, 2000.

Kinder, Patricia. "*Girardin et La Maison Nucingen.*" *L'Année balzacienne* (1979): 15–46.

Komur-Thilloy, Greta, and Anne Réach-Ngo, eds. *L'Écrit à l'épreuve des médias.* Paris: Classiques Garnier, 2012.

Krakovitch, Odile. *Censure des répertoires des grands théâtres parisiens (1835–1906).* Paris: Centre Historique des Archives Nationales, 2003.

———. *Hugo Censuré: La Liberté au théâtre au XIXe siècle* Paris: Calmann-Lévy, 1985.

———. *La Censure théâtrale (1835–1848): Édition des procès-verbaux.* Paris: Classiques Garnier, 2016.

———. "Robert Macaire ou la grande peur des censeurs." *europe: Revue littéraire mensuelle*, nos. 703–4 (1987): 49–60.

Kroen, Sheryl. *Politics and Theater: The Crisis of Legitimacy in Restoration France, 1815–1830.* Studies on the History of Society and Culture. London: University of California Press, 2000.

Lamartine, Alphonse de, Henry-Roch Dupuys, and Marie-Renée Morin. *Correspondance 1809–1858.* Études, guides et inventaires. Paris: Bibliothèque nationale, 1989.

Larousse, Pierre. *Grand dictionnaire universel du XIXe siècle français, historique, géographique, mythologique, bibliographique.* Paris: Slatkine, 1982.

Lassère, Madeleine. *Delphine de Girardin, journaliste et femme de lettres au temps du romantisme.* Paris: Perrin, 2003.

Laubriet, Pierre. "L'Élaboration des personnages dans *César Birotteau*: Enseignement des épreuves corrigées." *L'Année balzacienne* (1964): 251–70.

———. Introduction to *César Birotteau*, by Honoré de Balzac. Paris: Garnier, 1964.

Laurencin [P.-A. Chapelle] and Marc-Michel [Marc Antoine Amédée Michel]. *La Gazette des tribunaux, comédie-vaudeville en 1 acte*. Paris: Marchant, 1844.

Léal, Juli. "Le Discours du fait divers et des petites annonces dans le théâtre de Labiche." In *Les Genres insérés dans le théâtre*, edited by Anne Sancier and Pierre Servet, 109–24. Lyon: C.E.D.E.C., 1997, 109–23.

Lefranc, Auguste, and Eugène Labiche. *Le Club champenois, à-propos mêlé de couplets, en 1 acte*. Paris: Beck, 1848.

Le Hir, Marie-Pierre. *Le Romantisme aux enchères Ducange, Pixéricourt, Hugo*. Purdue University Monographs in Romance Languages. Amsterdam: J. Benjamins, 1992.

Lemaire, Marion. "Robert Macaire la construction d'un mythe: Du personage théâtral au type social; 1823–1848." Ph.D. diss., Université de Paris 8 St. Denis, 2015. http://www.theses.fr/2015PA080079.

Le Men, Ségolène. *Daumier et la caricature*. Paris: Citadelles et Mazenod, 2008.

———. "Les Images sociales du corps." In *L'Histoire du corps*, edited by Jean-Jacques Courtine Alain Corbin, and Georges Vigarello, 119–48. Paris: Seuil, 2005.

"Le Théâtre de Balzac." *fabula*, January 15, 2013. http://www.fabula.org/actualites/le-theatre-de-balzac_52913.php.

"Le Vaudeville." Special issue, *europe* 72, no. 786 (1994).

Lévrier, Alexis, and Adeline Wrona, eds. *Matière et esprit du journal: Du "Mercure Galant" à Twitter*. Histoire de l'imprimé. Paris: Presses de l'Université Paris-Sorbonne, 2013.

Lichtlé, Michel. "Balzac, *Illusions Perdues*." *Information littéraire 55*, no. 3 (2003): 58–61.

Lichtlé, Michel, Françoise Mélonio, and Sophie Marchal. *Balzac, le texte et la loi*. Paris: Presses de l'Université Paris-Sorbonne, 2012.

Lindenberg, Daniel. "La Tentation du vaudeville." In *Le Théâtre en France 2 de la Révolution à nos jours*, edited by Jacqueline de Jomaron-Leyvastre, 163–87. Paris: A. Colin, 1989.

Lojkine, Stéphane, ed. *L'Écran de la représentation*. Paris: L'Harmattan, 2001.

Loncle, Stéphanie. *Théâtre et libéralisme (Paris, 1830–1848)*. Paris: Classiques Garnier, 2017.

Lucas, Hippolyte. "Feuilleton." *Le Siècle*, August 4, 1845.

———. "Revue des théâtres." *Le Siècle*, March 15, 1843.

———. "Revue des théâtres." *Le Siècle*, January 24, 1848.

———. "Théâtres." *Le Siècle*, October 18, 1842.

———. "Théâtres." *Le Siècle*, January 18, 1847.

"M. de Girardin." *Le Charivari*, December 30, 1836, 1.

Mah, Harold. *Enlightenment Phantasies: Cultural Identity in France and Germany, 1750–1914*. Ithaca, N.Y: Cornell University Press, 2004.

———. "Phantasies of the Public Sphere: Rethinking the Habermas of Historians." In "New Work on the Old Regime and the French Revolution," special issue (in honor of François Furet), *Journal of Modern History* 72, no. 1 (2000): 153–82.

Malo, Henri. *La Gloire du vicomte de Launay: Delphine Gay de Girardin*. Paris: Émile-Paul frères, 1925.

Martin-Fugier, Anne. *Comédiennes: Les actrices en France au XIXe siècle*. Paris: Complexe, 2008.

———. *La Vie élégante ou La formation du Tout-Paris 1815–1848*. Paris: Points / Seuil, 1993.

Martin, Marc. *Trois siècles de publicité en France*. Paris: Odile Jacob, 1992.

Martin, Roxane. *La Féerie romantique sur les scènes parisiennes 1791–1864*. Romantisme et modernités. Paris: H. Champion, 2007.

———. "Les Parodies 'intra-dramatiques,' ou Les voix d'une critique en mouvement." In Bury and Laplace-Claverie, *Le Miel et le fiel*, 97–108.

Mason, Haydn T., ed. *The Darnton Debate: Books and Revolution in the Eighteenth Century*. Oxford: Voltaire Foundation, 1999.

Matharel, Charles de. "Feuilleton." *Le Siècle*, February 17, 1844, 3.

———. "Revue des théâtres." *Le Siècle*, April 4, 1843, 2.

———. "Revue des théâtres." *Le Siècle*, May 25, 1844, 2.

———. "Revue des théâtres." *Le Siècle*, December 27, 1844.

———. "Revue des théâtres." *Le Siècle*, January 6, 1845.

———. "Revue des théâtres." *Le Siècle*, July 6, 1846, 2.

———. "Théâtres." *Le Siècle*, May 17, 1847, 1–2.

———. "Théâtres." *Le Siècle*, December 29, 1847, 3.

Matlock, Jann. *Scenes of Seduction: Prostitution, Hysteria, and Reading Difference in Nineteenth-Century France*. New York: Columbia University Press, 1994.

Matthes, Lothar. *Vaudeville Untersuchungen zu Geschichte und literatursystematischem Ort einer Erfolgsgattung*. Studia Romanica. Heidelberg: C. Winter, 1983.

Maurice, Charles. *Histoire anecdotique du théâtre*. Vol. 2. Paris: Henri Plon, 1856.

McCormick, John. *Popular Theatres of Nineteenth-Century France*. New York: Routledge, 1993.

McCready, Susan. *The Limits of Performance in French Romantic Drama*. Durham, N.C.: Durham University Press, 2007.

Ménissier. *Une heure d'exposition, revue un acte*. Paris: Archives Nationales, 1839.

Michelot, Isabelle. "Récit romanesque et théâtralité dans les Scènes de la vie parisienne et le 'cycle de Vautrin' d'Honoré de Balzac." Ph.D. diss., Université Paris 4 La Sorbonne, 2002, http://www.theses.fr/2002PA040219.

Miner, Margaret. "Devouring Streets: Jules Janin and the Abjection of Paris." *MLN* 113, no. 4 (September 1998): 780–811. http://www.jstor.org/stable/3251403.

Mitchovitch, Jean-Pierre. "*Léo Burckart* entre histoire et politique." In *Quinze études sur Nerval et le romantisme*, edited by Hisashi Mizuno and Jérôme Thélot, 171–94. Paris: Kimé, 2005.

Moindrot, Isabelle, Olivier Goetz, and Sylvie Humbert-Mougin. *Le Spectaculaire dans les arts de la scène du romantisme à la Belle époque*. Arts du spectacle. Paris: CNRS éd., 2006.

Mollier, Jean-Yves, Philippe Régnier, Alain Vaillant, and Pierre Macherey. *La Production de l'immatériel: Théories, représentations et pratiques de la culture au xixe siècle*. Saint-Étienne, Fr.: Publications de l'Université de Saint-Étienne, 2008.

Moulin, Victor. *Scribe et son théâtre, études sur la comédie au XIXe siècle*. Paris: Tresse, 1862.

Mourier, Charles, and Paul de Kock. *La Concierge du théâtre, vaudeville en 1 acte*. Paris: E. Michaud, 1838.

Mozet, Nicole. "Au commencement est l'imprimérie." In *Balzac: Illusions perdues*, "*l'oeuvre capitale dans l'oeuvre*," 23–33. Groningen, Neth.: CRIN, 1988.

———. *Balzac au pluriel*. Écrivains. Paris: Presses universitaires de France, 1990.

Muhlman, Geraldine. *Du journalisme en démocratie*. Critique de la politique. Paris: Payot et Rivages, 2004.

Mullaney, Steven. *The Reformation of Emotions in the Age of Shakespeare*. Chicago: University of Chicago Press, 2015.

Muret, Théodore. *La Quotidienne*, December 31, 1839.

———. "Un grand homme de province à Paris par M. de Balzac." *La Quotidienne*, December 10, 1839, 1–2.

N. "Feuilleton du Siècle." *Le Siècle*, June 17, 1838.

Nablow, Ralph Arthur. *The Addisonian Tradition in France, Passion and Objectivity in Social Observation*. Rutherford, N.J.: Fairleigh Dickinson University Press, 1990.

Nerval, Gérard de. *Léo Burckart, scènes de la vie allemande*. Coeuvres-et-Valsery, Fr,: Ed. Ressouvenances, 1995.

———. *Lorely*. Edited by Jacques Bony. Paris: José Corti, 1995.

———. *Œuvres complètes*. Vol. 2. Paris: Gallimard, 1993.

Nerval, Gérard de. Edited by Jean Richer. *Œuvres complémentaires*, vol. 4. *Théâtre 2*. Nouvelle bibliothèque nervalienne. Paris: Minard, 1981.

Nesci, Catherine. *Le Flâneur et les flâneuses les femmes et la ville à l'époque romantique*. Bibliothèque stendhalienne et romantique. Grenoble, Fr.: ELLUG, Université Stendhal, 2007.

Nodier, Charles. *Feuilletons du Temps*. Vol. 1. Edited by Jacques-Rémi Dahan. Paris: Classiques Garnier, 2010.

Novak-Lechevalier, Agathe. "De la construction stratégique d'un cliché: Scribe vu par les romanciers." In Bara and Yon, *Eugène Scribe*, 413–28.

———. "La Théâtralité dans le roman: Stendhal, Balzac." Ph.D. diss., Université de Paris 3, 2007. http://www.theses.fr/2007PA030131

Nye, Robert A. *Masculinity and Male Codes of Honor in Modern France*. New York: Oxford University Press, 1993.

O. "Théâtre français." *Le Constitutionnel*, November 22, 1837, 1.

Ortel, Philippe. "Le Stade de l'écran: Écriture et projection au dix-neuvième siècle." In Lojkine, *L'Écran de la représentation*, 111–40.

Ourliac, Édouard. "Malheurs et aventures de *César Birotteau* avant sa naissance." *Le Figaro*, December 15, 1837.

Parent-Lardeur, Françoise. *Les Cabinets de lecture: La lecture publique à Paris sous la Restauration*. Paris: Payot, 1982.

Pelta, Corinne. *Le Romantisme libérale en France: 1815–1830, La représentation souveraine*. Critiques littéraires. Paris: L'Harmattan, 2001.

Péraud, Alexandre. "L'Ironie textuelle balzacienne ou l'art de composer avec le réel." In Bordas, *Ironies balzaciennes*, 237–58.

Piana, Romain. "Du dramaturge au feuilletoniste: Aristophane hors de la scène française au XIXe siècle." *Lieux Littéraires* 4 (2001): 185–203.

———. "L'Imaginaire de la presse dans la revue théâtrale." In Bara and Thérenty, *Presse et scène au XIXe siècle*. Médias 19. October 19, 2012. http://www .medias19.org/index.php?id=3005.

Pinson, Guillaume. *L'Imaginaire mediatique: Histoire et fiction du journal au XIX'siecle*. Paris: Classiques Garnier, 2013.

———. "Présentation du dossier." In *Presse, prostitution, bas-fonds (1830–1930)*. Médias 19. June 9, 2013. http://www.medias19.org/index.php?id=13457.

Popkin, Jeremy. *Press, Revolution, and Social Identities in France, 1830–1835*. University Park: Pennsylvania State University Press, 2002.

"Porte Saint-Martin." *Le Journal des théâtres*, May 15, 1847, 2.

Prasad, Pratima, and Susan McCready, eds. *Novel Stages: Drama and the Novel in Nineteenth-Century France*. Newark: University of Delaware Press, 2007.

Prémaray, Jules Regnault de. *Part à deux, comédie en 1 acte, mêlée de chants*. Paris: Gallet, 1844.

Prendergast, Christopher. *Balzac Fiction and Melodrama*. London: E. Arnold, 1978.

———. *The Order of Mimesis: Balzac, Stendhal, Nerval, Flaubert*. Cambridge Studies in French. New York: Cambridge University Press, 1986.

Prévost-Paradol, Lucien-Anatole. *Essais de politique et de littérature*. Paris: Michel Lévy frères, 1859.

Procès en diffamation de M. J. Janin contre M. F. Pyat, condamnation . . . réflexions de plusieurs avocats à ce sujet. Galeries de l'Odéon. Paris: Gazel, 1844.

"Prospectus." *La Presse*, June 15, 1836.

Przybos, Julia. *L'Entreprise mélodramatique*. Paris: J. Corti, 1987.

Pyat, Félix. *Le Chiffonnier de Paris*. Paris: Michel Lévy, 1847.

———. *Le Chiffonnier de Paris grand Roman dramatique*. Paris: A. Fayard, 1892.

———. *Marie-Joseph Chénier et le prince des critiques*. Paris: Leriche, 1844.

R. "Feuilleton du Constitutionnel." *Le Constitutionnel*, January 12, 1845, 3.

———. "Théâtres." *Le Constitutionnel*, April 11, 1846, 2.

———. "Théâtres." *Le Constitutionnel*, January 24, 1848, 1–2.

Rancière, Jacques. *The Emancipated Spectator*. Translated by Gregory Elliott. London: Verso, 2009.

———. *Le Spectateur émancipé*. Paris: La Fabrique éditions, 2008.

Ravel, Jeffrey S. *The Contested Parterre: Public Theater and French Political Culture, 1680–1791*. Ithaca, N.Y.: Cornell University Press, 1999.

Reclus, Maurice. *Émile de Girardin, le créateur de la presse moderne*. Paris: Hachette, 1934.

Reddy, William M. "Condotteiri of the Pen: Journalists and the Public Sphere in Postrevolutionary France (1815–1850)." *American Historical Review* 99, no. 5 (1994): 1546–70.

———. *The Invisible Code: Honor and Sentiment in Postrevolutionary France, 1814–1848*. London: University of California Press, 1997.

Reverzy, Éléonore. *Portrait de l'artiste en fille de joie*. Paris: CNRS éditions, 2016.

"Revue des théâtres." *Le Siècle*, November 13, 1843.

Robert, Vincent. "Theater and Revolution on the Eve of 1848: Le Chevalier de Maison Rouge." *Actes de la recherche en sciences sociales*, nos. 186–87 (2011).

Rosanvallon, Pierre. *Le Moment Guizot*. Bibliothèque des sciences humaines. Paris: Gallimard, 1985.

Rosenkranz, Karl. *Georg Wilhelm Friedrich Hegels Leben*. Berlin: Duncker und Humblot, 1844.

Rougemont, Martine de. *La Vie théâtrale en France au XVIIIe siècle*. Paris: H. Champion, 2001.

Rozan, Charles. *Petites ignorances de la conversation*. Paris: Lacroix-Comon, 1857.

Salvandy, M. de. "Une fête au Palais-Royal." In *Paris, ou Le livre des cent et un*, edited by Ladvocat. Paris, 1831–1834.

Saminadayar-Perrin, Corinne. *Les Discours du journal: Rhétorique et médias au XIXe siècle, 1836–1885*. Le XIXe siècle en représentation(s). Saint-Étienne, Fr.: Publications de l'Université de Saint-Étienne, 2007.

Samuels, Maurice. *The Spectacular Past: Popular History and the Novel in Nineteenth-Century France*. Ithaca, N.Y.: Cornell University Press, 2004.

Sancier, Anne, and Pierre Servet, eds. *Les Genres insérés dans le théâtre*. Lyon, Fr.: C.E.D.E.C., 1997.

Sand, George. *Correspondance*. Vol. 7. Edited by Georges Lubin. Paris: Garnier, 1970.

———. *Le Péché de Monsieur Antoine*. Paris: Hetzel, 1859.

Sarcey, Francisque. *L'Opinion nationale*, July 16 and 23, 1860, reprinted in *Quarante ans de théâtre*. Paris: Bibliothèque des annales politiques et littéraires, 1900–1902, vol. I, p. 54. Cited by Marianne Bouchardon, "Introduction" in *Francisque Sarcey: un critique dramatique à contre-courant de l'histoire du théâtre?* Université de Rouen: Publications numériques du CÉRÉdI, no. 12, 2015.

"Second-Théâtre-Français." *Le Charivari*, November 11, 1843, 2.

"Second-Théâtre-Français." *Le Charivari*, December 13, 1847.

Sicard, Monique. "Tekhnê et anonymat." In *Figures de l'anonymat Médias et société*, edited by Frédéric Lambert, 223–30. Paris: L'Harmattan, 2001.

Simonnin, Antoine-Jean-Baptiste. *Le Marchand de chansons, vaudeville en 1 acte, par MM. Vanderbuch et Simonnin . . . .* Paris: Morain, 1837.

Soulié, Frédéric. "Feuilleton." *Le Journal des débats*, July 16, 1839, 1–3.

Staël, Germaine de. *Considérations sur la Révolution française*. Edited by Jacques Godechot. Paris: Tallandier, 1983.

Stendhal [Marie-Henri Beyle]. "La Comédie est impossible en 1836." In *Œuvres complètes*, edited by Victor Del Litto and Ernest Abravanel, 265–78. Geneva: Cercle du bibliophile, 1972.

Strauss, Jonathan. *Subjects of Terror*. Stanford, Calif.: Stanford University Press, 1998.

Sussman, Hava. "La Datation du récit dans *Illusions Perdues*." *L'Année balzacienne* (1985): 339–42.

Terdiman, Richard. *Discourse-Counter-Discourse: The Theory and Practice of Symbolic Resistance in Nineteenth-Century France*. London: Cornell University Press, 1985.

Terni, Jennifer. "A Genre for Early Mass Culture: French Vaudeville and the City, 1830–1848." *Theatre Journal* 58, no. 2 (2006): 221–48.

"Théâtre de la Gaîté." *Le Constitutionnel*, September 11, 1837.

"Théâtre du Gymnase." *Le Charivari*, February 25, 1844, 2.

"Théâtre français." *Le Charivari*, January 24, 1848, 1–2.

"Théâtre français." *Le Constitutionnel*, October 17, 1836, 2.

"Théâtre français: L'École des journalistes." In *Commission d'examen, Ministère de l'intérieur, Division des beaux arts*. Paris: Archives Nationales, 1839.

"Théâtres." *Le Charivari*, April 21, 1843.

"Théâtres, fêtes et concerts." *La Presse*, December 21, 1841, 3.

"Théâtres, fêtes et concerts." *La Presse*, December 25, 1841, 3.

"Théâtres, fêtes et concerts." *La Presse*, December 29, 1841, 3.

Théaulon and Bayard. *Le Père de la débutante, vaudeville en cinq actes*. La France Dramatique. Paris: Barba, 1837.

Thérenty, Marie-Ève. *Mosaïques être écrivain entre presse et roman, 1829–1836. Romantisme et modernités*. Paris: H. Champion, 2003.

Thérenty, Marie-Ève, and Alain Vaillant. *1836 L'An I de lère médiatique: Analyse littéraire et historique de La Presse de Girardin*. Paris: Nouveau monde, 2001.

———, eds. *Presse et plumes*. Paris: Nouveau monde, 2004.

———. "Quand le roman [se] fait l'article: Palimpseste du journal dans *Illusions perdues*." In *Illusions perdues, actes du colloque des 1er et 2 décembre 2003*, edited by José-Luis Diaz and André Guyaux, 233–45. Paris: Presses de l'Université de Paris-Sorbonne, 2004.

Thomasseau, Jean-Marie. "Le Théâtre critique de lui-même dans les vaudevilles de l'époque romantique." In Bury and Laplace-Claverie, *Le Miel et le fiel*, 87–96.

———. "Le Théâtre et les révolutions." *Comédie française les cahiers* 13 (1994): 40–51.

Tournemine, Pierre. *La Révolte des coucous, comédie-vaudeville en un acte*. Paris: Michaud Pilout Barba, 1838.

Tournemine, Pierre, and Adolphe Guénée. *La France et l'industrie, vaudeville allégorique en 1 acte, à propos de l'exposition des produits de 1839*. Paris: L.-A. Gallet, 1839.

Tournier, Isabelle. "Portrait de Balzac en Shéhérazade." In Duchet and Tournier, *Balzac, œuvres complètes: Le moment de "La comédie humaine,"* 77–109.

Vanoncini, André. "Le Théâtre de Balzac: Triomphe et crise d'une esthétique d'identification." *Œuvres et Critiques* 11, no. 3 (1986): 297–311.

van Rossum-Guyon, Françoise. *Balzac La littérature réfléchie*. Edited by Stéphane Vachon. Paragraphes. Montréal: Département d'études françaises, Université de Montréal, 2002.

"Variétés." *Le Constitutionnel*, July 15, 1843, 5.

"VAUDEVILLE–PALAIS ROYAL–AMBIGU." *Le Charivari*, January 2 and 3, 1837, 2.

Vaulabelle, Eléonore Tenaille de, Clairville, Jules Cordier, and Dumoustier. *Ah ! enfin ! pièce d'ouverture en 3 actes et 2 entr'actes*. Paris: Beck, 1848.

Vielledent, Sylvie. *1830 aux théâtres*. Paris: Honoré Champion, 2009.

———. "Dumas Parodié." *Revue d'Histoire littéraire de la France* 4, no. 104 (2004): 851–69.

Wagneur, Jean-Didier. "La Place de la littérature dans l'univers des journaux," in *Les Écrivains et la presse*. Le Blog Gallica. January 22, 2018. https://gallica.bnf .fr/blog/22012018/la-place-de-la-litterature-dans-lunivers-des-journaux

Walton, Charles, Ed. *The Darnton Debate: Books and Revolution in the Eighteenth Century*. Oxford: Voltaire Foundation, 1999.

Wechsler, Judith. *A Human Comedy: Physiognomy and Caricature in Nineteenth-Century Paris*. Chicago: University of Chicago Press, 1982.

Weston, Helen. "The Light of Wisdom: Magic Lanternists as Truth-Tellers in Post-Revolutionary France." In *The Efflorescence of Caricature, 1759–1838*, edited by Todd Porterfield, 97–104. Burlington, Vt.: Ashgate, 2011.

Wicks, Charles Beaumont, and Jerome W. Schweitzer. *The Parisian Stage: III (1831–1850)*. University of Albama Studies.Tuscaloosa: University of Alabama Press, 1961.

Wild, Nicole. *Dictionnaire des théâtres parisiens au XIXe siècle*. Paris: Aux Amateurs de livres, 1989.

Y. "Théâtre des Variétés." *Le Constitutionnel*, October 30, 1837.

———. "Théâtres." *Le Constitutionnel*, January 2, 1837.

———. "Théâtres." *Le Constitutionnel*, December 13, 1841, 1.

Yon, Jean-Claude. "Balzac et Scribe: 'Scènes de la vie théâtrale'." *L'Année balzacienne*, (1999): 439–49.

———. "La Féerie ou le royaume du spectaculaire: L'Exemple de *Rothomago*." In *Le Spectaculaire dans les arts de la scène du romantisme à la belle époque*, edited by Isabelle Moindrot, 126–33. Paris: CNRS éditions, 2006.

INDEX